CLAR[illegible]ERIES

General Editors

J. L. ACKRILL AND LINDSAY JUDSON

Also published in this series

Categories and *De Interpretatione*
J. L. ACKRILL

De Anima Books II and III
D. W. HAMLYN

De Generatione et Corruptione
C. J. F. WILLIAMS

Eudemian Ethics Books I, II, and VIII
MICHAEL WOODS
Second edition

Metaphysics Books M and N
JULIA ANNAS

Physics Books I and II
W. CHARLTON
New impression with supplementary material

Physics Books III and IV
EDWARD HUSSEY

Other volumes are in preparation

ARISTOTLE
De Partibus Animalium I
and
De Generatione Animalium I
(with passages from II. 1–3)

Translated with Notes
by
D. M. BALME

With a Report on Recent Work
and an Additional Bibliography
by
ALLAN GOTTHELF

CLARENDON PRESS · OXFORD

Oxford University Press, Walton Street, Oxford OX2 6DP
Oxford New York Toronto
Delhi Bombay Calcutta Madras Karachi
Kuala Lumpur Singapore Hong Kong Tokyo
Nairobi Dar es Salaam Cape Town
Melbourne Auckland
and associated companies in
Berlin Ibadan

Published in the United States
by Oxford University Press, New York

First published 1972
Reprinted 1985
Reprinted with new material 1992

British Library Cataloguing in Publication Data
Data available

Library of Congress Cataloging in Publication Data
Aristotle.
[De partibus animalium. 1. English]
Aristotle's De partibus animalium I ; and, De generatione animalium I : (with passages from II. 1–3) / translated with notes by D. M. Balme ; with a report on recent work and an additional bibliography by Allan Gotthelf.
p. cm.
Originally published: Oxford : Clarendon Press, 1972.
Includes bibliographical references and index.
1. Zoology—Pre-Linnean works. 2. Reproduction—Early works to 1800. I. Balme, D. M. (David M.), 1912– . II. Gotthelf, Allan, 1942– . III. Aristotle. On the generation of animals. English. 1992. IV. Title: De partibus animalium I. V. Title: De generatione animalium I.
QL41.A727 1992 591—dc20 92–15167
ISBN 0–19–875128–1

Printed in Hong Kong

PREFACE

THESE two books show different but complementary sides of Aristotle's biology, one being a philosophical discussion of principles, the other an exposition of a particular problem (animal reproduction). *P.A.* I is intended as an introduction to zoology. It sets out Aristotle's principles of biological explanation, especially his teleological and hylomorphic theory and his views about defining and classifying species. In *G.A.* I Aristotle applies the hylomorphic analysis to 'generation', that is reproduction and embryology. In the course of it he criticizes the preformationist views then current in medical and philosophical circles.

Neither book is in a finished state. *P.A.* I consists of five papers strung together, partly in note form. *G.A.* I together with the first three chapters of Book II (from which long extracts are given here) presents a continuous argument, but has been interpolated and divided up by an ancient editor who evidently mistook it for a descriptive anatomy. The Greek MSS. are fairly well agreed in *G.A.* I–II, but less so in *P.A.* I. Both books have been edited and commented upon by several modern scholars, but there is still disagreement over details both of text and of interpretation, though not over major issues. The text of *P.A.* I chosen for translation, in the absence of an Oxford Classical Text, is the Berlin Academy edition by Bekker, which although questionable in details remains on the whole a sensible and likely version, and is easily available. The texts of Langkavel (Teubner) and Le Blond (Aubier) differ little from Bekker's; those of Bussemaker (Didot), Peck (Loeb), and Louis (Budé) differ more widely, especially the Loeb. For *G.A.* I the admirable O.C.T. of H. J. Drossaart Lulofs (1965) has been used.

Footnotes to the translation mark the few places where I have departed from these texts, as follows:

P.A. I: 642^{a}15 δῆλόν γε πειρᾶσθαι ποιεῖν, ⟨δῆλον,⟩
642^{b}8 δίπουν ⟨ἢ⟩ σχιζόπουν· ἄπουν.
643^{b}7 εἰ ⟨μὴ⟩ ὁμώνυμον
644^{a}5 δίπουν ⟨ἢ⟩ σχιζόπουν
645^{a}8 ὁμοίως

G.A. I: 717^{a}4 τὰ γὰρ
721^{a}11–12 τῶν . . . ἐστίν transp. post συνεώραται (17).
723^{a}31 οὕτως⟨,⟩
725^{b}32 πολύσαρκοι μᾶλλον ἢ πρότερον ἧττον
726^{a}8 ἑκάτεραι
728^{a}14–17 καὶ . . . σπέρμα transp. post φύσεως (21).
728^{b}3–4 ἐχόντων ⟨τισὶ πλὴν⟩ τοῖς

In addition, I have altered the paragraphing in *G.A.* I, to show the connection of the argument. Sentences that seem to be interpolations are in square brackets, and in general the use of brackets and punctuation is not always the same as in the O.C.T.

In conformity with the policy of this series, the translation is *not* explanatory, nor on the other hand is it a word-for-word rendering; it tries to be semantically faithful to what Aristotle says, remaining obscure or ambiguous where the Greek is obscure or ambiguous. For explanations please see the notes at the back, which also give a running summary of the argument.

I should like to express my sincere thanks to Professor J. L. Ackrill for many valuable criticisms and suggestions made in the course of revision.

D. M. BALME

Queen Mary College, London

EDITORS' NOTE

We are grateful to Professor Gotthelf for undertaking the preparation of the Report on Recent Work and the Additional Bibliography.

In this reprinting a few small changes have been made in the translation and commentary, as indicated in the Report (pages 168 and 173).

J.L.A.
R.L.J.

July 1991

CONTENTS

TRANSLATIONS

DE PARTIBUS ANIMALIUM I

CHAPTER 1

In relation to every study and investigation, humbler or 639a more valuable alike, there appear to be two kinds of proficiency. One can properly be called knowledge of the subject, the other as it were a sort of educatedness. For it is characteristic of an educated man to be able to judge successfully what is properly expounded and what is not. This in fact is the kind of man that we think the generally educated man is, and by being educated we mean being able to do just this—except that in his case we consider one and the same man capable of judging about practically everything, whereas we consider another capable in some limited field; for there may be another who is qualified in the same way as the former, but only in respect of part.

Clearly therefore the inquiry about nature, too, must possess certain principles of the kind to which one will refer in appraising the method of demonstration, apart from the question how the truth has it, whether thus or otherwise.

(*1*) I mean, for example, should one take each *being* singly and clarify its nature independently, making individual studies of, say, man or lion or ox and so on, or should one first posit the attributes common to all in respect of something common? For many of the same attributes belong to many different kinds of animal, for example sleep, breathing, growth, wasting, death, and any other affections and conditions of this sort (for at present we are not in a position to speak of them with clarity and precision). If we do speak of the animals severally, it is plain that we shall often be saying the same things about many of them. For each of the above attributes belongs to both horses and dogs and men, so that if one refers to each of their attributes one will have

to speak repeatedly about the same ones—all that are the same in different species of animal while having no differentia themselves. On the other hand there are no doubt others which, although they have the same dèsignation,
639b differ by the specific differentia. Animal locomotion, for example, is evidently not one in species, for there are differences between flying, swimming, walking, and creeping. Therefore we must not overlook the question how the examination should be made, that is whether one should first survey common general attributes and then later the peculiar ones, or take them individually straight away. At present this has not been clarified. Nor has the next question:

(*2*) Should the natural philosopher, like the mathematicians when they demonstrate astronomy, first survey the appearances in regard to the animals and their parts in each case, and only then go on to state the because-of-what (i.e. the causes), or should he proceed in some other way?

(*3*) And further, since we see more than one cause in connection with coming-to-be in nature, for example the cause *for the sake of which* as well as the cause *from which comes the beginning of the movement*, we must be clear about these too, as to which sort of cause is naturally first and which second.

First is evidently the one we call *for the sake of something*. For this is the definition, and the definition is the beginning alike in things composed according to an art and in things composed naturally. It is after defining health or house, either mentally or perceptually, that the doctor and the builder respectively expound the definitions and the causes of each thing they do and why it must be done thus. And the *for the sake of which* and the good exist to a greater degree in the works of nature than in those of art.

(*4*) The *necessary* cause is not present in all natural things in the same way. Nearly everyone tries to reduce explanations to it, not having distinguished in how many ways the necessary is spoken of.

The *absolutely necessary* is present in what is eternal, but it is the *hypothetically necessary* that is present in everything that comes to be, as it is in the artefacts such as a house and anything else of that sort. It is necessary that such-and-such matter be present if there is to be a house or some other end; and first this thing must come to be and be moved, then this, and so on successively as far as the end and that for the sake of which each thing comes to be and is. It is the same with things that come to be naturally.

But the mode of demonstration, i.e. the mode of necessity, differs as between natural science and the theoretical sciences. (We have discussed the latter elsewhere.) For the latter begin from what is, the former from what will be: "Because health or man is such, it is necessary that this be or come to be"—not "Because this is or has come to be, that of necessity is or will be". Nor can one link together the necessity in such a demonstration for ever, so as to say "Because this is, therefore that is". (These matters too have been clarified elsewhere; we have explained where necessity is present, where it is reciprocal, and for what reason.)

(*5*) Another question not to be overlooked is whether it is appropriate to speak, as the earlier scientists did, of the way in which each thing naturally *comes to be* rather than of the way in which it *is*. There is an important difference here.

It seems right that, even in dealing with coming-to-be, our starting-point should be the same as we said before: first to take the appearances in respect of each kind, and only then to go on to speak of their causes. For in house-building too it is more the case that *these* things take place because the form of the house is *such*, than that the house is such because it comes to be in this way. For coming-to-be is for the sake of being, not being for the sake of coming-to-be. Hence Empedocles was wrong in saying that many attributes belong to animals because it happened so in their coming-to-be, for instance that their backbone is such because it happened to get broken by bending. He failed to recognize, first, that the seed previously constituted must already possess this sort of capability, and secondly that its producer was prior not only in definition but in time; for it is the man that generates a man, and therefore it is because *that* man is such that *this* man's coming-to-be happens so.

The same applies to things that seem to come to be spontaneously, as it does also to artificial things; for in some cases the same things as come to be from an art also come to be spontaneously, for example health. Now there are some things whose producing agent pre-exists resembling them, for example the art of making statues: for they do not come to be spontaneously. And the art is the definition of the work without the matter. And so it is with chance products: as the art has it, so they come to be.

Hence we should if possible say that because this is what it is to be a man, therefore he has these things; for he cannot be without these parts. Failing that, we should get as near as possible to it: we should either say altogether that it 640b cannot be otherwise, or that it is at least good thus. And these follow. And because he is such a thing, his coming-to-be necessarily happens so and is such. And that is why this part comes to be first, and then this. And this is the way we should speak of everything that is composed naturally.

(*6*) Now those who in ancient times were the first to philosophize about nature were thinking about the material origin and that sort of cause—what and what kind of thing is matter, how does the universe come to be out of it, and with what cause of movement (such as strife or love or mind or spontaneity), assuming that the underlying matter has a certain kind of nature by necessity—fire a hot nature and earth a cold one, the former light and the latter heavy. For this is how they generate the universe. And they speak similarly of the coming-to-be of the animals and plants: they say, for example, that when the water flowed in the body a hollow stomach came to be, together with all the receptacles of food and residue, and when the breath made its way through, the nostrils were forced open. But the air and the water are the bodies' matter; for it is out of such bodies that they all construct nature. But if the existence of man and the animals and their parts is natural, we must have to say of each part—of flesh, bone, blood, and all the homoeomerous parts, and similarly of the non-homoeomerous such as face, hand, foot—in virtue of what, and in respect of what sort of capability, each is such as it is. For it is not enough to say what it is made of, for example of fire or of earth. If we were speaking of a bed or some such thing, we should be trying to define its form rather than its matter such as the metal or timber—or if not the form, at least the matter of the composite whole. For a bed is a *this in this*, or a *this such*, so that we should have to speak also of its shape and of what sort of thing it is in respect of its form. For its nature in respect of conformation is more important than its material nature.

But now if each animal and part exists by virtue of shape and colour, Democritus might be right; for this seems to be his assumption. At any rate he says it is clear to everybody what sort of thing man is in conformation, suggesting that he is known by shape and colour. Yet the dead man too has the same conformation of shape, but nevertheless is not a man. Moreover there cannot be a hand in any and every state, such as metal or wood, except homonymously like the doctor in the picture. For it will not be able to do its own work any more than stone flutes or the painted doctor can do theirs. In the same way none of the dead man's parts is such a part any longer, for example eye or hand. Therefore his statement is too simple: it is like a carpenter speaking about a wooden hand. For that is how the writers on nature state the coming-to-be and causes of the shape: they say by what powers things were fashioned. But no doubt the carpenter will say adze or drill where the other says air and earth—except that the carpenter's account will be better, for it will not be enough for him just to say that after the tool struck this became hollow and that became flat, but he will say why he made the blow so, and for the sake of what, giving the reason—so that it should come to have such or such a conformation. Clearly therefore their account is wrong. They ought to say that the animal is *such*, and to speak about that—what it is and what kind of a thing, and the same with each of its parts, just as in speaking of the form of the bed.

(7) Now if this is soul, or part of soul, or not without soul (at any rate when soul has gone there is no longer an animal, nor does any of its parts remain the same except in shape alone, like those turned to stone in the fable)—if then this is so, it will be for the natural philosopher to speak and know about soul (if not about all soul, then about just this part in virtue of which the animal is *such*); he will both say what the soul is (or just this part of it) and speak about the attributes that belong to the animal in virtue of its soul's being such. He must do so especially because nature is spoken of in two ways: in one way it is nature as matter, in the other it is nature as being. And the latter is also nature as moving cause and as end. And such, in the animal, is either its whole soul or some part of it. So in this way the student of nature will actually have to speak more about soul than about the matter, in proportion as it is more due to soul that the matter is nature than the other way round. For the timber too is bed and stool in that it is potentially these.

(8) The question may arise, in view of what has just been said, as to whether it belongs to natural science to speak about all soul or about some. For if about all, then no philosophy is left outside natural science. For the intellect 641b has the intelligibles as its object. So natural science would seek to know about everything; for it belongs to the same science to study intellect and the intelligible, if indeed they are correlative and if all correlatives are the object of the same study, just as it does with perception and the perceptibles.

The answer is that not all of the soul is an origin of movement, nor are all of its parts. Growth is originated by the same part as in plants, alteration by the perceptive part, and locomotion by some other part but not by the intellective; for locomotion is present in other animals too, but thought in none. Clearly therefore not all soul is to be spoken about; for not all soul is nature, but some part of it, either one part or several.

(*9*) A further reason why none of the abstract objects can be studied by natural science is that nature does everything *for the sake of* something. For as in the artefacts there is the art, so in things themselves there is evident another such origin and cause, which we grasp from the universe just as we grasp the hot and the cold. This is why it is more likely that the heavens have been brought into being by such a cause, if they have come into being, than the animals that are mortal. At any rate the ordered and the defined is far more apparent in the heavenly bodies than about us, while the inconstant and random is more apparent about the mortal bodies. Yet there are those who say that although each animal exists and came to be naturally, the heavens were constituted in this way by chance and spontaneity—in which there is not a sign of chance and disorder.

But we commonly say that "this is for the sake of that" wherever there is apparent some end which the movement reaches if nothing stands in the way. So it is evident that something of this sort exists (and it is precisely what we call *nature*). For what comes to be from each seed is certainly not the product of chance, but *this* comes from *this*; nor does any chance seed come from any chance body. The seed, then, is the origin and productive agent of what comes out of it. For these are natural: at any rate they grow naturally out of this. Yet still prior to this is that of which it is the seed; for the seed is a coming-to-be, but the end is a being. And still prior to both is that from which the seed is. For it is the seed in two ways, of that *out of* which it is and of that *of* which it is: it is the seed of that from which it came, e.g. a horse, and of that which will be out of it, e.g. a mule, not however in the same way but of each in the way we said. Further, the seed is potentially something; and we know 642a
how potentiality is related to actuality.

(*10*) There are then these two causes, the *for-the-sake-*

of-which and the *of-necessity*—for many things come to be because of necessity. Perhaps the question might arise as to what kind of necessity is meant by those who say "of necessity". For neither of the two modes defined in our philosophical treatises can be present. In things that have coming-to-be, however, there is the third kind. For we say that food is a necessary thing not according to either of those modes but in that it is impossible to be without it. This is as it were *ex hypothesi*. For just as there is a necessity that the axe be hard, since one must cut with it, and, if hard, that it be of bronze or iron, so too since the body is an instrument (for each of its parts is for the sake of something, and so is the body as a whole), therefore there is a necessity that it be *such* a thing and made of *such* things if that end is to be.

(*11*) Clearly[1] then there are two ways of causing, and our account should if possible arrive at both, or failing that at least try to make this clear; and all who fail to state this give virtually no account of nature. For nature is an origin more than matter is. Occasionally even Empedocles stumbles on it, led by the truth itself, and is compelled to say that the being and nature of a thing is its definition. For example, in expounding what bone is he does not say it is a particular one of the elements, nor two or three, nor all, but a definition of their mixture; clearly therefore flesh too and every other such part exists in the same way.

The reason why previous generations did not arrive at this way is that they lacked the notion of what-it-is-to-be and the defining of the being. Although Democritus was the first to touch upon it, it was not as something necessary to the study of nature but because he was carried away by the facts themselves. In Socrates' time, although this interest grew, the inquiry into nature ceased, and those who philosophized turned aside to the study of practical virtue and political science.

(*12*) Exposition should be as follows: for example,

[1] Reading *δῆλόν γε πειρᾶσθαι ποιεῖν*, ⟨*δῆλον*⟩, at 642a15.

breathing exists for the sake of *this*, while *that* comes to be of necessity because of *those*. Necessity signifies sometimes that if there is to be *that* for the sake of which, *these* must necessarily be present; and sometimes that this is their state and nature. For the hot necessarily goes out and comes in again when it meets resistance, and the air must flow in; so much is already necessitated. And when the inner hot beats back, 642b
in the cooling occurs the inflow of the outside air and the outflow. [This then is the manner of the investigation, and these and such are the things about which one must obtain the causes.]

CHAPTER 2

Some obtain the particular by dividing the genus into two differentiae. But this is in some respects not easy and in others impossible.

(*1*) For some things will have one differentia alone, the rest being superfluous, for example:

footed / *footless* OR[1] *footed* / *footless*
| |
two-footed *split-footed*

The latter differentia is valid by itself. Otherwise it is necessary to say the same thing many times.

(*2*) Further, it is correct to avoid splitting each kind, for example putting some birds in one division and others in another, as the written divisions have them; for there it comes about that some have been divided off with the water animals and others in another kind. Now this likeness has had a name put to it, *Bird*, and another has *Fish*. But others are unnamed, such as the blooded and the bloodless: no one name has been put to either of these. If therefore no animals of the same kind are to be split up, division into two must be fruitless; for this way of dividing necessarily separates

[1] 642b8: reading δίπουν ⟨ἢ⟩ σχιζόπουν (see note).

and splits. For some many-footed are among the land animals and others are among the water animals.

CHAPTER 3

(*3*) Further, it is necessary to divide by privation, and the dichotomists do so divide. But there is no differentia of a privation *qua* privation; for there cannot be species of what is not, for example of *footlessness* or the *featherless*, as there are of *featheredness* and of *feet*.

(*3a*) But the general differentia must have species, for otherwise what would make it a general differentia and not a particular one? Some differentiae certainly are general and have species, for example *featheredness*: the one feather is *unsplit*, the other *split*. And *footedness* similarly is *many-toed*, *two-toed* (the cloven-hoofed), and *toeless* and undivided (the solid-hoofed).

(*3b*) Now it is difficult enough to make a distribution even into differentiae such as the above, which possess species, in such a way as to include every sort of animal in them without having the same one in several, such as *feathered* and *featherless* (for the same animal exists as both, for example ant, glow-worm, and certain others). But it is most difficult of all, or impossible, to distribute into the bloodless kinds. For each differentia must belong to some
643a particular kind, and so its opposite must also. But if a single and indivisible species of being cannot belong to things differing in species, but will always be differentiated, as bird is from man (for their *two-footedness* is other and different), then if they are blooded the blood is different; otherwise the blood must be counted as no part of their being. But it will follow that one differentia belongs to two. If so, it is clear that a privation cannot be a differentia.

(*3c*) The differentiae will be equal in number to the indivisible animals, if it is true both that these are indivisible and that the differentiae are indivisible and if no differentia is common. But if one can belong not actually in common but indivisibly, clearly in virtue at any rate of its being common there are in the same class animals differing in species. So it is necessary, if the differentiae into which all the indivisibles fall are peculiar, that none of them should be common. Otherwise things that are other will enter the same differentia. But it is required that the same indivisible should not go now into one and now into another differentia in the division; that others should not go into the same; and that all should go into these. Plainly therefore one cannot obtain the indivisible species by dividing animals (or indeed any other kind) in the way the dichotomists do. For according to them too the last differentiae must be equal in number to all the specifically indivisible animals. For let there be a certain genus as follows: its first differentiae are the *white* ones, and of each side of these there are other differentiae, and so on down to the indivisibles; the final differentiae will be four or some other quantity obtained by doubling from one onwards, and that will be the number of the species.[1] It is the differentia in the matter that is the species. For just as there is no part of an animal without matter, so there is none that is only the matter; for it is not body irrespective of state that can be an animal or any part of one, as we have often said.

(*4*) Further, one should divide by what is in the being, and not by the essential accidents—as if one were to divide figures on the basis that some have their angles adding up to two right angles and others to more; for it is an accident of the triangle that it has its angles adding up to two right angles.

(*5*) Further, one should divide by opposites. For opposites

1

<table>
<tr><td colspan="5">genus</td></tr>
<tr><td colspan="4">white sub-genus</td><td rowspan="3"></td></tr>
<tr><td colspan="2">white *a*</td><td colspan="2">white *b*</td></tr>
<tr><td>sp.</td><td>sp.</td><td>sp.</td><td>sp.</td></tr>
</table>

are differentiated from each other, for example *whiteness* and *blackness*, *straightness* and *curvedness*. Therefore if one of two is differentiated, the division must be made by its opposite, not one by *swimming* and the other by *colour*.

(6) Nor again, in the case of the ensouled, should one divide by the common functions of body and soul, for
643b example *walkers* and *fliers* in the divisions mentioned above; for there are some kinds to which both belong, existing as fliers and as featherless, like the ant kind. And dividing by the *wild* and the *tame* would similarly seem to divide the same species. For practically all that are tame occur also as wild, for example men, horses, cattle, dogs in India, pigs, goats, sheep. Each of these, if it is not[1] homonymous, is undivided; and if these are one in species, *wild* and *tame* cannot be a differentiation.

(7) But in general this is the necessary result of dividing any sort of differentia by a single differentia. Rather one should try to take the animals by kinds in the way already shown by the popular distinction between *bird* kind and *fish* kind. Each of these has been marked off by many differentiae, not dichotomously. For by dichotomy either one cannot obtain them at all (for the same one falls into more than one division, and opposites fall into the same) or there will be only one differentia, and this either as a simple one or as a compound will be the final species. If on the other hand one does not take the differentia of a differentia, one can only make the division continuous in the way that one unifies speech by a connective. I mean the sort of thing that comes about if one divides off the *featherless* and the *feathered*, and among the *feathered* the *tame* and the *wild* or the *white* and the *black*; for *tame* or *white* is not a differentiation of *feathered* but begins another differentiation and is accidental here. This is why one should divide off the one kind straight away by many differentiae, in the way that we say. In this way too the privations will make a differentiation, whereas in dichotomy they will not.

[1] 643b7: reading μή for μέν (see note).

(*8*) It is in fact clear from the following that none of the particular species can be obtained by dividing the genus dichotomously as some have thought. The particulars divided off cannot have just one differentia, whether one takes them simple or compounded. I call them simple if they have no differentia, such as *toedness*, and compounded if they have, such as *the many-toed in relation to the toed*. For this compounded sense is intended by the continuity of the differentiae proceeding from the genus according to the division, showing that the whole is a one; but the manner of expression makes it seem that the final differentia is the only one, for example *many-toed* or *biped*, and that *footed* and *many-footed* are superfluous. And clearly there cannot be more than one such differentia; for by proceeding continuously one reaches the last differentia (though not the final differentia which is the species). And this is either the *toed* alone or the whole compound, if one divides off man, for example, putting *footed* with *biped* or[1] *toed*. If man were merely a thing with toes, this method would have shown it to be his one differentia. But since in fact he is not, he must necessarily have many differentiae not under one division. Yet more than one cannot belong to the same object under one dichotomy, but one dichotomy must end with one at a time. So it is impossible to obtain any of the particular animals by dichotomous division.

CHAPTER 4

The question arises why there is no popular designation which includes both the water animals and the fliers under one higher name, denoting a single genus which embraces both. For they have certain affections in common, and so have all the other animals. Nevertheless they have been rightly distinguished in this way. For all kinds that differ by

[1] 644^{a}5: reading δίπουν ⟨ἢ⟩ σχιζόπουν (see note at 642^{b}8).

degree and by *the more and the less* have been linked under one kind, while all that are analogous have been separated. I mean for example that bird differs from bird by *the more* or by degree (one is long-feathered, another is short-feathered), but fishes differ from bird by analogy (what is feather in one is scale in the other). But to do this for all is not easy, since the similarity in most animals is by analogy.

Since beings are the immediate forms, and these are formally undifferentiated, e.g. Socrates, Coriscus, we must either first state their general attributes or say the same thing many times, as we mentioned above. But the general attributes are common; for it is those that belong to more than one that we call general. The question is which should be our subject. For in so far as a being is what is indivisible in form, there would be most force in a separate survey (if possible) of those that are particular and formally indivisible—as of man, so of bird (for this is a genus possessing species) but of *every sort* of bird among the indivisibles, like sparrow or crane or such. But in so far as it will result in speaking frequently about the same affection because it belongs in common to more than one species, to this extent it is somewhat absurd and lengthy to
644b speak about each separately. Perhaps then the right course is to speak of some affections in common by genera, wherever the genera have been satisfactorily marked off by popular usage and possess both a single nature in common and species not far separated in them—bird and fish and any other that is unnamed but like the genus embraces the species that are in it; but wherever they are not like this, to speak of particulars, for example about man or any other such.

The genera have been marked off mainly by the shapes of the parts and of the whole body, wherever they bear a similarity, as the birds do when compared among themselves, and the fishes, cephalopods, and testaceans. For their parts differ not on the basis of analogous likeness, as bone in man is to spine in fish, but rather by the bodily affections such as largeness and smallness, softness and hardness, smoothness and roughness, and such—in general by *the more and less.*

[We have now said how the investigation into nature should be appraised, and in what way the survey of these matters may be most direct and easy; also concerning division, by what procedure the species can be usefully obtained, and why dichotomy is in some respects impossible and in others empty. Having clarified these matters, let us speak of what comes next in order, beginning as follows.]

CHAPTER 5

Of all beings naturally composed, some are ungenerated and imperishable for the whole of eternity, but others are subject to coming-to-be and perishing. It has come about that in relation to the former, which possess value—indeed divinity—the studies we can make are less, because both the starting-points of the inquiry and the things we long to know about present extremely few appearances to observation. We are better equipped to acquire knowledge about the perishable plants and animals because they grow beside us: much can be learned about each existing kind if one is willing to take sufficient pains. Both studies have their attractions. Though we grasp only a little of the former, yet because the information is valuable we gain more pleasure than from everything around us, just as a small and random glimpse of those we love pleases us more than seeing many other things large and in detail. But the latter, because the 645a
information about them is better and more plentiful, take the advantage in knowledge. Also, because they are closer to us and belong more to our nature, they have their own compensations in comparison with the philosophy concerned with the divine things. And since we have completed the account of our views concerning these, it remains to speak about animal nature, omitting nothing if possible whether of lesser or greater value. For even in the study of animals

unattractive to the senses, the nature that fashioned them offers immeasurable pleasures in the same way[1] to those who can learn the causes and are naturally lovers of wisdom. It would be unreasonable, indeed absurd, to enjoy studying their representations on the grounds that we thereby study the art that fashioned them (painting or sculpture), but not to welcome still more the study of the actual things composed by nature, at least when we can survey their causes. Therefore we must avoid a childish distaste for examining the less valued animals. For in all natural things there is something wonderful. And just as Heraclitus is said to have spoken to the visitors, who were wanting to meet him but stopped as they were approaching when they saw him warming himself at the oven—he kept telling them to come in and not worry, "for there are gods here too"—so we should approach the inquiry about each animal without aversion, knowing that in all of them there is something natural and beautiful. For the non-random, the *for-something's-sake*, is present in the works of nature most of all, and the end for which they have been composed or have come to be occupies the place of the beautiful. If anyone has thought the study of the other animals valueless, he should think the same about himself; for one cannot without considerable distaste view the parts that compose the human kind, such as blood, flesh, bones, veins, and the like. Just as in any discussion of parts or equipment we must not think that it is the matter to which attention is being directed or which is the object of the discussion, but rather the conformation as a whole (a house, for example, rather than bricks, mortar, and timber), in the same way we must think that a discussion of nature is about the composition and the being as a whole, not about parts that can never occur in separation from the being they belong to.

645b It is necessary first to divide off, in relation to each kind, the attributes that belong essentially to all the animals, and

[1] 645a8: reading ὁμοίως.

then to try to divide off their causes. Now we have said before that many belong in common to many animals, some simply (for example feet, feathers, scales, and affections too in the same way), but others analogously. (By 'analogously' I mean that some have lungs while others have not lungs but something else instead which is to them what lungs are to the former; and some have blood while others have the analogous part that possesses the same capability as blood does for the blooded.) To speak separately about each particular will, as we said before, often result in repetition when we speak of every attribute: the same ones belong to many. Let this then be determined so.

Since every instrument is for the sake of something, and each bodily part is for the sake of something, and what they are for the sake of is an activity, it is plain that the body too as a whole is composed for the sake of a full activity. For sawing has not come to be for the sake of the saw, but the saw for the sawing; for sawing is a kind of using. Consequently the body too is in a way for the sake of the soul, and the parts are for the sake of the functions in relation to which each has naturally grown. Therefore we must first state the activities, both those common to all and those that are generic and those that are specific. (I call them common when they belong to all animals, generic when they belong to animals whose differences among each other are seen to be in degree. For example, I speak generically of 'bird' but specifically of 'man' and of every animal that has no differentia in respect of its general definition. What they have in common some have by analogy, some generically, some specifically.)

Now where activities are for the sake of other activities, clearly the parts of which they are the activities are set apart in the same way as the activities. Similarly if some activities are prior and exist as the end of others, each part whose activity is such will have the same priority. And thirdly, the things whose existence necessitates attributes. (By 'affections and activities' I mean generation, growth, coition, waking,

sleep, locomotion, and all other such attributes of animals. By 'parts' I mean nose, eye, and the face as a whole, each
646a of which is called a member; and it is the same with the other parts.)

So much then for the manner of the investigation. And we should try to state the causes in respect both of the common and of the peculiar attributes, beginning, in the way that we have made clear, first with what is first.

DE GENERATIONE ANIMALIUM I

[Now that we have spoken about the other parts of animals, 715[a] both in common terms and separately about the parts (*Chap. 1*) peculiar to each kind, stating in what way each is due to this sort of cause, namely *for the sake of something*—for we have postulated four causes: the *for the sake of which as end* and the *definition of the being* (these should be taken more or less as one thing) and third and fourth the *matter* and that from which comes the *beginning of the movement*—and having spoken about the other three causes, for the definition and that for the sake of which as end are the same thing, and the matter for animals is their parts (the non-homoeomerous parts for every whole animal, the homoeomerous parts for the non-homoeomerous, and those bodies that we call elements for the homoeomerous), it remains for us to speak about the parts that contribute to generation in animals, which still await clarification, and about the source of the moving cause. To inquire about the latter and about the generation of each animal is in a way the same inquiry; which is why our exposition has brought them together, putting these parts at the end of our account of the parts, and the beginning of our account of generation next after them.]

Some animals are produced from a coupling of male and female, among such kinds as have male and female—for not all have. Among the blooded kinds, in all but a few the male on the one hand and the female on the other hand are perfected. But among the bloodless, while some have male and female in such a way that they generate the same kind, others generate offspring that are not in fact the same kind: such are all that come not from coupling animals but from rotting earth and residues. Speaking generally, (*a*) male and female exist in all animals capable of locomotion, whether

by swimming or flying or walking, not only in the blooded kinds but in certain bloodless kinds too. In some of the latter
715b they exist throughout the whole kind, for example in the cephalopods and the crustaceans; but in the insect kind they exist only in the majority. And of these last, all that come from coupling of animals of their own kind also generate according to their kind; but all that come not from animals but from matter that is rotting generate a kind different from themselves, and the offspring is neither male nor female: such are some of the insects. That this is so is reasonable. For if those that do not come from animals went on to produce animals themselves by coupling, then if the offspring were of the same kind the parents ought also to have been produced like this in the first place (this is a reasonable claim, for it is what we see happening in the other animals), but if the offspring were unlike them but able to couple, then from them in turn would come a different nature of animal, and from these in turn some other, and this would be going on without limit. But nature flees from the unlimited; for the unlimited is incomplete, but nature always seeks an end.

(*b*) In those without locomotion (like the testaceans and those that live by growing on something), because their being is almost like plants there is no male and female any more than in the plants; but they have come to be called male and female in virtue of resemblance and analogy, for they have a small differentiation of this sort. Among the plants too there are in the same kind of tree some that are fruit-bearing and some that do not bear themselves but contribute to the concocting of the others' fruit, as occurs with the fig and caprifig.

(*c*) It is the same with plants. Some come from seed, others as though by a spontaneous act of nature. The latter come from rotting earth or from rotting parts in plants: for some are not constituted separately by themselves but are produced on other trees, for example the mistletoe. [Now
716a plants must be studied separately by themselves.]

(Chap. 2) With regard to the generation of the other animals, we must speak of each as suits the course of the exposition, linking it with what has been said. Now in accordance with what we said, the male and the female might be considered among the chief sources of generation, the male as containing the source of the movement and generation, the female that of the matter. And this will seem most likely if one considers how the seed is produced and from where; for, accepting that animals produced naturally are constituted out of seed, we must not omit to observe *how* this comes to be produced from the male and from the female. For it is in virtue of the fact that such a part is secreted from the male and the female, and that the secretion is in them and out of them, that therefore the male and the female are sources of generation. Male is what we call an animal that generates into another, female that which generates into itself. That is why in the universe as a whole the earth's nature is thought of as female and mother, while the sky and sun or such others are called begetters and fathers.

Male and female differ by definition in having different capabilities, and by appearance in certain parts. They differ by definition in that the male is that which can generate into another, as was said above, while the female is that which generates into itself and out of which the generated offspring is produced while present within the generator. Since they are distinguished by capability and by particular function, and since there is need of organs for every performance of function, and the organs for the capabilities are the parts of the body, there must be parts both for producing young and for coupling, and these parts must be different from each other; it is in this respect that the male will differ from the female. For although male and female are predicated of the animal as a whole, nevertheless it is not male or female in respect of all of itself but in respect of a particular capability and a particular part, just as it is a seeing animal and a walking animal, and this is also evident by appearance. Such are in fact the parts which in the female

are called the uterus and in the male are those associated with testes and genitals in all blooded animals (some of them have testes while the others have channels of this sort).
716b There are differences between male and female also in all bloodless animals that have this opposition. And in the blooded animals the parts for mating differ in shape. But we must recognize that if a small source is disturbed, many of the things after the source usually change with it. This is clear in the case of castrated animals: although only the generative part is destroyed, almost the whole shape of the animal changes with it to such an extent that it looks female or not far short of that, showing that it is in respect of no ordinary part and no ordinary capability that the animal is male or female. Plainly then the male and the female are shown to be sources: at any rate many things change too when those parts change in virtue of which they are male and female, indicating that a source is being altered.

(*Chap. 3*) The arrangement of the parts associated with testes and uterus is not the same in all blooded animals. First, those associated with testes in males. Some blooded animals lack testes altogether, for example the fishes and the snakes, but have two spermatic channels only. Others, while having testes, have them inside the lower part of the back in the region of the kidneys, and from each of them a channel as in those that lack testes, the two channels uniting as also in those. Such are all birds together with those oviparous quadrupeds that take in air and possess lungs, for they too all have the testes inside the lower part of the back and two channels from them like the snakes, for example lizards and tortoises and all the horny-scaled animals. The viviparous animals on the other hand all have the testes in front, but some have them inside at the end of the belly, for example the dolphin, and not channels but a penis leading from them to the outside, as in oxen; others have them outside, some hanging free as in man, some at the fundament as in pigs. [A more precise clarification has been made about them in the *Historia Animalium*.]

The uterus is in two sections in all animals, just as the male testes are always two. Some have it by the genitals, as do women and all that are viviparous within themselves as well as externally, and all fishes that are externally ovi- 717a parous. Others have it by the diaphragm, as do all the birds and the viviparous fishes. The uterus is bifurcated also in the crustaceans and cephalopods, for[1] the membranes enclosing their so-called eggs are uterine. It is least distinct in the poulps, so that it looks single; but the reason for this is that the mass of the body is alike all over. It is bifurcated, again, in those insects that have some size; in the smaller ones it is not clearly visible, because of the smallness of the body. [This then is the arrangement of the above-mentioned animal parts.]

With regard to the differentiation of spermatic organs in *(Chap. 4)* males, if one is to study the reasons why they are there, one must first grasp the end for which the testes are constituted. Now if nature does everything either because it is necessary or because it is better, then this part too must be because of one or the other. That it is not necessary for generation is evident: for it would be present in all that generate, but as it is neither the snakes nor the fishes have testes (for they have been seen coupling and with the channels full of semen). It remains then that it is for the better in some way. Now it is true that most animals' function is virtually nothing but seed and fruit, like plants. But just as in the case of the nutritional parts the animals with straight intestines are more impetuous over their desire for food, so too those that have no testes but only channels, or have testes but have them within, are all hastier over performing coition. And in those that need to be more restrained, just as in the other case the intestines are not straight, so here the channels have convolutions tending to prevent their desire from being impetuous or hasty. And the testes are contrived in a way conducive to this; for they make the movement of the spermatic residue less continuous.

[1] 717a4: reading τὰ γὰρ with most MSS. and edd.

They do so (*a*) in the vivipara, for example in horses and the like and in man, by preserving the doubling-back of the channels [the manner of this should be studied in the *Historia Animalium*]. For the testes are no part of the channels but are attached, like the stones that weavers fasten to the 717b warp. When they are removed the channels are drawn up inside, and so castrated animals cannot generate, as they could if they were not drawn up; there has been a case of a bull that mated immediately after castration and impregnated the cow because the channels were not yet drawn up.

(*b*) In birds and oviparous quadrupeds the testes take in the spermatic residue, so that its emission is slower than in fishes. It is plain in the case of birds; for at the mating season their testes get much larger, and in those that mate at one season the testes are so small when this time has passed that they are practically invisible, though in the season they are very large. Now those that have internal testes are quicker at mating, for those that have them outside do not emit the seed until they have drawn up the testes. (*Chap.* 5) Further, whereas the quadrupeds have the organ for coition, since it is possible for them to have it, birds and footless animals cannot have it because the former have their legs up by the middle of the belly and the latter have no legs at all, while the nature of the penis is connected with the legs and its position is there (this is why in coupling there occurs the tension of the legs; for the organ is sinewy and the nature of the legs is also sinewy). And so, since they cannot have this, they must either not have testes or not have them there; for those that have them there have both penis and testes in the same position.

[Further, in those at least that have the testes outside, it is on the heating of the penis through the movement that the seed comes forward after being collected, not because it is ready on immediate contact as in fishes.]

[All the vivipara have the testes in front, either inside or outside, except the hedgehog. It alone has them in the lower part of the back, for the same reason as the birds: their coupling must be quick, because unlike the other quadrupeds they do not mount upon the back but unite upright because of the spines.]

[We have now said why those that have testes have them, and why some have them outside and others inside.]

Those that lack testes, as we have said, do so not because (*Chap. 6* it is good but only because it is necessary, and also because their mating must be quick. Such is the nature of the fishes and of the snakes. The fishes mate by falling alongside, and 718a are quickly detached. For just as men and all such must hold their breath to emit semen, so in fishes it depends on their not taking in sea water, and they are apt to perish if they do not take it in. Therefore they must not concoct the seed during coition like the footed vivipara, but the warmth of the season concocts the seed and they have it collected so that on touching each other they do not concoct it but emit it already concocted. This is why they have no testes but channels that are straight and simple, like a short section that the quadrupeds have near the testes. For in the doubling-back of the channel one section contains blood and the other is bloodless; the latter receives the fluid, which is already seed when it passes through it, so that when the seed has arrived there these animals too are quickly detached. In the fishes the whole channel is of the same sort as the second section of the doubling-back in man and such animals.

On the other hand the snakes mate by coiling round each (*Chap. 7*) other, and they have no testes nor penis as we said before. They have no penis because they have no legs; but they have no testes because of their length, and instead they have channels like the fishes. For since their nature is elongated, if there were further delay in the region of testes the semen would get cold because of the slowness. This actually happens in animals whose penis is large: they are less fertile than the moderate-sized, because seed that is cold is not fertile, and it gets cold if it has too far to go. [We have now said why some animals have testes and others have not.]

The snakes twine round each other because of the awkwardness of lying alongside. For the section at which they fit together is short, and they are too long to fit exactly with ease. And so, since they have no parts to grip with, instead they use the flexibility of the body by coiling round each other. This is why they seem slower to separate than the fishes, not only because of the length of the channels but also because of this elaborate method.

(*Chap. 8*) In females the *arrangement* of the uterine parts may seem puzzling, for there are many contradictions among them. Not all the vivipara have the same arrangement, but man and the footed vivipara all have the uterus below by the 718b genitals, while the viviparous selachians have it above by the diaphragm. Nor again are the ovipara alike, but the fishes have it below like man and the viviparous quadrupeds, while the birds and all oviparous quadrupeds have it above. Nevertheless these contradictions are actually in accordance with reason. For in the first place the egg-layers lay eggs differently. Some lay them unperfected, for example the fishes whose eggs are perfected and take on increase outside. The reason is that they are prolific: this is their function, as it is of plants. If they brought their young to perfection within themselves, they would have to be few in number; but as it is, they get so many that each of the two sections of the uterus looks like an egg, at any rate in the small fry. For these are the most prolific, just as is the case with others that have a nature analogous to them among both plants and animals, because the bodily increase is diverted to the seed in them. On the other hand birds and oviparous quadrupeds lay perfected eggs, which must be hard-skinned for protection (they are soft-skinned so long as they are increasing in size). The shell is produced by heat evaporating the moisture out of the earthy material, and so the place where this is to happen must be hot. Such is the region of the diaphragm, where the nutriment is concocted. So if the eggs must be in the uterus, the uterus must be by the diaphragm in those that lay their eggs perfected; but in those that lay them unperfected it must be below, where it will be on their way. Also the natural place of the uterus is below rather than above, provided that no other function of nature prevents this; for its terminus is below, and where the terminus is the function is too, and the uterus is where its function is.

The vivipara too differ from each other. Some produce live young not only externally but also within themselves, for example men, horses, dogs, and all that have hair, and also among water animals the dolphins and whales and such cetaceans. On the other hand the selachians and the vipers, although externally viviparous, produce eggs within themselves first. They produce a perfected egg, for only so is the animal generated from the egg, never from an unperfected one. But they do not produce the eggs externally, because they are cold by nature and not hot as some say. At any rate the eggs they generate are soft-skinned; for because they have little heat nature does not dry out the last part of them. Since then they are cold they generate soft-skinned eggs, and since the eggs are soft-skinned they do not generate them (719a) externally, for they would be destroyed. When the animal is produced from the egg, in most respects it happens in the same way as in chicks. The eggs descend below and animals are produced near the genitals just as in those that are immediately viviparous from the beginning. This is why such animals have the uterus unlike both the vivipara and the ovipara, because they participate in both kinds: all selachians have it both by the diaphragm and extending below. [The arrangement of this and the other kinds of uterus should be studied in the *Dissections* and the *Historia*.] So because they are egg-layers of perfected eggs they have the uterus above, but because they produce live young they have it below, thus participating in both.

(*Chap. 9*) (*Chap. 10*) (*Chap. 11*)

But those that are immediately viviparous all have the uterus below, for no function of nature prevents it nor do they generate in two stages. Besides, animals cannot be produced near the diaphragm; for the embryos necessarily have weight and movement, which this vital region could not tolerate. Further, there would of necessity be difficulty in birth because of the length of the passage; as it is, if women in childbirth draw up the uterus by yawning or some such action they have a difficult birth. And even when empty the uterus causes stifling if pressed upwards; for a uterus that is to hold an animal must be stronger, and therefore all of this sort are fleshy while those by the diaphragm are membranous. And this is clearly the case in the very animals that perform the double generation: they get the eggs above and to one side, but the animals in the lower part of the uterus. [We have now said why the arrangement of the uterine parts is contradictory in certain animals, and in general why some have the uterus below and others above by the diaphragm.]

(*Chap. 12*) As for the reason why the uterus is internal in all animals while the testes are internal in some but external in others, the uterus is internal in all because it contains the developing creature which needs protection and shelter and concoction, and the outside of the body is vulnerable and cold. The testes on the other hand are external in some and internal
719b in others because they too need shelter and a cover, both for protection and for the concocting of the seed; for if they are chilled and stiffened the animal cannot draw them up and emit the semen. That is why all that have the testes in the open have a shelter of skin called the scrotum; but all whose skin has a nature opposed to this use because of its hardness, so that it is not enwrapping and soft and skinlike (for example those with the fishy type of skin and the horny-scaled), must have them internally. Hence they are internal in the dolphins and in all cetaceans that have testes, and in the horny-scaled oviparous quadrupeds. Birds' skin too is hard and consequently does not fit well to a size so as to wrap it round, so that this is a reason applicable to all these animals in addition to those previously mentioned as arising from the necessary circumstances of their coition. And for the same reason both the elephant and the hedgehog have the testes internally, for their skin too is not well adapted to have the sheltering part separate.

The *position* in which the uterus lies is also contrary in the internal vivipara as compared with the external ovipara, and among the latter in those that have the uterus below as compared with those that have it by the diaphragm (for example in fishes as compared with birds and oviparous quadrupeds), and again in those that generate in both ways, producing eggs within themselves but live young into the open. Those that are viviparous both within themselves and externally have the uterus in the belly, for example man, ox, dog, and the other such animals; for it is expedient for the embryo's protection and growth that no weight be pressing on the uterus. (*Chap. 13*) Moreover these all have a channel for excreting the dry residue different from that for the wet. This is why all such animals both male and female have pudenda, through which is discharged the wet residue and also the seed in males and the foetus in females. This channel is above and in front of that for excreting the dry nutriment.

But all ovipara that lay an unperfected egg, for example the oviparous fishes, have the uterus not under the belly but in the lower part of the back. For the egg's growth does not prevent this, since the perfecting and progress of the growing egg takes place outside, and the channel is the same as for the dry nutriment in those without a generative pudendum, that is, all ovipara even including those with a bladder like the tortoises. For the double channel is for generation, not for the discharge of the wet residue; but since the nature of the seed is wet, the residue of wet nutriment has shared the same channel. This is clear from the fact that, although all animals bear seed, not all produce residue that is wet. Since then both the male spermatic channels and the female uterus must be fixed and not wandering, and the fixing must be either to the front of the body or to the back, the vivipara have the uterus in front because of the embryos while the ovipara have it behind in the lower part of the back.

All that are externally viviparous after producing eggs within themselves have it in both ways because they participate in both, being both viviparous and oviparous. The upper part of the uterus, where the eggs are produced under the diaphragm, is behind in the lower part of the back, but the lower part of it as it extends is in the belly, for at that stage they are producing live animals. But they too have one passage for both dry residue and coition, for none of these has a separate pudendum, as we said before.

The male channels, both in those that have testes and in those that have not, are placed like the uterus in ovipara: all have them attached at the back in the region of the spine. For they must not wander but stay fixed, and such is the region behind: it provides continuity and stability. Now in those that have the testes inside, the channels are fixed at once; and it is the same with those that have them outside. Then they join into one towards the region of the penis. In dolphins too the channels are similarly arranged, but they have the testes concealed under the abdominal cavity. [We
720b have now said how the parts contributing to generation are positioned, and for what reasons.]

(*Chap. 14*) In the other animals, the bloodless, the arrangement of the parts contributing to generation differs both from the blooded animals and among themselves. There are four kinds remaining: first the crustaceans, second the cephalopods, third the insects, and fourth the testaceans—but there is no certainty about all of the latter, though it is evident that the majority do not copulate; the way they are constituted is to be stated later.

The crustaceans couple like the retromingent animals, one on its back and one on its front fitting the tail parts together; for the tails with their attachment of long flaps prevent mounting front to back. The males have narrow channels for semen, and the females have a membranous uterus, divided along each side of the gut, in which the egg is produced.

(*Chap. 15*) The cephalopods intertwine in the region of the mouth, pushing at each other and spreading their tentacles. They must intertwine in this way, because nature has bent back the outlet of the residue and brought it round beside the mouth [as we have said before in the accounts of the parts]. In each of these animals the female clearly has a uterine part. An egg is formed, which at first is not distinctly divided but afterwards separates out into many eggs, each of which is laid unperfected as in the oviparous fishes. The channel belonging to the uterine part is the same as for the residue in these animals, as well as in the crustaceans; †it is where they discharge the ink through the channel. This is†[1] in the under part of the body where the mantle stands open and the sea goes in. This is why the male couples with the female at this part; for if he does emit something, whether seed or part or some sort of capability, coition must be at the uterine channel. But the putting of the male's tentacle through the female funnel in the case of poulps, by means of which the fishermen say they mate by tentacle, is done for the sake of intertwining and not for use as an organ of generation; for it is outside the channel and the body. Sometimes the cephalopods couple also by mounting on to the back; but it (721^{a}) has not yet been observed whether this is for generation or for some other reason.

(*Chap. 16*) Of the insects which couple, some are themselves generated out of animals synonymous with themselves just as the blooded animals are, for example the locusts, cicadas, spiders, wasps, ants. Others couple and generate, but do not produce a kind like themselves but only grubs; and they themselves are not produced from animals but from rotting liquids or in some cases solids, for example the fleas, flies, beetles. Others neither come from animals nor couple, like gnats, mosquitoes, and many such kinds.[2]

The males are not seen with channels for semen, and generally speaking the male does not put any part into the female, but the female puts a part up into the male from below. This has been observed in many cases [and similarly about the mounting], and the opposite in a few cases; but

[1] $720^{b}26$–7: the words between daggers are doubtful, but the version translated (Lulofs O.C.T.) agrees with *P.A.* IV. $679^{a}1$–4, *H.A.* IV. $524^{a}12$, $^{b}20$.

[2] $721^{a}11$–12 *τῶν . . . ἐστίν* transposed to 17 after *συνεώραται*.

not enough has been seen over all to make a distinction by kinds in this respect.

In most of those that couple the females are bigger than the males. This is largely true too of most oviparous fishes and oviparous quadrupeds; the females are bigger than the males because it is expedient in view of the bulk produced in them by the eggs in gestation. In the female insects the part analogous to the uterus is divided along the gut, as in the others too, and in it the embryos are produced. This is clear in the locusts and in all insects of some size, among those that naturally couple; most insects are too small to observe.

[This then is the arrangement of the animals' organs of generation, about which we did not speak before. Of the homoeomerous parts we omitted semen and milk, about which it is now opportune to speak, about semen now and about milk in what follows.]

(*Chap. 17*) For some animals evidently emit seed, for example all that are blooded by nature, but it is not clear in which of the two ways the insects and cephalopods act. We must therefore consider whether all males emit seed, or not all; and, if not all, why some do but others do not; also whether
721b the females contribute any seed or not, and if not seed, whether they contribute nothing at all or something that is not seed. We must consider further, in the case of those that emit seed, what they contribute by means of the seed to generation, and altogether what is the nature of the seed and of the fluid called menses in those animals that emit this.

It seems that they all come from seed, and the seed from those that generate. Therefore it is part of the same argument whether both male and female emit seed or one only, and whether it comes from all the body or not from all; for it is reasonable, if it does not come from all the body, that it may not come from both the generators either. Since some say that it comes from all the body, we must first examine how this matter stands.

There are roughly four pieces of evidence that might be adduced to prove that the seed comes away from each part.

(1) The intensity of the pleasure. For the same affection becomes pleasanter if there is more of it, and that which occurs in all the parts is more than that which occurs in one or a few. (2) The fact that mutilated parents have mutilated offspring. For it is said that because the part is missing no seed comes from it, and that the part from which no seed comes is consequently not produced. (3) Likenesses to parents. For just as offspring resemble them in the body as a whole, so they do part for part; therefore if the reason for the whole's likeness is that the seed came from the whole, the reason for the parts' likeness must be that something came from each part. (4) It would also seem reasonable that just as there is some first thing in the whole out of which the whole develops, so there is in each part; hence if the whole has a seed, each part must have a seed of its own.

These opinions are also plausibly supported by such evidence as the following. Children are born resembling not only their parents' innate characteristics but also their acquired ones. There have been parents with wound-scars, some of whose children got the impression of the scar in the same places. In Chalcedon a man with a tattooed arm had a son on whom a trace of the picture showed, though it was run together and not clearly articulated.

These are roughly the main grounds for believing that the seed comes from all the body. But if we test the argument, we 722a
come rather to the opposite opinion. For it is not difficult to (*Chap. 18*)
refute what has been said, and in addition other consequences follow which are impossible. First, to show that resemblance is no indication that seed comes from all the body, there is the fact that resemblance occurs in voice, nails and hair, and movement, but from these nothing comes away. And there are some things that men do not have by the time they generate, for example grey hair or a beard. Further, there are resemblances to distant ancestors from whom nothing has come; these resemblances occur at intervals of several generations, for example the woman at Elis who had intercourse with the Ethiopian—it was not her

daughter but her daughter's son that became Ethiopian. And the same argument holds of plants; for clearly their seed too would be produced from all the parts. But many parts are absent in some cases, others could be removed, and others are later growths. Further, the seed does not come also from the seed-case; yet this too is produced in the same form.

Further, does the seed come only from each homoeomerous part like flesh, bone, sinew, or does it come also from the non-homoeomerous like face and hand? If from the former only, we object that resemblance to parents lies rather in the latter (the non-homoeomerous, like face, hands, feet); if then the latter's resemblance is not due to seed's coming from all, why should the former's resemblance be due to seed's coming from all and not to another cause? But if it comes only from the non-homoeomerous, then it is not from all parts. And it ought to come rather from the homoeomerous, because they are prior and the non-homoeomerous are composed of them, and just as resemblances occur in face and hands so they do also in flesh and nails. But if it comes from both, what could be the manner of generation? For the non-homoeomerous are composed of the homoeomerous, so that to come from the former would be to come from the latter *and* from the composition; in the same way if something came from a written word, then if it came from all the word it must come from each syllable, and if from them then it must come from the letters *and* from the composition. So if flesh and bones are in fact constituted of fire and such elements, the seed would come rather from the elements.
722b For how can it come from the composition? Yet without the composition the resemblance would not be there. If the composition is fashioned by something later, the resemblance must be caused by that thing and not by the coming of seed from all the body.

Further, if the parts are separate from each other in the seed, how are they alive? Yet if they were connected they would be a little animal.

And what of the parts belonging to the pudenda? For what comes from male and from female will not be alike.

Further, if it comes equally from all of both parents, two animals are produced; for they will have every part of each parent. Therefore, if this is the right way to speak, Empedocles' account seems the most consistent with it (just to this extent; but if a different way is right, his account is not good). For he says that the male and the female contain as it were a tally, and that neither produces a whole,

'But sundered is limbs' nature, part in man's . . .'

Otherwise why do not the females generate from themselves, if in fact the seed comes from all the body and they have a receptacle?

But, as it seems, it either does not come from all the body, or comes in the way that Empedocles says, not the same things from each parent, and this is why they need intercourse. Yet this too is impossible. For they cannot survive and be ensouled if "sundered", any more than when they are large, as Empedocles generates them in the period of "Love"—

'Where first there sprouted many neckless heads'

—and then says that the parts grew together. But this is plainly impossible. For without soul and without some kind of life they could not survive; nor, if they were like several living animals, could they grow together so as to become one instead. Yet this is what follows from asserting that seed comes from all the body: what happened then in the earth in the period of Love must on this view happen in the body. (For the parts cannot be *produced* already connected and go off together to one place.) Then again, how are the upper and lower and right and left and front and back parts "sundered"? All this is illogical.

Further, some parts are distinguished by capability and others by affections—the non-homoeomerous by their ability to do something (for example, tongue and hand), the homoeomerous by hardness and softness and the other affections of this sort. So they are not blood or flesh irre-

spective of their state. Clearly therefore that which has come away cannot be synonymous with the parts, blood from
723a blood or flesh from flesh. But if it is something else and blood is produced from it, the cause of resemblance will not be the coming of seed from all parts, as those who assert this say; for it is enough that it should come from one part alone, if in fact blood is produced not from blood. Why should not all be produced from one? Their argument seems to be the same as that of Anaxagoras, in holding that none of the homoeomerous parts comes into being: except that he asserted it of "all things" while they assert it in the generation of animals. Secondly, in what way will these parts that have come from all the body be made bigger? For Anaxagoras is consistent in saying that flesh from the nutriment comes to the flesh. But if they do not say this, and yet assert that seed comes from all, how do they account for something growing through the addition of something different, unless that which is added changes? But now if that which is added can change, why is not the seed right from the outset such that blood and flesh can be produced from it without itself being blood and flesh? They cannot of course say that later growth is brought about by admixture, as wine is increased by pouring in water. For each part would have been itself most at the beginning while still unmixed; but in fact it is later on that it is flesh and bone and each other part. And to assert that some of the seed is sinew and bone is really going too far.

Again, if male and female are differentiated during gestation as Empedocles says—

> 'Poured into clean vessels, some become women
> Having encountered cold . . .'

—however that may be, it is evident that just as men and women change from infertile to fertile so they change from female-bearing to male-bearing, which suggests that the cause does not lie in the seed's coming or not coming from all, but in the proportion or disproportion between what comes from the woman and what from the man, or some other such cause. If we are to put it so,[1] then it is clear that the female is not the result of the seed's coming from a particular thing, and consequently that the characteristic male or female part does not come from a particular thing either—if it is true that the same seed can become either male or female, implying that the part is not in the seed. What difference then is there between saying it of this part and saying it of the others? For if seed is not produced even from the uterus, the same argument will apply to the other parts too.

Further, certain animals are produced neither from the same kind nor from a different kind, for example the flies and the kinds called fleas; and from these come animals that are not of like nature but a sort of grub. Clearly offspring that are of a different kind are not produced from seed that comes from every part; for they would be like them if likeness is a sign that seed comes from every part.

Further, from one coition certain animals generate several young (and plants do so universally, for clearly they bear all their annual fruit as the result of one movement). Yet how could they, if the seed were secreted from all the body? For one coition and one separating-off of seed must produce one secretion. It could not be divided up in the uterus, for by then the division would be as it were from an animal and not from seed.

Further, plant cuttings bear seed from themselves; clearly then before they were cut, too, they bore the fruit from the same amount of plant, and the seed did not come from all the plant.

But a stronger proof than all of these is what we have sufficiently observed in insects. For if not in all, at any rate in most cases the female in mating extends a part of itself into the male. (This is why they mate in this way, as we said before: the ones underneath are seen inserting a part into the ones above, not in all but in most of those observed.) This must show that even in those males which emit semen

[1] 723^{a}31: comma after οὕτως.

generation is not caused by the seed's coming from all the body, but in some other way which must be considered later. For even if it were the case that it came from all the body, as they assert, they ought not to claim that it comes from *everything* but only from that which does the fashioning, as it were from the carpenter but not from the matter. But by their account it might as well come from the shoes too; for usually a son like father is shod like father.

The reason why pleasure is intensified in sexual intercourse is not that the seed comes from all but that there is strong titillation. That is why if this intercourse takes place often,
724a the enjoyment becomes less for those who consort. Further, the pleasureableness occurs where the completion is; but it ought to be in each part, and not simultaneously but earlier in some and later in others.

Mutilated offspring come from mutilated parents for the same reason that they resemble them. But mutilated parents also have unmutilated offspring, just as some are unlike them. The cause of these things is to be studied later, for the one problem is the same as the other.

Further if the female does not emit seed, by the same argument it does not come from all. And if it does not come from all, it would not be inconsistent that it should not come from the female but that the female should be a cause of generation in some other way. This is the next matter to examine, now that it is clear that the seed is not secreted from all the parts.

As starting-point both of this inquiry and of what follows, the first thing to grasp about seed is *what it is*. For so we shall be better able to study both its functions and the concomitant facts.

To be seed means to be by nature the sort of thing *out of which* naturally constituted things are produced in the first place, not inasmuch as something that makes them comes out of that thing there (e.g. that man): they are produced out of this thing inasmuch as this is the seed. But there are several ways in which one thing comes out of another. One is the way that we say night comes out of day and man out of boy, in that this is after this. In another way, like a statue coming out of bronze and a bed out of wood and all other products that we speak of as produced out of matter, the whole is produced out of something that remains within it in altered shape. Another is the way that unmusical comes out of musical, sick out of healthy, and generally opposite out of opposite. Again, besides these, the way that Epicharmus composes his 'build-up': out of the insult came abuse, and out of that came the battle; in all these the beginning of the movement comes out of something. Some of this sort contain the beginning of the movement in themselves, for example those just mentioned (the insult is a part of the whole disturbance); but in others it is external, for example the beginning of movement in artefacts is the arts, in the burning house it is the torch.

The seed is plainly in one of these two classes: it is either as out of matter or as out of proximate mover that the product comes out of it. For it is certainly not as this after this, like the voyage that comes out of the Panathenaea, nor as out of an opposite; for one opposite is destroyed when the other comes out of it, and there must be something else underlying and remaining present, out of which it will come proximately. We must grasp, then, in which class to put the seed, whether as matter and passive, or as form somehow and active, or indeed as both. At the same time it will perhaps be clear too how generation out of opposites holds good of everything that comes out of seed. For generation out of opposites is natural too: some things come out of opposites (out of male and female), but others out of one thing alone, for example plants and all those animals in which male and female are not distinguished and separate.

Now semen is the name for that which comes away from the generator in animals that naturally couple, the first container of the source of generation. But seed is that which contains the sources from both the coupled animals (like the seeds of plants and of certain animals in which male and female are not separated), as it were the first mixture produced out of male and female, being like a sort of foetus or egg; for these already contain what has come from both parents. Seed and fruit differ by the prior and posterior: fruit in that it is out of another, seed in that another is out of it; both are in fact the same thing.

[We must now in turn say what is the primary nature of that which is called seed.]

Everything that we find in the body must be either a natural part (and that either non-homoeomerous or homoeomerous), or an unnatural part like a growth, or a residue, or a colliquation, or nutriment. (Residue is what I call the surplus nutriment, colliquation that which has been secreted out of the incremental material by unnatural decomposition.) Now clearly it would not be a part, since although it is homoeomerous nothing is composed of it as of sinew and flesh. Nor again is it separate, whereas all the other parts are. Nor on the other hand is it an unnatural part nor a deformity, since it is present in all and nature comes into being out of it. And nutriment is plainly an imported thing. So seed must be either a colliquation or a residue. Now the ancients seem as if they thought it a colliquation; for to say that it comes from all the body because of the heat arising
725a from the movement has the force of a colliquation. But colliquations are something contrary to nature, and out of things contrary to nature nothing comes that is in accordance with nature. Therefore it must be a residue. But now every residue is, of course, either of useless nutriment or of useful. I call useless that from which nothing further is contributed to nature, but much harm is done by using up too much of it; I call useful the opposite. Clearly it cannot be the former sort, because those in worst condition through age or sickness have most of that sort within them but least of seed; for either they have no seed at all or it is infertile through being mixed with useless and morbid residue.

The seed then is some part of a useful residue. The most

useful is the last, that out of which each part is immediately produced. For there is earlier and later residue. That from the first nutriment is phlegm and the like (for even phlegm is a residue of useful nutriment: an indication is that when mixed with pure nutriment it is nourishing and is used up in illness). But the final residue is the smallest in proportion to the amount of nutriment. It must be borne in mind that the material used for the daily growth of animals and plants is small: a tiny addition of the same material would result in excessive size.

We should say therefore the opposite of what the ancients said. They called the seed that which comes from all: we shall call it that which naturally goes to all. They thought it a colliquation, but we find it rather a residue. For it is more reasonable that the final material which goes to the parts should resemble what is left over from it, just as portrait painters often have flesh-coloured paint left over which resembles what they used. But everything that colliquesces is destroyed and departs from its nature.

A proof that seed is not a colliquation, but rather a residue, is that large animals have few young while small animals are prolific. For there must be more colliquation in large animals, but less residue, since the body being large uses up most of the nutriment so that little residue is produced.

Further, there is no place naturally allotted to a colliquation, but it flows wherever it finds an easy way in the body. But the natural residues all have a place; for example, that 725b
of the dry nutriment is the lower belly, that of the wet is the bladder, that of the useful is the upper belly, and for the spermatic residues there are uterus and pudenda and breasts; into these places they collect and flow together.

The concomitant facts too are evidence that seed is what we have said: they happen because the nature of the residue is such as it is. The lassitude produced by the smallest loss of seed is obvious, and suggests that the body is being deprived of the end product of the nutriment. A few individuals for a brief period in youth obtain relief through its loss when the seed is excessive; similarly if the primary nutriment is excessive in quantity, on its loss too the body is more at ease. Relief is also obtained when other residues depart with it; for what goes is not only seed, but other capabilities mixed with it also go in these cases, and these are morbid. That is why in certain cases the emission is actually infertile through having little spermatic content. But in most cases and as a general rule the result of sexual indulgence is rather lassitude and incapacity, for the reason stated.

Further, no seed is present either in earliest youth or in old age or in ill health. It is absent in sickness because of incapacity, in old age because nature does not concoct a sufficient quantity, and in childhood because the body is growing and everything is used up first; for it seems that in about five years, in the case of man, the body gains half of the total size that is attained in the rest of the lifetime.

In many animals and plants there occurs a difference in this respect both between one kind and another and between specifically similar members of the same kind, for example between man and man or vine and vine. Some have much seed, some little, some none at all, not through weakness but the opposite, in some at any rate; for it is all used up on the body, as in some men who through being in good condition and putting on more[1] flesh than before emit less seed and have less desire for sexual indulgence. It is like the affection in 'goaty' vines which rampage because of their nutriment
726a (for goats too mate less when they are fat, which is why they are thinned down beforehand; and the vines are called 'goaty' from the affection of the goats). Fat people too, both men and women, appear to be less fertile than those that are not fat, because the residue when concocted in well-nourished bodies becomes fat; for fat too is a healthy residue caused by good feeding. But some bear no seed at all, for

[1] 725b32: reading πολύσαρκοι μᾶλλον ἢ πρότερον. Lulofs (O.C.T.) reads "more flesh or more fat".

example the willow and the poplar. This affection too has both[1] kinds of cause. For through weakness they do not concoct, and also through strength they use it up, as we have said. Similarly abundance of emission and abundance of seed are due in some cases to strength but in others to weakness; for much useless residue is mixed with it, so that some people even become ill when there is no easy way for the discharge. Some recover but others actually perish. For colliquations flow by this way as also into the urine; this too is an ailment that has befallen some people.

Further, the channel is the same for the excrement as for the seed. In those that excrete both wet and dry nutriment the semen is discharged by the same way as the wet excretion (for it is a residue of wet, since all animals' nutriment is wet rather than dry), but those that do not have wet excretion discharge the semen by the way of the dry excretion.

Further, colliquescence is always noxious, whereas the removal of a residue is beneficial; but the discharge of the seed has both qualities because it takes with it some of the non-useful nutriment. But if it were a colliquescence, it would always do harm; as it is, it does not.

What has been said makes it plain that the seed is a residue of useful nutriment in its last stage, whether or not all animals emit seed. But next we must distinguish what sort (*Chap. 19*
of nutriment it is a residue of, and the same with regard to the menses; for menses occur in some vivipara. Thereby it will also be evident whether the female emits seed like the male and the product is a mixture of two seeds, or whether no seed is secreted from the female; and if no seed, whether she contributes nothing else to generation but only provides a place, or contributes something, and if so how and in 726b
what manner.

Now we have said before that the last stage of nutriment is the blood in blooded animals and the analogous part in the bloodless. Since the semen is a residue of nutriment in

[1] 726a8: reading ἑκάτεραι (Wimmer).

its last stage, it will be either blood or the analogous part or something out of these. And since each bodily part is produced out of the blood as it is being concocted and somehow particularized, and since the seed (although quite different from blood when it is secreted *after* concoction) when unconcocted and when forced out by too frequent sexual indulgence has sometimes come out still bloodlike, it is evident that the seed must be a residue of the nutriment which has become blood and is being distributed to the parts in its final stage. And because of this its capability is great (for the withdrawal of the pure and healthful blood is also weakening) and the resemblance of offspring to parents is reasonable; for what has gone to the parts resembles what is left over. Consequently the seed that produces the hand or the face or the whole animal is in an undifferentiated way hand or face or whole animal: as each of those is in actuality, such is the seed potentially, either in respect of its bodily mass or in that it contains a certain capability within itself (for what has so far been elucidated does not yet show us whether the body of the seed is the cause of generation, or whether it contains some disposition and source of movement which is generative); for the hand also, or any other part, if without the capability of soul or some other capability, is no hand or part except homonymously.

[1]It is also plain that whenever a colliquescence is produced which is spermatic, this too is a residue. This occurs when it is dissolved into the previous secretion, just as when a fresh coat of plaster falls off at once; for the part that comes away is the same as what was first applied. Similarly the final residue is the same as the first colliquation. [Such are the clarifications to be made in these matters.]

Since the weaker animal must produce residue that is more abundant and less concocted, and being such it must consist of a quantity of bloodlike fluid, and since the weaker is that which has naturally the smaller share of heat, and the female is such (as previously stated), it must follow that

[1] 726^{b}24–9 should be read after 726^{a}25.

727a the bloodlike secretion produced in the female is a residue too. Such a production is the discharge called the menses. Plainly then the menses are a residue and are analogous in females to the semen in males.

That this is a correct statement is indicated by the concomitant facts. For at about the same age the males begin to produce and emit semen and the females first discharge the menses; the voice changes and signs appear at the breasts. Again at the decline of life the ability to generate ceases in the one, and the menses in the other.

There are also the following indications that this discharge in females is a residue. As a rule neither blood-flows nor nose-bleeding nor anything else occurs in women unless the menses are suspended, and if any of these do occur the purgation becomes more difficult, showing that the secretion is being diverted to the former. Further, the females have neither such prominent blood-vessels nor so much hair and roughness as the males, because the residue that would go to these is discharged along with the menses. This too must be accounted the cause of the smaller physical bulk of the females compared with the males in vivipara; for it is only in them that the menses are discharged externally. Among them it is most conspicuous in women, for woman discharges more secretion than other animals. That is why she is conspicuously pale and lacking in prominent blood-vessels, and has an evident bodily deficiency compared with men.

Since this is what is produced in females corresponding to the semen in males, and since two spermatic secretions cannot be produced at once, it is plain that the female does not contribute seed to generation. For if there were seed there would be no menses; but as it is, because the latter comes into being, the former does not exist.

[We have now said why the menses are a residue just as the seed is.]

Supporting evidence can be found in some of the concomitant facts. Fat animals produce less seed than those without fat, as we said before (the reason is that fat too is a residue like seed; it is concocted blood, but not concocted in the same way as seed; hence it is reasonable that when 727b the production of residue has been used up on fat there is a deficiency with regard to semen). And among bloodless animals the cephalopods and crustaceans are at their best when gestating; for since they are bloodless and produce no fat, that which is analogous to fat in them is secreted to make the spermatic residue.

A sign that the female does not emit the kind of seed that the male emits, and that generation is not due to the mixing of both as some hold, is that often the female conceives without experiencing the pleasure that occurs in intercourse; and on the other hand she may experience it no less, and both male and female may reach it concurrently, and yet nothing is generated unless the moisture of what we call the menses is present in proportion. This is why the female does not generate either when the menses are wholly absent or (usually) when they are present and being discharged, but after the purgation. For at the former times she has no nutriment or matter out of which the animal will be able to be constituted by the capability that comes from the male and is present within the semen, while at the latter times it is washed out because of the amount of fluid. But when the menses have been produced and discharged, what remains is constituted into an embryo. Any females that conceive when the menses are not being produced, or during their production but not later, do so because in the former case they produce only so much moisture as remains after the purgation in fertile females, but no excess residue to be discharged externally as well, while in the latter case the mouth of the uterus closes up after the purgation. Therefore when the amount discharged has been considerable but the purgation is still taking place, though not enough to wash away the seed, that is when they conceive if they have intercourse. And there is nothing strange in its continuing after conception. (The menses even recur later up to a point, but in small quantity and not throughout the time. But in this case

it is morbid, which is why it occurs in few females and
infrequently. It is what occurs in the majority that is the 30
most natural.)

It is clear then that the female's contribution to generation is the matter, and that this is in the constitution of the menses, and that the menses are a residue.

As for the opinion that seed is contributed by the female (*Chap. 20*)
during intercourse on the grounds that a pleasure comparable 35
with that of the males is sometimes produced in them
together with a fluid discharge, this fluid is not spermatic
but is peculiar to the region in particular females. It is a 728a
secretion from the uterus and occurs in some but not in
others: it occurs in the fair-skinned and feminine of appearance as a rule, not in the dark and masculine-looking. Its
quantity, where it occurs, is sometimes out of proportion to 5
the emission of seed and far exceeds it. Moreover, different
foodstuffs make a great difference in diminishing or increasing this kind of secretion; for example, some of the bitter
foods increase it to an amount that is noticeable. But the
occurrence of pleasure in intercourse is due to the emitting 10
not only of seed but also of pneuma, the constituting of
which results in the emission. It is evident in boys who are
not yet capable of emission but are near the age, and in
infertile men: in all these pleasure is produced by friction. 14

[1]In appearance too a boy is like a woman, and the woman 17
is as it were an infertile male; for the female exists in virtue
of a particular incapacity, in being unable to concoct seed
out of the nutriment in its last stage (which is either blood 20
or the analogous part in the bloodless animals) owing to the 21
coldness of her nature.

Also, in those whose genital organs have been destroyed 14
the bowels are sometimes loose because residue which cannot 15
be concocted and become seed is discharged into the bowel. 16
Therefore just as in the bowels lack of concoction causes 21
diarrhoea, so in the blood-vessels it causes the blood-flows,
in particular the menses; for they too are a blood-flow, but
whereas the others are due to disease this one is natural. 25

[1] 728a14–17 καὶ . . . σπέρμα transposed to 21 after φύσεως.

And so it is clearly reasonable that generation takes place out of this. For the menses are seed that is not pure but needs working on; similarly in the production connected with crops, when the nutriment has not yet been sifted, although it is present within it needs working on to purify it. That is why, when the former is mixed with semen and the latter with pure nutriment, the one generates and the other nourishes.

A sign that the female does not emit seed is that the pleasure in intercourse is produced by touch in the same region as in males; yet they do not emit this moisture from there.

Further, this discharge is not produced in all females, but in those with plenty of blood, and not even in all of them but in those that do not have the uterus by the diaphragm
728b and do not lay eggs; nor again in those that have not blood but the analogous part (for they possess a different compound which corresponds to blood in the others). The reason why the purgation is produced neither in them nor in certain[1] blooded animals with the above-mentioned exceptions (those that have the uterus below and do not lay eggs) is the dryness of their bodies, which leaves little residue, enough only for generation but not for external emission. But those that have live young without first producing an egg [(these are man and all quadrupeds that bend the hind leg inwards; all these have live young without first producing an egg)] all produce menses unless they are deformed in generation like the mule, but the purgation is not superficially abundant as in man. [A detailed description of the way this occurs in each animal has been given in the *Historia Animalium*.] The greatest amount of purgation in animals is produced in women, and in men the emission of seed is the greatest in proportion to size. The cause is their bodily constitution, which is wet and hot; in such there is bound to be the greatest amount of residue produced.

[1] 728^b3–4: reading ἐχόντων ⟨τισὶ πλὴν⟩ τοῖς and retaining the words bracketed by Lulofs (O.C.T.).

Further, they have not the sort of bodily parts to which residue is diverted, as the others have; for they have not a large amount of hair about the body nor outcrops of bones and horns and tusks.

A sign that the seed is in the menses: at the same time of life, as we said before, the males produce this residue and the females show a trace of the menses, implying that the regions receptive of the residue in each of the two cases are drawn apart at the same time; and as the neighbouring regions in each become less dense, the pubic hair grows up. When they are about to be drawn apart, the regions are swelled up by the pneuma, in males more conspicuously about the testes though it shows also about the breasts, in females more about the breasts (when they are two fingers high, then the menses are produced in most females).

Now in all living things in which male and female are not separated the seed is a sort of foetus. By 'foetus' I mean the first mixture derived from male and female. This is why one body comes from one seed, for example one stem from one wheat grain, just as one animal comes from one egg (for the double-yolked are two eggs). But in all kinds in 729a
which male and female are distinct several animals can come from one seed, because seed differs in nature as between plants and animals. A sign of this is that several young come from one mating in animals that can generate more than one. Thereby it is also clear that the semen does not come from every part; for the same part would not immediately secrete separated parts, nor would they become separate in the uterus having arrived together. But it comes about as is reasonable, since in fact the male provides both the form and the source of movement while the female provides the body, i.e. the matter. Just as in the setting of milk, while the body is the milk, the curdling-juice or rennet is the container of the source that constitutes it, so is that which comes from the male when it is partitioned in the female. Why it is partitioned here into a larger number, here into fewer, and here remains single, will be part of a separate argument.

But since there is no difference of form in it, the only condition for generating more than one offspring is that the amount divided off should be proportionate to the matter, and be neither too little to concoct and constitute it nor too much so as to dry it up. But from the proximate constituting agent, inasmuch as it is one, there comes one offspring only.

Now, that the female does not contribute semen to generation, but contributes something, and that this is the constitution of the menses (and the analogous part in bloodless animals), is clear both from what has been said and according to reason on general considerations. For there must be that which generates and that out of which. Even if these are one, they must at least differ in form and in having separate definitions. But in animals that have the capabilities separated, both their bodies and their nature must be different as between the active one and the passive one. If therefore the male exists as active and causing movement, and the female as passive, the female's contribution to the male's semen will be not semen but matter. And this is evidently the case; for the nature of the menses is in accordance with the proximate matter.

(*Chap. 21*) [Let these matters be clarified in this way.] At the same time these considerations throw light on the questions that
729b follow upon them: how is it that the male contributes to generation, and how is the seed from the male a cause of what is produced? Is it by being present within and by being immediately a part of the body that is being produced, mingling with the matter from the female? Or does the body of the seed not participate, but only the capability and movement that is in it? For it is the latter that is the agent, while that which becomes constituted and takes the shape is the remainder of the female residue. This is evident both according to reason and on the facts. For (*a*), considering it generally, we do not see one thing being produced *out of* agent and patient in the sense that the agent is present within the product, nor indeed (to generalize) *out of* mover and moved. But now the female *qua* female is the patient,

while the male *qua* male is the agent and is that from which comes the beginning of the movement. So that if we take the extremes of each, whereby the one is agent and mover while the other is patient and moved, the one thing being produced is not *out of* these except in the way that the bed is out of the carpenter and wood or the sphere out of the wax and the form. Clearly then it is not necessary that something should come away from the male; and if something does come away, it does not follow that the offspring is made out of it as out of something present within, but only as out of mover and form, in the way that the cured invalid is the product of the medical art.

(*b*) On the facts too, what happens agrees with this argument. For this is why certain males, even though they couple with the females, are seen to put no part into the female, but on the contrary the female is seen to put a part into the male, as is the case in certain insects. For the effect that the seed, in those that emit, brings about in the female, is brought about in these insects by the heat and capability in the animal itself when the female brings into it the part that is receptive of the residue. This is also why such animals are joined for a long time, but when separated generate quickly. For they remain coupled until they have constituted the matter in the way that semen does; but after separating they emit the foetus quickly because they generate an unperfected offspring; for all of this sort produce grubs.

But what occurs in birds and in the oviparous kind of fishes is the best evidence that the seed does not come from all the parts, and that the male does not emit any part such 730a
as will remain present within the offspring, but generates an animal merely by the capability in the semen, just as we said of insects in which the female puts a part into the male. For if a hen is gestating wind-eggs and is then mated before the egg has changed from being entirely yellow to turning white, the eggs become fertile instead of wind-eggs; and if it is mated with a second cock while the egg is still yellow, the chicks turn out to be of the same kind in every respect

as the second cock. This is why some who are concerned with the highly bred birds act in this way, changing the first and subsequent matings. It implies that the seed is not mixed in and present within, and that it did not come from every part; for it would have come from both cocks, so that the same parts would have been contained twice. But by its capability the male seed puts the matter and nutriment that is in the female into a particular kind of state. The seed that came in later can do this by heating and concocting, since the egg takes nutriment so long as it is increasing in size. The same occurs in the generation of the oviparous fishes too. When the female has laid the eggs, the male sprinkles the semen over them; those that it reaches become fertile, but those that it does not are infertile, implying that the male's contribution to the animals is not quantitative but qualitative.

It is clear then from what has been said that, in those animals that emit seed, the seed does not come from every part; and that the female does not contribute in the same way as the male to the generation of the offspring that are constituted, but the male contributes a source of movement and the female the matter. This is why the female does not generate by itself; for it needs a source and something to provide movement and definition (though of course in certain animals, for example hens, nature can generate up to a point; for these do constitute, but the products are
(*Chap.* 22) unperfected, the so-called wind-eggs). It is also why the generation of the offspring takes place in the female: neither the male itself nor the female emits the semen into the male, but both contribute into the female that which is produced
730b from them, because it is the female that contains the matter out of which the product is fashioned. And some matter must be present immediately, already collected, out of which the foetus is constituted in the first place; other matter must continually be added so that what is being gestated may grow. Therefore birth must take place in the female; for the carpenter too is by the timber, the potter is by the clay,

and in general every act of working-upon and proximate movement takes place by the matter, for example building takes place in what is being built.

One may also grasp from these examples how the male contributes to generation. For not every male emits seed, and in those that do emit it the seed is no part of the foetus that is produced, just as nothing comes away from the carpenter to the matter of the timber, nor is there any part of carpentry in the product, but the shape and the form are produced *from* the carpenter *through* the movement *in* the matter. His soul (in which is the form) and his knowledge move his hands or some other part in a movement of a particular kind—different when their product is different, the same when it is the same—the hands move the tools, and the tools move the matter. Similarly the male's nature, in those that emit seed, uses the seed as a tool containing movement in actuality, just as in the productions of an art the tools are in movement; for the movement of the art is in a way in them. Those then that emit seed contribute in this way to generation. But those that do not emit, where the female inserts some part of itself into the male, act like one bringing the matter to the craftsman. For because of the weakness of such males their nature is not capable of acting through other means, but even when it applies itself direct the movements have barely enough strength; it acts like modellers, not carpenters, since it fashions the thing being constituted not by touching it through something else but directly by using its own parts.

Now in all animals that have locomotion the female is (*Chap. 23*)
separated from the male: female is one animal and male is another, but they are the same in form (for example, each is a man or a horse). But in the plants these capabilities are 731a
mingled and the female is not separated from the male. This is why they generate out of themselves and emit not semen but a foetus, what we call seeds. This is well said by Empedocles in his poem:

'Thus do tall trees bear eggs: first olive-trees . . .'

For the egg is a foetus, and the animal is produced out of part of it while the remainder is nutriment; the growing plant too is produced out of part of the seed, while the remainder becomes nutriment for the shoot and the first root. In a way the same happens also in those animals that have the male and the female separated. For when they are due to generate they become unseparated, as in plants, and their nature wants to become one; this indeed is visibly evident when they unite and couple, that both become a single animal. It is natural for those that do not emit seed to remain joined for a long time until they have constituted the foetus, for example the insects that couple; but others, for example the blooded animals, remain only until they have discharged some part that the male introduces, which will take further time to constitute the foetus. The former remain connected for some part of a day; in the latter the semen takes several days to constitute the foetus, but they separate when they have emitted such semen. Animals are just like divided plants, as though one were to take plants apart whenever they bear seed and were to separate them into the male and female that are present within.

Nature fashions all this reasonably. For plants have no other function or activity in their being except the generation of seed, so that since this is done through the coupling of male and female nature has arranged them together by mingling them; that is why male and female are inseparate in the plants. [Now plants have been examined elsewhere.] But the animal's function is not only to generate (for that is common to all living things), but also they all participate in some sort of cognition, some of them in more, some in less, some in very little at all. For they have perception, and perception is a sort of cognition. Its value or lack of value in our eyes differs greatly according as we compare it with intelligence or with the soulless kind of things. Compared
731b with being intelligent, merely to participate in touch and taste seems like nothing; but compared with plant or stone it seems wonderful. One would welcome even this share of

cognition, rather than lie dead and non-existent. It is by perception that animals differ from things that are merely alive. But since it must also be alive, if it is an animal, when it is due to accomplish the function of the living thing it then couples and unites and becomes as if it were a plant, as we said. But the testacean animals, which are between animals and plants, through being in both kinds perform the function of neither. For as plants they do not have male and female and do not generate into another, while as animals they do not bear fruit out of themselves as plants do, but are constituted and generated out of a certain earthy and wet compound. [But we are to speak about their generation later.]

DE GENERATIONE ANIMALIUM II

(*Extracts from Chapters 1–3*)

731b18 (*Chap. 1*) It has been stated previously that the female and the male are sources of generation, and what is their capability and the definition of their being. As for the reason why the one becomes and is female and the other male—that it is due to necessity and the proximate mover and a certain sort of matter, our argument must try to explain as it proceeds. But that it is for the better, and due to the cause *for the sake of something*, derives from a prior principle.

For since some existing things are eternal and divine, while the others are capable both of being and of not being, and since the good and the divine is always according to its own nature a cause of the better in things that are capable, while the non-eternal is capable both of being [(and not being)] and of partaking in both the worse and the better, and since soul is a better thing than body, and the ensouled than the soulless because of the soul, and being than not being, and living than not living,—for these reasons there is generation of animals. For since the nature of such a kind cannot be eternal, that which comes into being is eternal in the way that is possible for it. Now it is not possible in number (for the being of existing things is in the particular, and if this were such it would be an eternal) but it is possible in 732a form. That is why there is always a kind—of men and of animals and of plants.

Since their source is the male and female, it must be for the sake of generation that male and female exist in those that have them. But the proximate moving cause (in which is present the definition and the form) is better and diviner in its nature than the matter; and it is better that the more excellent be separated from the worse. Because of this the male is separated from the female wherever possible and as far as possible.

The difference between an egg and a grub is that an egg 29 is that out of which the product is produced out of part (the remainder being food for the product), while a grub is that out of which the product is produced whole from whole.

Much overlapping between kinds comes about. For the 732b15 bipeds are not all viviparous (for the birds are oviparous) nor all oviparous (for man is viviparous); and the quadrupeds are not all oviparous (for horse, ox, and countless others are viviparous) nor all viviparous (for lizards, crocodiles, and many others are oviparous). Nor does the possession or non-possession of feet differentiate them; for there are viviparous footless animals such as the vipers and the selachians, and oviparous ones such as the fish kind and the other kinds of snakes. . . .

. . . There is no dividing in this way, then, nor is any of 26 the locomotive organs the cause of this difference. Rather, the viviparous are those animals that are more perfected in nature and partake in a purer source; for none is internally viviparous unless it takes in the breath and breathes. The more perfected are those that are hotter in nature and wetter and not earthy. And the mark of natural heat is the lungs.

We should note how well and consecutively nature brings 733a32 forth generation. The more perfected and hotter animals 733b bring forth their young perfected in respect of what sort they are (though no animal at all does so in respect of size, for all increase their size after birth), and these are the ones that generate animals within themselves immediately. The second grade do not generate perfected animals within themselves immediately (for they bear live young after first producing eggs) but externally they bear live. The next generate not a perfected animal but an egg, and this egg is perfected. The next, having a nature still colder than those, generate an egg, but it is not perfected: it becomes perfected outside, in the manner of the scaly kind of fishes and the crustaceans and cephalopods. The fifth and coldest kind does not even lay eggs out of itself, but this kind of affection comes about in this case outside, as we have said: the insects bear grubs in the first place, but the grub after development becomes egglike (for what is called the chrysalis has the capability of an egg) and then out of this there comes an animal, gaining the end of its generation in the third change.

31 The question now is not *out of* what but *by* what the parts are produced. For either something outside makes them, or something present within the semen and seed, and this is
734a either some part of soul, or soul, or it must be something possessing soul. Now, that something outside should make each of the viscera or other parts would seem unreasonable. For it is impossible to move a thing without touching it, and if it does not move it the thing cannot be affected by it. . . .

16 . . . The parts are all produced either simultaneously (heart, lungs, liver, eye, and all) or consecutively as in the so-called poems of Orpheus: there the animal is said to be produced like "the plaiting of the net". Now it is plain even to observation that they are not simultaneous; for some parts are seen to be already within while others are not. . . .

734b4 . . . We must try to resolve this problem. Perhaps something that we have said is not unambiguous, namely in what sense exactly the parts cannot be brought into being by what is outside. For there is a sense in which it is possible, and a sense in which it is not. Now whether we speak of the seed, or of that from which the seed has come, makes no difference in respect of the fact that the seed contains the movement caused by that other. And it is possible for this to move this, and this this, and for it to be like the automata in the 'marvels'. For their parts stand there containing somehow a capability when they are at rest; and when something outside has moved the first of them, immediately the next one becomes actualized.

Everything produced naturally or by an art is produced *by* a thing existing actually *out of* what is potentially of that sort. Now the seed, and the movement and source which it contains, are such that as the movement ceases each part is produced having soul. For it is not face nor flesh unless it has soul: after their death it will be equivocal to say that the one is a face and the other flesh, as it would be if they were made of stone or wood. The homoeomerous parts and the instrumental parts are produced simultaneously. We would not say that an axe or other instrument was made by fire alone: no more would we say it of hand or foot. The same applies to flesh, for it too has a certain function. Now heat and cold would make them hard and soft and tough and brittle, with all other such affections that belong to the parts containing soul, but would not go so far as giving them the definition in virtue of which the one is now flesh and the other bone: that is due to the movement derived from the generator, which is *actually* what the thing out of which the product comes is *potentially*. It is the same with things produced according to an art. Heat and cold make the iron hard 735a
and soft, but the *sword* is made by the instruments' movement which contains a definition belonging to the art. For the art is source and form of the product, but in another thing; but the movement of nature is in the thing itself, being derived from another nature which contains the form actualized.

And has the seed soul or not? The same reasoning applies to it as to the parts. For there can be no soul in anything except in that of which it is in fact the soul, nor can there be a part unless it has some soul (except homonymously, like a dead man's eye). Clearly therefore it does have soul and exists—potentially. But it is possible to be relatively nearer and farther in potentiality, as the geometer asleep is farther than the one awake, and the latter is farther than the one studying.

Now this generative process is not caused by any of its parts, but by that which proximately moved it from outside. For nothing generates itself. But once it has been produced, it proceeds to increase itself. Therefore some first thing is produced, not everything at once. And the first thing to be produced must be that which contains the source of increase; for all alike, whether plant or animal, possess this, the nutritive. (And this is what is generative of another like oneself; for that is the function of every naturally perfected thing, both animal and plant.) It must be so, because once a body has been produced it must be increased. Therefore although it was generated by that which is synonymous (a man by a man), it is increased by means of itself. It itself must be something, therefore, if it causes increase. Now if it is one particular thing, and this is first, it must be the first to be produced. Consequently if the heart is the first to be produced in certain animals (and the part analogous to it in those that do not have a heart), the source must be from the heart in those that have one, and from the analogous part in the others.

735b37 The seed, then, is a combination of pneuma and water,
(*Chap. 2*) and the pneuma is hot air.

736a13 The reason for the seed's whiteness is that the semen is foam.

736a24 If, in the case of those that emit semen into the female,
(*Chap. 3*) that which enters is no part of the foetus produced, where is its bodily part diverted, if it is true that it works through the capability that is within it? We must make clear (i) whether that which is constituted in the female takes over anything from that which enters, or nothing; (ii) concerning soul in virtue of which it is called an animal [(it is animal in virtue of the perceptive part of the soul)], whether it is present within the seed and the foetus or not, and where it comes from. One could not class the foetus as soulless, in every way devoid of life; for the seeds and foetuses of

animals are no less alive than plants, and are fertile up to a point. It is plain enough that they have nutritive soul [(and why they must obtain this first is evident from what we have made clear elsewhere concerning soul)], but as they 736b
progress they have also the perceptive soul in virtue of which they are animal. For they do not become simultaneously animal and man, or animal and horse, and so on; for the end is the last to be produced, and the end of each animal's generation is that which is peculiar to it. This is why the question of intellect—when and how and from where it is acquired by those that partake in this source—is especially difficult, and we must try hard to grasp it according to our capabilities and to the extent that is possible.

Now seeds and foetuses which are not yet separate must clearly be classed as possessing the nutritive soul *potentially*, but not *actually* until they are drawing in their food like the separated foetuses and are performing the function of this sort of soul; for at first all such seem to live a plant's life. And what we say of the perceptive and intellective souls should clearly conform with that; for all souls must be possessed potentially before actually.

And either they must all be produced in the body without existing beforehand, or they must all pre-exist, or some must but not others; and they must be produced in the matter either without having entered in the male's seed, or having come from there; and in the male they must either all be produced from outside, or none from outside, or some but not others.

Now it is evident from the following that they cannot all pre-exist: all principles whose actuality is bodily are clearly unable to be present without body (for example, walking without feet). Hence too they cannot enter from outside. For they can neither enter by themselves, since they have no separate existence, nor enter in a body; for the seed is a residue produced by a change in the nutriment. It remains then that the intellect alone enters additionally from outside

and alone is divine; for [the] bodily actuality is in no way associated with its actuality. Now the capability of all soul seems to be associated with a body different from and diviner than the so-called elements; and as the souls differ from each other in value and lack of value, so too this sort of nature differs. For within the seed of everything there is present that which makes the seeds to be fertile, the so-called hot. This is not fire or that sort of capability, but the pneuma enclosed within the seed and within the foamy part, and more precisely the nature in the pneuma, being analogous
737a to the element of the stars. This is why fire generates no animal, and none is seen to be constituted in things subjected to fire, whether wet things or dry. But the heat of the sun and the heat of animals do generate—not only the heat conveyed through the seed, but also if there is some other residue of their nature, even this too contains a vital source. Such things make it plain that the heat in animals neither is fire nor has its origin from fire.

But the body of the semen, in which there also comes the portion of soul-source—partly separate from body in all those in which something divine is included (and such is what we call the intellect) and partly inseparate—this body of the semen dissolves and evaporates, having a fluid and watery nature. That is why one should not look for it always to come out again, nor to be any part of the constituted form, any more than the curdling-juice which sets the milk: it too changes and is no part of the mass that is being constituted.

Since the seed is residue, and is being moved in the same movement as that with which the body grows when the final nutriment is being particularized, when it comes into the uterus it constitutes and moves the female's residue in the same movement in which it itself is actually moving. For that too is residue and contains all the parts potentially, though none actually. It even contains potentially the sort of parts whereby there is a difference between male and female. For just as the offspring of deformed animals are sometimes deformed and sometimes not, so that of a female is sometimes female and sometimes not—but male. For the female is as it were a male deformed, and the menses are seed but not pure seed; for it lacks one thing only, the source of the soul. This is why in all animals that produce wind-eggs the egg that is being constituted has the parts of both, but has not the source, and therefore does not become ensouled; for the source is brought in by the male's seed. But once it has acquired such a source, the female's residue becomes a foetus.

NOTES

DE PARTIBUS ANIMALIUM I

The book in its present form, which must go back at least to Andronicus' edition in the first century B.C., is a general introduction to zoology, complete in itself and independent of the remaining three books of *P.A.*, which are factual studies. The abrupt differences of style and lack of overall continuity suggest that it is a collection of five separate papers. The topics are discussed in a reasonable order, however, and are all required. Aristotle probably used the papers as his lecture notes, but did not write them up into a connected book. Chapter 1 is a single paper setting out the principles of zoological explanation, and showing what 'causes' must be brought into the account. Chapters 2 and 3 evidently originated as a polemical critique of Academic dichotomy, but serve here as an analysis of the problem of defining species. Chapter 4 explains the grouping of animals in genera and species, distinguishing the two sorts of resemblance that are now called 'analogy' and 'homology'. Chapter 5 is two papers: first an exhortation to zoology, warning against a feeling of revulsion; secondly an analysis of the relation between bodily parts. This chapter at last brings the audience to the study of details (including dissections) repugnant to Greek taste, and one can see why the exhortation was put in where it is. The actual account of the bodily parts begins in Book II.

Chapter 1

The Principles of Zoological Explanation

Aristotle's introductory paragraph makes it clear that he is not setting out to discuss scientific *method*. His views on that are given in the *Posterior Analytics*, which must be taken as read. Here he is not considering how to arrive at an explanation (how to investigate facts and establish theories) but how to judge an explanation when it is made. That is to say, he is considering what natural principles and factors must be recognized in accounting for zoological phenomena. His approach may seem indirect, but it enables him to make the point that zoology *has* very important principles and deserves the educated man's attention. The whole discussion amounts to a philosophy of zoology: what are the causes operative in living nature and how they relate to each other. To elucidate the argument, the principles identified by Aristotle have been numbered 1 to

11 in the translation; but the divisions are not clear cut, and the original Greek is continuous as one topic leads into the next. Section 12 is a brief model exposition illustrating these principles.

639a1–15 *Introduction: Every scientific exposition should be judged by the principles appropriate to the subject.*

By 'study' (θεωρία) and 'investigation' (μέθοδος) Aristotle here refers not to the *making* of the investigation but to its completed results. Every scientific exposition can be judged (i) by the specialist, as to its facts, (ii) by the educated man, as to its general principles and procedure. It follows that a biological exposition too, at however humble a level, has a judgeable procedure as well as facts. Into (ii) Aristotle has inserted a distinction between the man so educated that he can judge all expositions and the man so educated that he can judge some. This distinction has two useful implications. First, biological principles may be peculiar to biology; secondly, they are none the less as fundamental as the principles of other subjects. As Chapter 5 shows, Aristotle is recommending biology to an audience that considers itself educated but is ignorant (and perhaps contemptuous) of it. He is also taking his usual stance against Plato and Speusippus, who held that the educated man must have an all-embracing knowledge of general principles, and that without knowing the whole one cannot know a part. Aristotle on the contrary holds that each science proposes its own axioms and can therefore be known independently of other sciences. Consequently its general principles and procedure are independent too. Hence the judging of them does not require the whole of educatedness: it is a *sort* of educatedness (παιδεία τις 639a4).

The principles or 'marks' (ὅροι 639a13) are of this kind: that common attributes should be expounded before peculiar ones, that 'appearances' (i.e. data) should be stated before their causes, that final causes are prior to necessary causes, and so on. These are methodological principles, not the hypotheses and axioms of the science. The latter would be those discussed in *De Generatione et Corruptione* concerning alteration, acting upon and being acted upon, combination, transformation of elements, and such. They are reached by dialectic or by induction, and are part of the 'appearances' of natural science. As such, they are the province of the specialist.

(Some interpreters hold that at 639a8–11 Aristotle is identifying the 'other man, qualified in respect of part' with the specialist who knows the subject matter (a3). But at a14 he repeats the distinction between judging the procedure and judging the truth, which implies that the former is the province of the 'man qualified in respect of part' and not of the specialist. Therefore Aristotle has distinguished three people: (1) the specialist who knows the data; (2) the educated man who, whether or not he is also a specialist, can see whether a scientific explanation is based on the appropriate principles; (3) the man who can do this for one science but not for others. He distinguishes (2) and (3) also at *E.N.* I. 1095a1.)

Zoology is 'humble' (639a1) presumably because its data are imprecise, perishable, and disgusting. The objects studied by the 'more valuable' sciences, such as astronomy and theology, are exact, eternal, beautiful, divine; their value derives primarily from their inability to cease being what they are (*G.A.* II. 731b25). Aristotle returns to this contrast in Chapter 5. It is not a question here of Plato's distinction between philosophic and banausic studies. That distinction did, however, play a part in a controversy about the relation between knowledge of facts and educatedness (Plato, *Gorgias* 485, *Protagoras* 312B; Isocrates, *Antidosis* 261 f.). Aristotle probably alludes to the controversy at 639a3, and this would help his audience to take the point that general principles are different from observational data.

'Nature' (639a12) includes everything that comes to be and perishes, roughly everything sublunary. The subject matter of *P.A.* and *G.A.* is in fact zoology, but Aristotle does not separate it from physics systematically: its principles are the same as those of natural science as a whole, and much of the argument of *P.A.* I is the same as that of *Physics* II. 8–9. Nor does Aristotle set up *biology* as a subject at all. He speaks of the study of animals and the study of plants, and says that these differ from other things in having soul and life. The soul is the living organism's capability (see note at 641a27); it is neither an entity independent of body, nor a function of the constituents of the body, but exists only when these constituents are organized in a living animal or plant. The bodily constituents themselves are composed of the same elements as the constituents of non-living things. The only suggestion of a special material comes in Aristotle's theory of *pneuma*, the heated air which conveys soul-movements (see note at *G.A.* II, 736b29, p. 162). Otherwise the chief factor that he invokes to explain biological phenomena is 'vital heat', which he does not distinguish from the action of fire (one of the ordinary four elements) except when it is associated with pneuma in effecting reproduction. Even there it is doubtful whether he means more than heat of the greatest purity, though on this question interpreters differ. Aristotle seems able to assume that natural materials initiate movements and form complexes without prior mechanical causes. There may be some unconscious 'hylozoism' in his theory, as in so much of Greek science. This may be why the later 'problem of life' hardly seems to have troubled the classical philosophers. Though there is an occasional suggestion in Stoicism and in medieval philosophy, the concept of biology does not really appear before the seventeenth century; the word itself, according to Charles Singer, was first used in this sense in 1802 by Treviranus and Lamarck. Therefore although it is convenient to speak of Aristotle's 'biology', referring to the field of study, this must not be taken to connote the modern problem of 'organic' materials.

639a15–b7 (*1*) *Should we first state specific attributes or general attributes?*

This question again shows that Aristotle is speaking of scientific explanation, not method of investigation; for one cannot investigate a genus apart from its species. He does not answer it formally until Chapter 4, but the answer is implied here at 639a24—that to repeat common attributes in the case of each species would involve saying the same things many times, which would be both absurd and lengthy (cf. 644b1, 645b11).

Aristotle is not saying (as he has been accused since Bacon) that the scientist should make general statements without first *examining* all the facts. Since Plato described 'Collection and Division', it was a commonplace that the scientist first collects all the specific instances and then analyses and groups them generically. Aristotle makes this clear in the *Analytics*. He criticizes Democritus because "he states a general cause without having examined all the instances . . . but an examination of all is necessary, because a general statement is a statement about all" (*G.A.* 788b11; cf. 756a5, 760b31, 765a28, *De Caelo* ii. 293a25). True, he admits intuitive induction: the examination of some instances may bring about direct insight into a general principle (*An. Post.* ii. 100a15–b15; cf. Ross, *Aristotle's Prior and Posterior Analytics*, p. 49). But if induction is to prove demonstratively, it is necessary to know all the species that fall under the genus (*An. Pr.* II. 68b27).

Assuming, then, that the zoologist has investigated all available species of bird, when he comes to give his *reasoned account* (*logos*) of birds he need not—indeed should not—say of each species that it has two legs. Aristotle makes this point three times in *P.A.* I, giving no reason other than the avoidance of repetition. Granted that it would be tedious, what makes it absurd or out of place (ὑπάτοπον 644a35) and how does this principle deserve to stand first in the list? It may be that Aristotle has a deeper motive, which I should like to suggest briefly.

Elsewhere Aristotle often shows that generic attributes are especially important in that they may reveal—or be—the causes of specific attributes. At *An. Post.* II. 14 he says that by picking out what is common to animals and seeing what further attributes are implied by it, we shall see the cause of the specific attributes: for example, bone and fish-spine and the squid's pounce are analogous, and certain things are implied by them. Here he must mean that these features all contribute rigidity, which implies certain material processes in their formation and in the body as a whole. Again, he says, horned animals have additional stomachs but lack upper incisor teeth. This example can be followed in more detail in *P.A.* III (662b23 f., 674a30 f.). Horns grow for defence; but their growth diverts material from the teeth; hence additional stomachs are needed to complete the mastication of food. But the case of the camel casts doubt on this analysis, for he has the additional stomach and fewer teeth, but no horns. In his case it is because his natural food of thorns requires extra digestion; having more stomachs he needs fewer teeth, and accordingly their material is diverted to his defence—which in the camel takes the form not of horns but of greater bodily size. Other defences are claws (hence many hornless animals are polydactylous, but all the horned are either cloven or solid-hoofed), or speed or tusks (hence the hornless solid-hoofed are either speedier or grow extra teeth as tusks). Such a discussion is clearly an attempt to pick out the significant causal factor and to show how other features flow from it.

In another passage Aristotle criticizes classification by limbs because it cuts across classification by modes of reproduction, and concludes that the cross-division occurs because differences of limbs are not the *cause* of the other differences: the real cause is differences of heat, indicated by the possession or non-possession of lungs (*G.A.* II. 732^{b}15). Breathing is for the sake of cooling (*Resp.* 478^{a}11), which leads Aristotle to suggest that lung-possessors could be recognized as a genus (*P.A.* III. 669^{b}10).

Aristotle evidently does not regard classification as arbitrary, serving only tidiness and convenience of reference. Its aim is to reveal the common causal attributes, and the specific attributes flowing from them. But it is also evident that he is not ready to say which are the fundamental attributes. His suggestions about heat and lungs and reproduction remain tentative and are not embodied in a scheme: Aristotle commits himself to no classification beyond naming the major genera (note at 644^{a}12).

Since he takes it for granted that the aim of a zoological *logos* is not merely to describe but to explain, he may also assume that the first necessary step is to pick out correctly the fundamental generic attributes, because they either are, or point to, the causes of the specific attributes: without the generic attributes, explanation cannot begin. Having once stated a generic attribute, one would obviously not want to repeat the explanation for every instance: that would be absurd because it would show that the expositor had not understood the fundamental character of the cause. If this is what was in Aristotle's mind it is admittedly odd that he did not say so. But it could be because he was not ready with evidence. So he leaves it with an apparently trivial reason—the tediousness of repetition—which may be ironical.

639^{a}16 "Being" (*οὐσία*): traditionally translated 'substance'. It is the verbal noun of 'to be'. To show its occurrence, I have translated it 'being' throughout. Aristotle uses it ambiguously for (i) a real object, as here, (ii) what is real in a real object, as at *G.A.* I. 715^{a}5, II. 731^{b}34 (what an object really is).

The *object* in sense (i) is always the *infima species* in Aristotle's zoological works, not the individual animal (except where he explicitly points to individuals, as at *G.A.* II. 731b34).

639a19 "In respect of something common" (κατά τι κοινόν) is syntactically ambiguous here, and may be construed either with 'posit' or with 'common to all'. So the meaning may be *either* "should one first posit the attributes which they all share through a common characteristic" *or* "should one first posit, in terms of some common characteristic, the attributes which they all share".

639a20 "Kind" (γένος). The root-meaning is kinship-group. It is Aristotle's usual word for a type of animal, at every level from *infima species* to major genus. But he uses it for *genus* as opposed to *species* (εἶδος, on which see note at 639a28) when he requires this distinction: this is rare in the biological works as a whole, but occurs in several places in *P.A.* I, where it is translated accordingly. In other passages *genos* and *eidos* are interchangeable, and each is translated 'kind' where the reference is simply to a type of animal as distinct from other types.

639a22 "Affections" (πάθη). Those mentioned are explained in the *Parva Naturalia*, locomotion in *De Incessu Animalium*. Other affections would probably include keenness of sense organs, coloration, hair, voice, which are dealt with in *G.A.* V.

639a26 "Refers to each of their attributes (καθ' ἕκαστον τῶν συμβεβηκότων λέγῃ): this is the MSS. reading, literally "speaks in respect of each of their attributes". Some editors write τὰ συμβεβηκότα: "if one states the attributes in respect of each kind of animal".

639a28 "Species" (εἶδος). The root-meaning is *apparent shape*. Aristotle uses it for (i) *a kind*, as distinct from other kinds—the cat kind, the dog kind; (ii) *kind*, as distinct from numerical instances of a kind—the cat as distinct from cats; (iii) *form*, as distinct from matter—a cat's catness as distinct from its flesh and bones; (iv) *species*, as distinct from genus—the lion or tiger kinds as distinct from the overarching Cat kind. These senses are not clearly distinguished. For the closeness of (iii) and (iv), see note at 643a24.

639b1 "Specific differentia" (τῇ κατ' εἶδος διαφορᾷ). For *diaphora* see 642b6 note. Here Aristotle may mean no more than 'the difference in respect of kind'—i.e. animal kind.

639b4 "Common general attributes": literally 'survey the attributes in common by kinds' (κοινῇ κατὰ γένος)—i.e. by kinds of animal.

639b7–10 (*2*) *Should we survey appearances before expounding their causes?*

'Appearances' (*φαινόμενα*) include both the facts established by observation and the facts and general statements established by argument (cf. G. E. L. Owen, "*Τιθέναι τὰ φαινόμενα*", *Aristote et les problèmes de méthode*, Louvain 1961, pp. 83 f.). The answer is assumed to be 'yes', as is shown by the reference at 640a14. There it becomes clear that Aristotle means that we should expound what features exist and what is their nature, before expounding why the animals possess them. His reason is probably that the feature's nature points to its cause; knowing the *what* may even entail knowing the *because-of-what* (*An. Post.* II. 90a14–23). For example, lungs (*P.A.* III. 6). In some animals they are large and filled with blood, while in others they are small and spongy. The cause of their presence is that land animals cool their vital heat by breathing; hotter animals have larger lungs into which much hot blood can go, while colder animals have smaller and drier lungs. Knowing the feature, therefore, one may be led to the cause. But one could not argue from the cause to the feature: that because all animals need cooling, therefore this animal will have lungs and that animal will live in water. The possibilities would be too undetermined.

Such statements of function explain the features' *being* (what the features are). Their *coming-to-be* (*γένεσις*) is explained partly by function and partly by the material factors affecting their development. Aristotle takes this point separately at 640a10 f. Meanwhile he explains in the coming section (639b11) why it is right to separate them, and why 'being' must be considered before 'coming-to-be'.

639b11–20 (*3*) *The definition and the final cause are prior to the moving cause.*

The definition defines the *being*, and usually consists of a statement of function. Lungs are defined as the organ of breathing, eyes as the organ of sight. Development is for sake of this, i.e. towards this state of being. This holds of all biological definitions: even where they are not directly statements of function, they define a state of being towards which growth naturally tends. In the case of an animal, what is defined is the complete adult state of its species—what the animal typically is when it is fully grown and functioning in its natural environment. Aristotle always refers to this state when explaining development—see for example his discussion of birds' necks and beaks, *P.A.* IV. 692b19–693a23.

The definition is logically prior because the movement is directed towards it and therefore presupposes it. But Aristotle will also insist that it is chronologically prior (640a24): the egg came from a hen. The movement is embodied in the male parent: he makes the seed, which transmits the movement to the female material, causing it to develop into an embryo growing towards the male parent's *eidos* (*G.A.* I. 729b1 f., II. 737a18).

In *Physics* II Aristotle says that the final, formal, and moving causes often coincide (as they do in the male parent) over against the material cause (198a24). Yet here he is saying that the moving cause is secondary, and in the coming discussion he treats it as including the 'necessary' movements of the material. This suggests that the natural growth of an animal is partly *final* (teleological, directive) and partly *necessary* (automatic), i.e. that natural movements fall into two classes, the automatic actions of materials *and* the super-imposed goal-seeking movements (imposed by what?). It will be argued below (note at 639b21) that this is untenable, and that Aristotle's apparently inconsistent statements can be reconciled with the view that *all* natural movements are either directly or ultimately teleological.

639b12 "Beginning" (ἀρχή). The ambiguity in this word contributes to the confusion about moving causes. ἀρχή may signify any one, or two, or all three of the following: (i) *a beginning*, i.e. the first part of a movement, as at 639b12; (ii) the *source* of a movement, itself perhaps unmoving as at 639b15 (for the definition is not a moveable); (iii) a governing *principle*, something that exercises continuous influence or control, as at 642a17, *G.A.* II. 736b22.

Its verb ἄρχειν, which signifies 'to be first', may denote either ruling or starting.

639b16 "Mentally or perceptually" (τῇ διανοίᾳ ἢ τῇ αἰσθήσει): i.e. mentally in words or image, perceptually with an example or drawing.

639b19 "To a greater degree" (μᾶλλον). In Chapter 5 (645a25) Aristotle says that in nature directiveness takes the place that beauty has in art. He does not make this point in *Physics* II, but at *E.N.* II. 1106b15 he says that nature is "more exact and better than art". He clearly means (1) that nature achieves ends more successfully: animals come nearer to their perfect states (as defined) than artefacts do, because the artist less often manages his material skilfully enough to achieve his own defined aim. He *may* also mean (2) that finality penetrates nature more completely: even the materials in nature are composed for the product, whereas in art they are used contrary to their own natures; hence the marble man, even if more beautiful, is less man-like, and ships swim less well than fishes.

639b21–640a9 (*4*) *Distinguish absolute necessity from hypothetical necessity: it is the latter that applies to natural coming-to-be.*

The absolute necessity of the eternals is that they cannot be other than what they are (*Met. E* 1026b27, cf. *G.A.* II. 731b25). Aristotle extends this sense to the conclusions of proofs which deduce the properties of unchanging objects: his stock example is the fact that the interior angles of a plane triangle add up to two right angles. He refers to this deductive necessity at 640a3 below: in the theoretical sciences (concerned with unchanging or abstract objects) we start with what is and prove that something else necessarily belongs to it (cf. *Phys.* II. 200a15; *Met.* Δ 1015b7, Z 1034a31; *An. Post.* II. 90b31). He contrasts this with natural science, in which we show that the end necessitates the means: the means is necessitated *only* by the end (not by prior mechanical causes), and it is necessitated only conditionally—on the hypothesis that the end will come about. He presents this point most fully at *Phys.* II. 199b34:

"Is that which is of necessity, of necessity only on some hypothesis, or can it also be simply of necessity? The general view is that things come to be of necessity, in the way in which a man might think that a city wall came to be of necessity, if he thought that since heavy things are by nature such as to sink down, and light to rise to the surface, the stones and foundations go down, the earth goes above them because it is lighter, and the posts go on top because they are lightest of all. Now without these things no city wall would have come to be; still, it was not on account of them, except as matter, that it came to be, but for the protection and preservation of certain things. Similarly with anything else in which the 'for something' is present: without *things which have a necessary nature* it could not be, but it is, not on account of them, except in the way in which a thing is on account of its matter, but for something. . . . The necessary, then, is necessary on some hypothesis, and not as an end: the necessary is in the matter, the 'that for which' in the account." (Trans. Charlton, italics mine.)

The phrase "things which have a necessary nature" raises the question whether the nature of the materials determines mechanically, to any extent, both the coming-to-be and the character of the product. Aristotle often deduces physical characteristics from the materials used, not from the end served. The materials are composed ultimately from the elements (air, earth, fire, water) which have their own properties. Why should we not say that their properties are absolutely necessitated by their nature, and that they in turn absolutely necessitate the character of their products in so far as it is deducible from the material's properties? How does the case differ from the triangle whose attributes are deducible and are therefore said to be absolutely necessary?

Now the relation between X and the matter-of-X rules out two possible ways in which matter might be thought to necessitate the product. (1) The essential X-properties are not deducible from the matter-of-X, because the matter-of-X is by definition lacking in X-properties. True, the proximate matter must include all the properties needed to compose the product, but they still do not add up to the product's own character. The tissues out of which an eye grows must be translucent, tough, watery, etc., but the eye's ability to see is not necessitated by them. The ability to see is deducible only from the eye's definition and function, and it is the function that necessitates the translucence, etc., not vice versa.

(2) The presence of the proximate matter does not necessitate the coming-to-be of the product. Horns do not grow unless a movement directed towards horns takes place in the materials, and this movement is only necessitated by the animal's growing horns: some grow horns, but others may grow teeth or tusks or claws or simply nothing out of the same material (*P.A.* III. 663b34). Although the powers of hot and cold, etc., are 'necessary', and the material for horns moves up the body 'of necessity', these powers and materials do not bring about the product unless 'nature uses' them. Only exceptionally does a train of events, of the kind that is normally directed towards an end, come about by accident (cf. 640a27 f.).

But there is a third possibility (3) that matter necessitates the non-essential or non-definitory properties of X. The case for this is made as follows. "Granted that the matter-of-X is itself X-less, nevertheless the stuff that provides the matter-of-X is itself a thing having properties. Some of these properties are necessary to X (if the stuff had not got them it could not act as the proximate matter of X), but other properties may be irrelevant or even disadvantageous. All of its properties, useful or not to X, are liable to continue on into the product X, and Aristotle calls them all equally 'necessary because of the material cause'. Those that are necessary to X are therefore doubly caused—*both* for the sake of X *and* of necessity because of the matter (more strictly: not the matter, but the properties housed in the stuff which provides or acts as the matter). Thus a limb is rigid *both* for the sake of locomotion *and* because the bone that it is made of is rigid. But those that are irrelevant to X are caused solely by the matter (i.e. by the concomitant properties of the stuff which acts as proximate matter). Thus the limb is breakable because the bone, being rigid, is breakable in a way that flesh is not. Hence the properties that are not hypothetically necessitated by the product's function are absolutely necessitated by the proximate matter because of what it is made of; and so there is an ultimate dualism between the teleological tendency in growing things and the simple tendencies in the elements and their compounds."

I believe that this argument is correct except for its conclusion. Aristotle certainly distinguished two classes of properties: (1) those that are both necessary for an end and due to the material, (2) those necessary because of the material. Those in class (2) are necessitated because the material has its own 'necessary nature'. He makes this kind of distinction in several careful statements, and it is worth observing exactly what he does and does not say. He never says that the necessity of the necessary properties is absolute and non-hypothetical; he says that it is due to the materials. The chief statements are as follows, *P.A.* I. 642a32: "Necessity signifies sometimes that if there is to be that for the sake of which, these things must be the case; and sometimes that this is their state and nature." *An. Post.* II. 94^b37: "Necessity is of two sorts: one is according to nature and the impulse, the other by force contrary to the impulse, e.g. a stone is borne both upwards and downwards of necessity but not because of the same necessity." *G.A.* II. 743^a36: "Nature uses heat and cold, which possess of necessity the capability to do this and that; in forming animals the cooling and heating take place for an end . . . flesh becomes soft, in one respect of necessity and in another respect for an end." (Cf. ibid. 739^b29, 755^a22; *P.A.* III. 663^b34.) *P.A.* IV. 677^a17: "One should not seek an end in every case; some things are for an end, while many others are necessary consequences of them." At *G.A.* V. 778^a33 he explains that the eye is for the sake of something, but its being blue is not; and that some things do not belong to the definition of the being but their causes must be referred to the matter and the moving cause: "the animal will have an eye of necessity, because it is by hypothesis such an animal, but it will have *such* an eye of necessity too but not that kind of necessity—but because of such natural action and reaction." (778^b16–19.)

This last statement is the nearest that Aristotle gets to saying that material necessity is absolute. Against this, I would suggest that such a dualism is untenable (but see Charlton's defence of it, *Aristotle Physics I and II*, Oxford 1970, pp. 115 f.). It would mean that in the case of class (1) properties, for example, flesh is softened (*a*) for an end, (*b*) automatically by heat. But if the action of heat is absolutely necessitant, what meaning is left for (*a*)? We should have to suppose that a ghost in the machine switches the heat on and off, but in that case what becomes of the absolute necessity? Horns are formed out of material which is 'flowing upwards of necessity' (*P.A.* III. 663^b34): are we to suppose that the necessary movement stops at a point and some other force takes over, and if so what force? If class (2) properties are absolutely necessary, then class (1) is make-believe.

Now Aristotle seems to see no problem here, and it may be that an artificial problem has been created by transferring the necessity that relates propositions to the relationship between events, a thing that Aristotle has not done. He does not speak of absolute necessity in this connection, and our only warrant for doing so is that the necessary properties are deducible from the materials. But if this is expressed rigorously, a confusion between propositions and events becomes apparent. (i) If such materials produce an eye, it will be a blue eye; (ii) but such materials are about to produce an eye; (iii) *ergo* they will produce a blue eye. Aristotle deals with this mistake at *G.C.* II. 337^b3 f., where he says that things that come-to-be are capable of not being, and therefore 'about to happen' does not entail 'will happen'. We are not entitled to say more than: *if* an eye comes to be from these materials, it will be a blue eye. We can never say that an eye *will* be blue without the if-clause. The coming-to-be of the blueness is not necessitated absolutely by the materials, but is contingent upon the coming-to-be of an eye, and this is necessitated hypothetically by the development of sight. Consequently the necessity of class (2) properties is not absolute but in some way hypothetical, though not directly hypothetical in the way that class (1) properties obviously are. This is in fact what Aristotle often says—that hypothetical necessity belongs to things that come to be (as here at 639b24; cf. 642a5 where he seems to correct *An. Post.* 94b37). True, he does not say precisely that things that come to be are always and only hypothetically necessary; but this must be so if hypothetical necessity and teleology are more than "*als ob*" explanations—as he perfectly clearly believes. (Here I disagree with W. Wieland, *Die Aristotelische Physik*, Göttingen 1962, pp. 261 f.).

It is because biological properties come to be—because they are events—that their relationship differs from the relationship between mathematical properties, even though both are deducible when reported in propositions. The parallel to the blue eye would be a blue triangle. We can say that *if* somebody draws triangles with blue ink, there will necessarily be some blue triangles. *If* an eye is made out of blue-eye-producing material, it is necessarily a blue eye. But this is mere tautology. We are never in a position to say *either* that if there are triangles, some must be blue, *or* that if there is blue ink, there will be some triangles drawn with it. On the other hand the necessity by which a triangle's angles add up to two right angles is absolute and non-tautologous. In biology we might say that from the definition of an eye it follows necessarily that it consists of material that is translucent, protective, etc. But there is no absolute necessity that the eye should come to be, and if it does not come to be its material will not come to be. The biological case is still one of hypothetical necessity. (There is also this way of looking at it. We need only consider the triangle mentally to see that its angles add up to two right angles: the triangle exists without being drawn, unlike the blue triangle which exists only in ink. The concept of sight, however, does not necessitate an eye until it is realized in an event. We could consider a putative sixth sense without knowing what its sense organ might be.) Hence all biological properties, whether essential or accidental, are necessitated hypothetically but not absolutely. This raises the question, how are the class (2) properties necessary for an end?

First, as to the scope of hypothetical necessity: is there any reason to limit it to living things? Whenever Aristotle discusses it, he refers to *natural* coming-to-be. 'Nature' excludes artefacts, but includes not only living things but all things that have natures—that is, all given sublunary substances down to and including the elements (*Phys.* II. 192b9). The difference between living and non-living things is that the former have soul; but Aristotle never suggests that hypothetical necessity applies only to ensouled things. Moreover, he says that nature is continuous from non-living to living (*P.A.* IV. 681a12; *H.A.* VIII. 588b4), and the implication is that the same principles operate throughout sublunary events. He makes this pretty clear at the outset of *P.A.* II: "there are three compositions [he means, three stages of composition], of which the first is composition out of the elements earth, air, water, fire . . . which are the matter of the composite bodies; the other differences follow upon these differences, for example heaviness and lightness, denseness and looseness. . . . The second composition is out of the first things, and is the nature of the homoeomerous things in animals, for example bone, flesh. The third and last is that of the non-homoeomerous things, for example face, hand. Now the order in coming-to-be is the opposite of the order in being, for what is later in coming to be is prior by nature, and the first is what is last in coming to be. The house is not for the sake of bricks and stones, but they are for the house: and similarly with the rest of matter. . . . Hence we see that the matter consisting in elements is necessary for the sake of the homoeomerous things, for the latter come to be after the former. Later still come the non-homoeomerous. These reach the end and the conclusion, having received their composition at the third count." (646a12–b9; cf. *G.A.* I. 715a9–11; *Meteor.* IV. 12.)

In this statement the elements bear the same relation to flesh and its properties as flesh does to limbs and their properties. The same arguments apply, except that the elements are not *proximately* but *ultimately* necessary for the limbs. This difference is enough to account for the distinction that Aristotle draws between class (1) and class (2) properties. For example, locomotion necessitates limbs, and limbs proximately necessitate certain material properties—a rigid lever, a joint. These in turn necessitate flesh and bone, which necessitate the action of heat and cold upon foodstuff, which itself necessitates other actions of heat and cold upon earth and water; but these last actions are proximately necessitated not for feeding animals but for growing plants, and plants may necessitate indigestible parts like thorns and wood. Therefore the more remote a material is from the end, the more irrelevant properties it may bring, because of the complexity of nature. Some, like the breakableness of bone, are even disadvantageous (examples at *P.A.* 648a16, 659a19, 663a11, 694a20). Such disadvantages are not failures of teleology, nor defects due to refractoriness in matter. They are the inevitable self-limitation of a creative process, brought about by the teleological development itself; as such, they are hypothetically necessitated, but ultimately not proximately. Aristotle probably likes to distinguish properties necessary for the end from properties necessary because of the matter, because he wishes to distinguish proper characteristics from accidental characteristics. But this line is notoriously difficult, perhaps impossible, to draw.

He often uses the expression 'necessary concomitants', which aptly describes them and does not deny their ultimately hypothetical necessity (ἐξ ἀνάγκης συμβαίνοντα, cf. *P.A.* IV. 677ᵃ18, ᵇ22, 679ᵃ27, 692ᵃ4, 694ᵃ22, ᵇ6; *G.A.* V. 782ᵃ23, 789ᵇ19). The hypothesis which necessitates them is that natural ends are to come to be at all; this necessitates the very existence and properties of the elements. Aristotle does not suggest (as Plato seems to in the *Timaeus*) that the elements are there first as a given, and that a teleological force then comes along and makes the best of them. (It is questionable whether Plato meant this literally either.) What he does say is that nature makes the best possible out of available conditions, referring to the complex properties of the proximate matter in a given situation. The further one gets from immediate ends, the less easy is it to detect finality and the more finality is disturbed, but finality is present even in the elements (*Meteor.* IV. 390ᵃ4; cf. *Met. Λ* 1075ᵃ19–22).

What makes the elements combine into compounds, and these into animals—i.e. what drives the teleological tendency—is a separate question (see note at 641ᵇ10 f.). Meanwhile it seems clear that hypothetical necessity covers the whole of the relation between matter and product in things that come to be.

What then are we to say about the deducibility of properties from the material? The eye is blue because of the material. Granted that the production of the eye is necessitated only conditionally, nevertheless when the production takes place is there not an absolute necessity that the eye produced from *this* material be blue? Are there not absolutely necessary sequences within the hypothetically necessary sequences? Aristotle deals with this question in *G.C.* II. 11, calling it 'reciprocal necessity': if *F* is necessary for the sake of *G*, and if *G* must take place (for any reason), may we say that *G* necessarily follows *F* as well as necessitating *F*? He answers that this is the case only where the sequence as a whole is necessitated absolutely. This could not apply to an individual animal. (His answer in fact seems to be mistaken. For even if the whole sequence is absolutely necessitated, the necessity by which *G* follows *F* still does not flow from the nature of *F*, but from the facts that *G* can only occur after *F* and that *G* is necessary. But this does not affect the point at issue.) Aristotle bases his argument there on the difference between 'about to happen' and 'will happen'. The matter that is potentially an eye is also capable of not becoming an eye, and the matter that is potentially blue may not become blue. As he says at *G.A.* IV. 778ᵃ4, nature is irregular because matter is undetermined. There is never an absolute necessity that *this* will follow *this* in nature. The interactions of natural materials are not in his view a closed nexus, partly because he does not attempt to measure physical and chemical actions (even the actions of the elements are not quantifiable, cf. *De An.* II. 416ᵃ15), and partly because he holds that fresh beginnings of motion are always occurring (*G.A.* IV. 778ᵃ7). Hence the conditional and non-absolute character of the necessity is grounded in the character of natural substances, not in either our own state of ignorance or our preference for expressing certain sequences teleologically.

But when abstracted from coming-to-be and reported in propositions, the conclusion that such a product *may* have such properties is itself absolutely deducible from the premiss that it is made of such material. This is a logical necessity, similar to that of mathematical proofs, whereby a conclusion is self-evidently entailed by the premisses. It does not imply the same necessity in the events reported. The sequence 'this is blue-eye-producing material, therefore it must produce a blue eye' does not correspond to anything in nature. In order to correspond, it should be expressed 'this material usually produces blue eyes, therefore any eye produced from it will probably be blue'. This conclusion, as a logical conclusion, follows with absolute necessity, but nobody would say it reports an absolute necessity in natural coming-to-be.

Now a logical conclusion, like most things, can be analysed, if one wishes, into matter and form. Aristotle does apply this analysis to the relations between concepts and also between propositions. (For genus as the matter of species, see note at 643ᵃ24.) The matter of a conclusion is that which is potentially the conclusion, that is, its grounds or premisses. At *Phys.* II. 195ᵃ18 the premisses of syllogism are cited as one among several examples of the material cause, and the reason given is that they are that out of which (ἐξ οὗ) comes the conclusion (cf. *Top.* VIII. 160ᵃ36). This explains the apparently anomalous statement at *An. Post.* II. 94ᵃ21, where Aristotle purports to quote the four causes, but in place of the material cause puts the grounds which necessitate a consequent (τὸ τίνων ὄντων ἀνάγκη τοῦτ' εἶναι . . . τὸ οὗ ὄντος τοδὶ ἀνάγκη εἶναι). Does he thereby imply that matter in nature similarly necessitates the product, in spite of all that he says elsewhere about hypothetical necessity? To avoid this, Ross (*ad loc.*) argues that Aristotle cannot have meant the material cause here. But it seems inescapable that he did mean it. The passage reads literally: "since we think we have knowledge when we know the cause, and causes are four—(1) the what-it-means-to-be something, (2) the given-what-things this must be, (3) he what-first-moved-it, (4) the for-the-sake-of-what—all these are demonstrated through the middle. For although the 'given-which this must be' does not hold if one premiss is taken but only if at least two, still it then holds whenever the two have one common middle term." He refers to the four-cause doctrine as known; he expresses the other three in usual form; and there is the other precedent for calling premisses matter (*Phys.* II. 195ᵃ18 just quoted). Now in this passage he is not setting out to show that each of the four causes is *always* the *causa cognoscendi*, but that each *can* be. Sometimes (but by no means usually) the efficient cause can be, as in the example he proceeds to give of the raid that began a war. But, as we know, he does not usually regard efficient causes as fully explanatory. In the case of the material cause, he has selected a particular area (possibly the sole area) where matter does necessitate its product, that is, the premisses of a logical conclusion. The example that he proceeds to give is a mathematical proof, in which the premisses in fact report the formal cause—as he immediately remarks (94a34). All that 94a21 does, therefore, is to select a case in which matter *is* fully explanatory of what comes out of it, and this is when it is the matter of a logical conclusion. It does not follow that other matters necessitate their products. What is common to every kind of matter is that it is that out of which the product is produced.

639b24 "but it is the hypothetically necessary that is present" (*τὸ δ' ἐξ ὑποθέσεως καὶ τοῖς ἐν γενέσει πᾶσιν*). *καί* here means not 'also' but 'actually' (cf. Denniston, *Greek Particles*, p. 317).

640a1 "differs as between". By 'theoretical sciences' here Aristotle means those, such as mathematics, that study objects in abstraction from matter (cf. 641b10). He distinguishes them from natural science in *Phys.* II. 2 and 9 (to which 640a2 probably refers).

The Greek literally signifies "different *both* (*τε*) in the case of natural science *and* of the theoretical sciences", which Düring takes to mean that natural science and the theoretical sciences together differ from some other—presumably the productive crafts just mentioned (I. Düring, 'Aristotle's Method in Biology', *Aristote et les problèmes de méthode*, Louvain 1961, p. 215). It is true that in *Met. E* 1 and *K* 7 Aristotle lists natural science with mathematics and metaphysics as theoretical sciences in contrast with the practical sciences (ethics, politics) and the productive sciences (crafts). But even there he points out that natural science differs from mathematics and metaphysics in that it does not study abstracts. Here the context shows that Aristotle is contrasting the hypothetical necessity of nature with the absolute necessity of the eternal objects studied by theoretical sciences, and the example 'health or man' (640a4) shows that he is still bracketing crafts and natural science as exhibiting hypothetical necessity (cf. the parallel passage at *Phys.* II. 194a22). To avoid difficulty, Ogle deleted the *τε* at 640a1. But this is unnecessary, for *τε* can connect things which are being contrasted (cf. *G.A.* I. 719b18, 20, 29, *passim*).

640a3 "Begin from what is": this argument is filled out at *Phys.* II. 200a15–30. In mathematics we deduce from something that exists, e.g. a straight line, that something else necessarily holds, e.g. that the angles of a triangle add up to two right angles. But in the case of things that come to be we deduce from something that *will* exist, e.g. a house, that something else must come to be first, e.g. bricks. In either case the deduction starts from the definition (of straight line or house) and shows what this entails. The difference is that in coming-to-be (which consists of activities, πράξεις, 200a24) the end necessitates the prior means, and what is there first chronologically does not necessitate what follows, whereas mathematics is not about activities but about unchangeable objects, so that there we argue from what is to what else is.

The reasoning is in both cases from premiss to conclusion. But if a coming-to-be is reported in such reasoning, it will be found that the premisses report the product while the conclusion reports the matter. 'If an eye is to be, there must first be tissues', but *not* 'if there are tissues, there must then be an eye'. In natural science the deduction is absolutely necessary, but it reports sequences of events that are only hypothetically necessitated. In mathematics the deduction is absolutely necessary, and it reports coexistent properties that are absolutely necessitated.

640a6 "Nor can one link". In *G.C.* II. 11 (to which 640a8–9 refers; cf. also *An. Post.* II. 12) Aristotle argues that a hypothetically necessary sequence cannot proceed *ad infinitum* either into the future or into the past; there must be a starting-point that is itself absolutely necessitated, since without it there will be infinite regress of causes. If *P* is necessary in order that *Q* may come to be, and if *Q* is necessary in order that *R* may come to be, and so *ad infinitum*, there will be no cause for the process to start at all and *P* will not happen. Similarly, looking to the past, if *A* presupposes B which presupposes *C* and so *ad infinitum*, the sequence cannot start.

In the same chapter Aristotle asks whether the necessity in a hypothetical sequence can be 'reciprocal' (ἀντιστρέφειν), as mentioned above, p. 82. He answers that here too there must be one member of the sequence that is absolutely necessitated. That is to say, hypothetical necessity is never a sufficient explanation by itself.

This seems to be the point at 640a6, and this is why explanations of nature cannot be reduced to 'necessity' (639b22), for the necessity in nature is only hypothetical. It is not clear what he has in mind at 640a7, "because this is, therefore that is". Presumably he is speaking of hypothetical sequences, but his usual expression is 'because this *will be*, therefore that is'. Possibly he is referring to sequences whose members go on existing together. For example, a man necessitates organs, which necessitate blood, which necessitates a liver . . . but however far you go with such a sequence you never reach a sufficient cause of the existence of any of the members, because the whole sequence is contingent upon the man's existence, which is not necessitated absolutely. The same applies to a future sequence. (See also Kirwan's note on *Met.* *E* 3 in *Aristotle's Metaphysics, Books Γ, Δ, E,* trans. by Christopher Kirwan, Oxford 1971, p. 196.)

640a10–b4 (5) *We should state the manner of a thing's existence before stating the manner of its coming-to-be.*

Just as we should expound what a thing is before we expound why it is there (639b7–10), so we should expound the state of an animal part when it does exist before we expound its growth in the animal. The animal's development is explained primarily by its adult state. This principle is the basis of Aristotle's teleology and is often repeated (e.g. 641b31; *G.A.* V. 778b2; see note at 641b10–642a1). In *G.A.* I and II he explains that the adult state is contained potentially in the male seed, which transmits it to the female material which becomes the embryo.

640a13 "as we said before": presumably at 639b8, though he did not actually answer his own question there.

640a18 "For coming-to-be . . . of coming-to-be": perhaps a deliberate quotation of Plato, *Philebus* 54A8 and C4; he repeats it at *G.A.* V. 778b5.

640a21 "backbone . . . broken": presumably in the uterus. Ogle says that Herbert Spencer proposed a similar explanation. For others of this type cf. 640b13, *G.A.* IV. 764b32.

640a23 "seed previously constituted" (*συστὰν*): this is the reading of all MSS., and is accepted in the Berlin and Teubner editions. Platt suggested *συνιστὰν*, "that constitutes it" (transitive), which gives a sharper point and has been accepted by recent editors. But the traditional reading also fits Aristotle's theory.

640a27–33: these lines answer a possible objection at this point. Why must we infer that the hen came from an egg and the egg from a previous hen, when we see some animals spontaneously generated? Aristotle's answer, which is almost in note form, is an analogy which he puts more fully at *Met. Z* 1032b23 and 1034a9. Health is produced by the physician who prescribes massage, which causes warmth which causes balance of humours which causes health. The same health can be produced accidentally by unprescribed warmth, which starts the same train of events. But there are other products, like statues, which cannot be spontaneous. In their case there is no question but that they are produced only by a pre-existing artist, whose mind contains the art of sculpture which consists of imagined sculptures together with the knowledge how to make them. The spontaneous production of health does not disprove the existence of the physician's art. When the product is spontaneous, it still comes about in the same sequence of events as defined by the art. (Cf. *An. Post.* II. 95a4; *Phys.* II. 199b19.) The spontaneous animals (testaceans, eels, some fishes, many insects) are generated when the conditions of a foetus happen to arise: a portion of mud warmed by the sun gets separated off, enclosing a foamy bubble of *pneuma* which sets movement going and makes a foetus (*G.A.* III. 11; cf. note at *G.A.* II. 736^{b}29).

640a33 "Hence . . .": resumes the argument from ^{a}26. The best explanation is to be able to say (1) that because a man is such (e.g. perceptive) therefore he must have these parts (sense organs). If we cannot argue so, we may be able to show (2) that he cannot survive without this part (e.g. heart or liver, *P.A.* III. 670^{a}23), or at least (3) that he is better with this part than without (e.g. kidneys, 670^{b}23). And given those parts, these necessarily accompany them (e.g. spleen, which is the necessary concomitant of the liver, 670^{a}30). The difference between (2) and (3) is between living and living well (cf. *G.A.* I. 717^{a}15). Aristotle uses almost the same words about the hollowing of bone-joints, without which movement would be "either impossible or not well done" (*P.A.* II. 654^{b}22).

640b4–641a17 (*6*) *The early philosophers spoke of matter and its necessary movements, but one should also speak of form and function.*

640^{b}8 refers to Empedocles (strife and love), Anaxagoras (mind), and Democritus (spontaneity); these are the three that Aristotle quotes most in biology. At ^{b}9 the quotation about fire and earth might come from any of several pre-Socratics. At ^{b}13 the explanation of stomach and nostrils is not otherwise known but could well be from Empedocles; a similar account in terms of water and fire occurs in the Hippocratic treatise *Regimen* I. 9. (VI. 482, L.).

640b14 "residue" (*περίττωμα*): not only excreta but all by-products of blood such as phlegm, bile, milk, etc. (*G.A.* I. 717^{a}30 note).

640b16 "bodies . . . bodies": the argument seems to be that air and water are no more than elements in their scheme, as is shown by the fact that they are also the materials of everything else; hence they treat the elements as what animal bodies are made of, when they should speak of flesh etc. If so, 'bodies' (*σώματα*) has different references in ^{b}16 and 17, but this is tolerable since it is a very ordinary word. At ^{b}17 it refers to air and water; Aristotle himself regularly uses it of the elements, 'the simple bodies'.

640b19 "homoeomerous" (*ὁμοιομερῆ*): those which divide into parts like the whole, as flesh divides into flesh, i.e. the tissues. The non-homoeomerous parts (i.e. organs) divide into unlike parts, as a nose divides not into noses but into flesh and bones. Aristotle uses this distinction to establish analogies and homologies (Chapter 4). It depends upon identifying organs by function, for morphology alone will not show that an organ is an organ (640^{b}29 f.).

640b26 "composite" (*συνόλου*): the whole *and* its parts, i.e. the form or structure of the whole *and* the proximate matter (cf. *Met. Z* 10–12). If asked what a bed is, our best reply is to describe a structure. If this is not possible (because we cannot divorce the structure from the material, cf. *Met. Z* 11. 1036^{b}2–7), then we state the matter but not baldly as 'wood': we say 'such pieces of wood shaped so and joined so', i.e. we cannot avoid stating the bed's conformation.

At 640^{b}24–8 Aristotle refers to the *eidos* (form) of the bed as *σχῆμα, ἰδέα, μορφή*, all of which signify the visible external shape. His point becomes clear at 640^{b}29 f.: the *suchness* of a bed is definable morphologically, but the *suchness* (i.e. the form when adequately defined) of a living thing includes being alive and able to function.

640b30 "exists": i.e. "is what it is".

640b36 "homonymously": equivocally named (cf. *Cat.* 1^{a}1, Ackrill's note).

641a6 What does the carpenter say? Possibly (1) that the hand he has cut out is a real hand: Democritus is equally mistaken in thinking that living things differ from other things, whether living or dead, only in shape and colour, i.e. that living phenomena are sufficiently accounted for by simple mixture of materials (cf. *G.A.* II 740^{a}15). But this makes the carpenter rather a simpleton. More probably he says (2) that this is how he shaped the hand. Democritus says that it was shaped by the automatic movements ('powers') of air and earth. The carpenter's account is better because he at least recognises that the adze and drill had to be directed (cf. *G.A.* II. 734^{b}27–30).

641a16 "speak about that": i.e. about the animal as *such a thing* (*περὶ ἐκείνου=περὶ τοῦ ζῴου ὡς τοιούτου*).

641a17–32 (7) *The animal's form and being is its soul: hence the natural philosopher must include some account of soul.*

'If this is soul' (^{a}17): 'this' (*τοῦτο*) is the *suchness* just referred to (^{a}16 *ἐκείνου* and ^{a}17 *εἶδους*, form). Aristotle argues in full for this concept of soul in *De An.* II. 1. It is the animal's ability to function, considered in abstraction from materials: that is, the condition of possessing the appropriate structures and of being able to live and grow. As the animal becomes more highly diversified, its soul has more varied powers. A plant has no more than the power to nourish and reproduce itself, and this is also the state of the animal foetus. The lowest animals develop the capacity to perceive through touch, the next lowest to move, the next to perceive through other senses. Each higher power presupposes the lower, so that what happens is a progressive differentiating of the soul rather than the addition of new 'parts' (cf. *G.A.* II. 736^a35 f., *De An.* II. 3). However, it was a commonplace since Plato to speak of 'parts' of the soul, and Aristotle often does so (cf. *De An.* III. 9).

641^a22 "if not about all soul": cf. 641^a32 f. The only 'part' of soul that is in doubt is the human intellect (*nous*): it is the one power of soul that is not a bodily function but enters the human being 'from outside' and may exist independently of body (*G.A.* II. 736^b28; *De An.* III. 4–5). It is strange that Aristotle should say that the intellect is not included in man's nature (641^b9) nor in that part of soul 'in virtue of which the animal is such' (641^a23). Taken generally, it is an overstatement, because although Aristotle never attempts a precise definition of man, he clearly regards intellect as the chief feature differentiating man from other animals. But he gives in effect three reasons for excluding it from natural science. (1) 'Nature' means the natures of things that come to be, that have matters and movers. But intellect consists solely of its own objects, that is universals and forms; although it has both potential and actual states, these states are not produced by anything outside intellect itself. It is not a function of body; nor is it a function of other powers of soul, for although it may acquire general concepts through perception, the intellectual apprehension of concepts is not a function of perception nor of the other mental powers such as imagination and memory. Therefore neither the existence nor the exercising of the intellect is the end of any process. We cannot say that man is so composed as to be capable of intellect, because intellect is not the product of any composition. Nor is it a moving cause of man except indirectly, in the way that the universe's prime mover moves it, by arousing desire. Consequently man is as complete and explainable a thing as other animals are, without taking account of intellect; similarly, as an animal, he is complete without happiness, even though this is most clearly his proper end as a man. Throughout his zoology Aristotle treats man just as one other animal (albeit the most 'perfected' animal); but this is because he deliberately excludes from zoology what he himself thinks the most important aspects of man. The other two reasons follow from this. (2) If zoology included the study of intellect, it would include all intelligibles (641^b1). But these are not part of *nature*, i.e. of things that come to be: intellect is not a moving cause (641^b7). (3) The intelligibles are not 'for the sake of something' (641^b10 f.) as everything in nature is.

641^a27 "moving cause and end". This is one of the places where Aristotle unequivocally puts together two roles of the soul that seem conflicting.

The soul is *both* form *and* mover (cf. *De An.* II. 415b8–12). In view of such a statement it is difficult to argue that Aristotle did not hold these theories simultaneously but 'developed' his doctrine from one to the other (Nuyens, *L'Évolution de la psychologie d'Aristote*, Louvain, 1948).

(1) As the *form* of the body, the soul is the animal's being (*ousia*) considered in abstraction from flesh and bones. It is the animal's functioning, including its ability to function (at times when it is not actually functioning). In his most careful discussion (*De An.* II. 1) Aristotle makes it clear that the soul is not a ghost sitting in the heart and dispatching *pneuma* to work the muscles, as some of his less careful expressions elsewhere suggest (e.g. *De Mot. An.* 10). The soul *is* the working of the muscles, the perceiving through sense organs, the nourishing and growing. It is not merely a resultant of such working; this is shown by his rejection of the epiphenomenon (ἁρμονία) theory (*De An.* I. 4).

(2) As the *mover* of the body, the soul is the animal's ability and tendency to grow, change, move. Again, it is not something distinct from flesh that makes the flesh grow. It is the nature of flesh and blood, once they have been constituted into a foetus, to continue to grow and function as a coherent organism; this includes diversification into the various parts of the developing animal. The tendency was implanted in the foetal material by soul-movements transmitted in the sire's semen (*G.A.* II. 3). These movements must become more complex as the animal develops, and they must be self-coordinating in the direction of the complete adult state, the 'end'. From the outset, therefore, the soul is potentially this end, which is the definition of the animal.

What unites these two aspects of soul is Aristotle's teleological theory (see note at 641b10 f.). He does not hold that a directive tendency has to be superimposed upon normal physical and chemical interactions, but that the normal interactions include a directive tendency. By 'cause' he means an explanatory factor, not necessarily a separate item (cf. Charlton, *Aristotle's Physics I, II*, pp. 98 f.). The soul is both the movement and a *cause* of the movement in the sense that functioning-*so* is (partly) explanatory of the animal's functioning.

The relation between soul and life is briefly stated in *De An.* II. 1 (cf. 412a15, 20, 27, b25–26). When an animal or foetus or seed is sufficiently equipped (including heat) to live, then it has soul. Soul is therefore a precondition of life; but if the body ceases to be capable of life (e.g. through loss of heat or of vital structures) then it no longer has soul. The formal definition of soul is "the first actuality [which is to the second actuality as sleep is to waking] of a natural body which has life potentially" (*De An.* II. 412a27).

641a31 "the other way round": i.e. that the soul is nature due to matter. Matter *enables* soul to exist, but does not determine the animal's nature except accidentally. The matter can be said to *be* the animal only in the sense that it becomes it when organized by soul. Similarly loose timber is potentially a bed in that it can become a bed actually if appropriately organized.

641a32–b10 (*8*) *Natural philosophy does not study the intellect and the intelligibles.*

For the argument, see note at 641a22. Aristotle's account of the intellect and its objects in *De An.* III leaves it uncertain how much he included among intelligibles, in fact he seems to have vacillated over this. He is always clear, however, that they are confined to human and divine minds. The animals can be clever and intelligent (φρόνιμος) but cannot contemplate (θεωρεῖν), i.e. apprehend universals and reason from them to discursive knowledge (ἐπιστήμη, cf. *Met. A* 1). Here he considers intelligibles merely as objects that do not move or change, i.e. abstracted forms and mathematical concepts.

641b5 "Growth . . . alteration . . . locomotion": a summary of theories explained elsewhere.

Nutritive soul is the ability to concoct foodstuff into flesh, etc. (using heat as the instrument). Since nutrition comes from the same materials as the embryo was constituted from, nutritive soul causes reproduction as well as growth (*G.A.* II. 740b35, cf. *De An.* II. 415a26). Aristotle holds that this is the only kind of soul possessed by plants (contrary to Plato, *Tim.* 77B). He does not report sensitive land plants but he knows of sensitivity in sponges, which he quotes to show that there is no clear borderline between plants and animals (*H.A.* I. 487b9; V. 548b10, 549a8; VIII. 588b11).

Perceptive or sensitive soul is said to be the source of alteration in the restricted sense of alteration which Aristotle uses in *Phys.* VII. 2–3 (244b2–248a6). It is a change of quality (ποιότης), but of only one of the four kinds of quality described in *Cat.* 8. Changes of shape and of state are excluded (σχῆμα, ἕξις, 245b9, 246a10 f.), and change of capacity (δύναμις) is simply omitted. Aristotle confines alteration to change of affections (πάθη), such as becoming hot, sweet, dense, dry, white (244b7, cf. 245b13, 246a7). These are changes in the sensible quality of an existing thing, not changes of substance or being. In his zoology Aristotle calls such qualities variously affections (πάθη), or affective conditions (παθήματα), or powers arising from the elements, or cases of 'the more and less' (cf. 644b13) such as denseness, roughness, hardness, colour. In *G.A.* V he attributes some of them to such causes as climate, soil, water, heat. But the point at 641b5 is that the cause of the *movement*—that is, the efficient cause of the alteration—is soul. Aristotle says this at *G.C.* I. 321b6: the moving cause of the alteration is in that which is altered, just as the cause of nutrition is within the body nourished but not within the food that enters (cf. 322a12: potential flesh is made into actual flesh by that within the body which causes growth, τὸ ἐνὸν αὐξητικόν).

Aristotle's distinction between the external stimulus and the internal cause of alteration seems correct. If my hand becomes sunburnt, the alteration is provoked by sunshine but caused by something in my body. If I get paint on my hand, that is not an alteration but a covering-up of its colour. If I warm myself at the fire, two separate things happen: one is a superficial warming of my hands which lasts while the fire warms them but fades afterwards, the other is that my hands 'warm up' and the muscles work freely again. This warming-up is the renewal of natural warmth which was lost faster than it was replaced while I was in the cold, but can be retained now that I am in a warm place. Its cause is within, and it is a real alteration which it would not be reasonable to call the same kind of change as the warming that came directly from the fire. The latter was accidental to what really happened, as we can see by comparing the warmth that my hands still have when the other objects in the room have cooled.

Alteration, then, may be brought about in sensible qualities by contact with sensible objects, but not mechanically: it is caused by soul. Since soul does not react mechanically, it must be through the exercise of its own power. It is not by nutritive nor by intellective power, so it must be by perception. If a change of food brings about a change in affective conditions, this must be due to perception of the body's internal processes. The same will apply to the perception of perceptions: this will be why a man can blush with shame (*Cat.* 9b30; *E.N.* IV. 1128b13) when his memory or expectation of certain pains or pleasures causes his perceptive soul to originate a movement of heat into his cheeks (*Probl.* 905a12).

Therefore the argument to be supplied here must be: alteration is a change of proper (not accidental) affection (*Phys.* VII. 245b4, *G.C.* I. 321b4), occasioned by contact with sensible objects (245b5) but caused by the internal source of change (321b6); this source is soul, which, if it is moved by sensible objects, must be perceptive soul. This sounds too doctrinaire. Moreover it would follow that plants do not have alteration since they have no perception. But probably Aristotle would not mean to departmentalize the soul so rigidly, but merely to show that perception *is* a source of movement while intellect is not.

The 'other part, not the intellective' (641b7), which originates locomotion, is desire (ὄρεξις, *De An.* III. 10). In *De An.* Aristotle distinguishes contemplative from practical intellect. The latter reasons about how to achieve ends, and he considers whether it originates movement; but he concludes that while either it or imagination occasions desire, the true source of movement is desirous soul (ὀρεκτική). He may have this problem in mind when he expresses the matter so evasively here.

In the zoological works Aristotle divides the soul simply into nutritive (common to plants and animals), perceptive (animals only), and intellective (man).

641b9 "nature": *qua* being, moving cause, or end (641a27).

641b10–642a1 (9) *Nature always acts for the sake of ends.*

Aristotle's argument for teleology has two bases: (i) we see ends in nature; (ii) we see that nature is regular, not random.

(i) We do not see only interacting elements, but composed wholes having their own properties, which are not simple additions of the properties of their ingredients. We see that animals grow from seed to adult; this is a movement towards a goal, and such a movement is not attributable to simple interaction of elements.

(ii) We see that animals breed true, which shows (a) that their kind is predetermined in the parent's seed, (b) that their growth is organized in a determinate direction; in neither case do we see random results.

Aristotle assumes that random conditions must produce disorder. Therefore he does not consider a mechanical solution, such as that put forward later by Epicurus, that random movements of a sufficiently large number of elementary particles will throw up a self-preserving orderly cosmos (Lucretius I. 1021 f.). If there is order, therefore, he thinks there must be a sustaining cause of order. The 'other such origin and cause' (641b15), which we see in nature comparable with an art, is a teleological tendency which modifies the interactions of elements so that they combine to form animals instead of producing chaos. What modifies them? Does Aristotle mean an 'extra factor' in nature, such as some modern teleological arguments posit?

There seem to be two reasons why one might think so: (1) Aristotle separates the causes, calling the teleological movement *another* cause over against the hot and the cold and the 'necessary' causes; (2) his language often suggests an *over-all* economy of nature, as though controlled by a presiding genius.

Now (1) is not a valid reason because, although Aristotle has taken over the language of the 'good' and the 'necessary' causes from Plato's *Timaeus*, his own stricter statements leave no room for any absolutely necessary causes in nature: there are on the one hand *ends* such as complete animal states, and on the other hand everything that makes such ends achievable—from the animal's organs down to the elements, all of which are either immediately or ultimately necessitated for the sake of ends (see note at 639b21). Therefore all natural actions and reactions are teleological. True, there still remains a difference between the action of heat in simply burning away stuff so long as the stuff is there, and its action in concocting food into flesh but not so far that it becomes marrow —i.e. a limited action. In an animal the action is limited by soul, which is in the flesh and controls the addition of new flesh from food *and* therefore causes the heat to concoct the food into so much flesh. But soul is not something other than this activity (see note at 641a27). It *is* the animal's activity, within which the activity of the flesh is part of the animal's activity, and within that again the activity of hot and cold is part of the activity of the flesh. Heat acts *so* in this part, and *so* in that part, and *so* when it is not in any part. All its actions are natural, in two senses: (i) they are what it can do, (ii) they are what it does in given conditions. Soul is a special case of nature: actions within a living organism coordinate themselves.

When Aristotle calls nature's teleology 'wonderful', he means that it should excite admiration, not surprise. He does not treat directiveness as an awkward mechanical problem—how to explain, as it were, the bending of the laws of nature. In fact directiveness, which is the chief concern of modern teleology, is not his most important evidence. At *Phys.* II. 8 he quotes a few stock examples from popular teleology, like the spider spinning webs, but only in order to generalize from them to the statement that nature does things for ends. He does not enter into contemporary discussions of supernatural causes (cf. Xenophon, *Memorabilia* IV. 3 for crude providential teleology), because he argues that it is *natural* for things to behave so. He does not ask what makes heat act differently in different conditions, and this must be because in each case the conditions are a sufficient explanation. There is no bending of natural interactions.

The evidence that Aristotle relies on is the existence of ends. He criticizes his materialist predecessors not for ignoring directiveness but for failing to distinguish between parts and wholes, and for failing to see that growth is intelligible in the light of adult states but not vice versa. When he says that nature is the efficient cause of teleological movements, unless we suppose that he means two natures (one directing the other) the more straightforward sense of his words is that the teleological tendency is part of the natural movement. Natural processes naturally move towards natural ends. If this does not seem enough to us, it may be because we are the victims of mechanical models.

What then should be said of (2) Aristotle's apparent suggestions that there is a unified over-all teleology in nature? He certainly suggests this when he compares nature with a prudent householder who diverts materials from one use to another, when he compares natural processes with craft-processes, and when he seems to subordinate some ends to other ends—especially when he says that the individual reproduces itself for the sake of the species. But each of these suggestions, on examination, turns out to afford little ground for so large a conclusion.

First the personification of Nature, and the craft model. Aristotle provides no overt place in his cosmology or theology for a unified creative force in sublunary nature, so the question really is whether he has allowed the craft model to mislead him into hypostasizing a Dame Nature like Plato's Demiurge (supposing the Demiurge to be meant literally, which is doubtful). We can see why he wants the model, apart from having inherited it from Socrates, because it usefully portrays a teleological sequence while separating the factors in it: the craftsman as source of movement, the craft as the abstracted forms of products and instruments, the material to be shaped, the physical tools to be used. Thus it clarifies the ambiguities of 'nature', which Aristotle constantly points out: nature *qua* being, *qua* abstracted form, *qua* actualization, *qua* mover or proximate matter or coming-to-be. But, just because it has this use, the analogy could be misleading at the point where it breaks down, which is precisely this separation of determinant factors which are not separate in nature. In natural coming-to-be (e.g. the growth of an animal) there is no stage at which the matter is separate from the teleological movement, so that you could say 'here is the matter with its own movements and there is the superimposed movement'. The parts cannot be examined in isolation from the whole, because if they are not joined in the whole they have no behaviour as parts but only a behaviour as something else (disintegrating flesh). There is no situation comparable with that in which a craftsman takes materials, then puts them into order, and thus makes something. Has Aristotle fallen into this trap? No, because he keeps warning us of it. "The art is the product's source and form, but in a different body, whereas the movement of nature is in the thing itself" (*G.A.* II. 735^{a}3; *Cael.* 301^{b}17, *Met.* *Λ* 1070^{a}7)—i.e. there is no separation of mover from material in nature, as there is in art. In nature it is as though the ship-building art were within the timber (*Phys.* II. 199^{b}28). There is no deliberating in nature, just as there is none in the craft (*Phys.* II. 199^{a}20, ^{b}28). Since it is the craftsman who deliberates, this last statement shows that the analogy lies between nature and craft rather than between nature and craftsman. In all such statements Aristotle seems to be consciously guarding against one false feature of the craft analogy—that it suggests a dualism between constructive force and material. Thus he denies any support that the analogy might give to his personification of Nature who 'does nothing in vain', who 'fashions' things and acts like a householder. Such language may be due to popular habit, but it is also convenient. For there are many modern biologists who, though far from admitting teleology, personify nature and speak of the 'purpose' of animals' structures. At least Aristotle never speaks of 'purpose' in zoology.

Secondly, there is the question whether particular ends are subordinated to general ends. The good in the whole cosmos depends upon the unmoved mover ('God'), and all things are somehow ordered together (συντέτακταί πως, *Met.* *Λ* 1075^{a}16). Now the general cause of sublunary growth and decay is the movement of the sun in the ecliptic, which produces seasonal variations of temperature; these cause mingling and separating, and hence coming-to-be and perishing. To this extent the growth and decay of particular animals is linked with the movement of the heavens. But natural bodies initiate their own movements (hence Aristotle can call nature 'a beginning of movement'), and within animals there are continually fresh starts of motion. Therefore the general good order of the universe does not imply an over-all control of particular cases. Most of Aristotle's comments on natural economy in fact refer to the economy within a particular animal, not to a general economy of nature. There are, however, two anomalous statements. At *Pol.* I. 1256^b16 he says that plants are for the sake of animals, and animals are for the sake of men. At *P.A.* IV. 696^b26 he says that sharks have their mouth underneath, both for the sake of other animals whose lives are thereby saved by the shark's delay in turning upside down to take them, and to avoid overeating. Now, to build a theory of over-all teleology upon these two passing remarks would be hazardous. At *Phys.* II. 198^b9 Aristotle says that the natural philosopher must explain how it is "better so, not absolutely, but in respect of each thing's being". This cannot be reconciled with a doctrine that the function of grass is to be eaten by sheep, and of sheep to be eaten by men. It is more likely that the strong meaning of these two statements is not intended, but that Aristotle means only that *A* is for the sake of *B* in the sense that *B* cannot happen without *A*. Man depends upon animals for food, and animals upon plants; if the latter were not present, the former could not be. Similarly the successful existence of smaller fishes implies that sharks cannot take them too easily.

Thirdly, does Aristotle's theory of the preservation of species imply that the individual animal's good is subordinated to the good of the species? Aristotle holds that a primary function of each animal and plant, other than those generated spontaneously, is to generate another like itself (*G.A.* II. 735^a18, *passim*). This is the nearest that mortal beings can get to living permanently (*G.A.* II. 731^b31; *De An.* II. 415^a29; *G.C.* II. 336^b30; cf. Plato, *Symposium* 207D). Some fishes that live in a hostile environment are especially prolific, 'for nature retrieves the wastage by quantity' (*G.A.* III. 755^a31). In plants nature has 'arranged' that the sexes are combined, to facilitate reproduction (*G.A.* I. 731^a25); but in animals the sexes are separate for other reasons, so nature ensures a sufficient production of females even though the female is a deviation from correct reproduction (*G.A.* II. 732^a2, III. 767^b9).

Now none of these statements implies that an individual's good is overridden or replaced or diminished by a greater good of the species. No animal is prevented thereby from achieving its own end. What 'nature has arranged' is that the inevitable death of individuals, and the inevitable separation of sexes, do not result in the annihilation of their species. This need be no more than a way of saying that there is a natural compensation in numbers. The fact that species survive in hostile circumstances *implies* that there are enough individuals to make good the losses. But the one kind of loss that numbers cannot circumvent is natural death, and this fact makes reproduction a special case. Here it is important to follow Aristotle's order of argument in *G.C.* II. 10–11. He does *not* say that the species is more important than the individual, nor that the individual exists for the sake of the species, nor even that reproduction is primarily for the species. He starts from the premiss that coming-to-be is ceaseless, and shows why it must be cyclical—growth, completion, waning, death, growth . . . Then he asks why the same individual does not grow again (338^b6), and answers that its being is destructible. What we see growing again is not itself but its kind. That is, Aristotle again takes it as a premiss that reproduction of the kind is ceaseless, and gives as reason for it that renewal or continuance of the individual is impossible. Therefore continuance of the species is a second-best, not the prior consideration. But why should it not be achieved by spontaneous generation? Aristotle answers that individuals reproduce themselves because they naturally seek to be rather than not to be, and thus they share in continuance as best they can. When he says that in this way "the god completed the universe in the only way left, by making coming-to-be ceaseless" (*G.C.* II. 336^b31), and that plants and animals 'desire' (ὀρέγεται, *De An.* II. 415^b1) to share in the divine, this is figurative language; for plants have no desire, and there is no creative god in Aristotle's system. His statements therefore reduce to this: reproduction is part of self-preservation, and its continuance is part of the continuance of the universe.

The *fixity* of species is a different matter, not entailed by the continuance of species. It was important to the Neoplatonists and later Stoics, and to Linnaeus, on theological grounds that are not relevant to Aristotle (they held species to be thoughts in God's mind). There is room to doubt whether Aristotle in fact believed that species do not change. He accepts the possibility of new species arising from fertile hybrids (*G.A.* II. 746^a30). He draws attention to animals that overlap generic classifications, and emphasizes the continuity of the *scala naturae* so that one cannot say whether certain testaceans are animals or plants (*P.A.* IV. 681^a10, 697^a29). The *G.A.* is not about reproducing species but about reproducing the parents. The natural product is a male resembling the sire, but defects may cause a progressive deterioration—a male resembling the dam, a female offspring, then offspring resembling remoter ancestors, and finally one resembling merely the species or even the genus (*G.A.* IV. 3). A species is a set of properties, a *suchness*, that is handed on from sire to offspring with changes due to physical circumstances. There is nothing in Aristotle's theory to prevent an 'evolution of species', i.e. a continuous modification of the kinds being transmitted. But he had no evidence of evolution, having no palaeontology, and therefore had no occasion to consider such a theory, of which there was no proponent in ancient philosophy. (The theories of Anaximander, of Empedocles, and of the atomists were not evolutionary, but explained how animals capable of reproducing themselves originated spontaneously.)

There seems to be insufficient ground, therefore, for holding that Aristotle believed either in an 'over-all teleology' or in an 'extra factor' in living things. 'Nature' does not seem to be more than a collective name for the natures of particular things. The efficient cause of teleology is clearly said to be 'nature', by which he must mean, therefore, that when particular things behave naturally they tend towards ends. 'Purpose' is never mentioned, and 'desire' is a rare metaphor; Aristotle makes it clear that teleology operates where there is no deliberating or seeking, for example when trees grow leaves for the sake of the fruit (*Phys.* II. 199^a20). Nor is there sufficient ground to limit this tendency to living things: Aristotle's considered statements clearly include the elementary properties in natural coming-to-be, which is subject to hypothetical but not absolute necessity. By hypothetical necessity he means the necessity of implication: the end *T* implies the previous sequence *a*, *b*, *c*, . . . What brings the sequence about? In replying 'nature' (or 'soul' in the case of living organisms) Aristotle is saying simply that *it is the case*—this is how the laws of nature operate. Within an organism, actions are interdependent and tend towards a coherent pattern—the form of the completed organism. In nature over all there *is* a balance, not only in the sense of equilibrium but of a good and expedient order, in which each animal is able to grow towards its own completion, within necessary limits. Underlying Aristotle's theory there may be an unconscious assumption of hylozoism. But all that he says explicitly is that this good order and these patterns can only be brought about if certain teleological sequences regularly occur: and they *do* occur.

641^b10–12. This transitional argument, condensed to note form here, can be filled out from *Phys.* II. 194^a1–12, *Met.* *B* 996^a22–32, *K* 1061^a28, *M* 3, *De An.* I. 403^b15. The mathematician considers abstracted curves, whereas the natural scientist considers curves in flesh (e.g. snub noses). Why is *snub* not abstractable? Not simply because it is in matter, for mathematical objects have matter too (extension). Aristotle says it is because natural objects are in movement (*Phys.* II. 194^a5) and because this movement is for the sake of ends (*Met.* *B* 996^a22). He illustrates his meaning from borderline cases. A study such as optics considers mathematical lines, but considers them as they are in nature; on the other hand mechanics considers natural quantities and bodies but treats them as mathematical objects. Aristotle does not necessarily imply that natural movements cannot be quantified, but that 'applied mathematics' is of no use in zoology. His reason is not like that of the practical engineer who criticizes the theoretician for envisaging weightless pieces of string. It is rather that natural movement is *for ends*. This implies that the behaviour of bodies in nature cannot be reduced to the mechanics of bodies abstracted from nature, since the explanation has to include the teleological tendency. You can abstract the curve of the snub nose, but the construction by which you produce it mathematically will not present the interacting forces which produced it in nature. It does not follow that these forces could not be so presented, giving the snub-nose curve as the resultant. But to do this you must know all the material factors, and Aristotle regards this as impracticable since matter is irregular and undetermined (cf. p. 82). Nevertheless it was his own suggestions about optics (*Meteor.* III) that eventually led Grosseteste and Roger Bacon to attempt mathematical analyses of nature (cf. A. C. Crombie, *Augustine to Galileo*, 1961, vol. i, chap. iii. 3). Since the teleological movement is towards a predictable form, it could be precisely stated if only one knew the exact state of the materials. Consequently Aristotle's distinction between natural science and mathematics (p. 84) rests ultimately on the difference in the amount of quantifiable data available.

641^{b}14 "another such origin . . . grasp": i.e. a cause comparable with the art, which is the producing of ends out of materials. For ἔχειν = 'grasp mentally' cf. *Meteor.* IV. 389^{b}24, 390^{b}14, 18. Just as we have generalized a concept of the hot and the cold from our experience of the perceptible universe, so we have gained a concept of the achievement of ends—especially from observing the stars, which exhibit a more perfect and direct achievement of ends than mortal animals do. The stars are alive and immortal, and seek the unchangeableness of the unmoved mover, achieving it as nearly as any material object could by moving eternally in perfect circles. Aristotle points to the materialists' inconsistency similarly at *Phys.* II. 196^{a}25 f.

641^{b}24 "we commonly say": i.e. not just we Aristotelians, but *it is common usage*, which shows that it is apparent to all that a final cause exists (^{b}25 ὥστε εἶναι φανερόν). It is an 'appearance' (φαινόμενον) or datum (cf. 639^{b}8 note).

Aristotle defines a teleological sequence not in terms of conative behaviour but as a sequence that reaches or terminates at an end (περαίνει, ^{b}25; cf. *Phys.* II. 194^{a}29, 199^{a}8–11, ^{b}15–17). He explains at *Phys.* II. 194^{a}32 that 'end' is not always chronological. An animal's growth is completed when it reaches not death but 'the best'; this *acme* is followed by wasting (cf. *De An.* I. 411^{a}30; *Resp.* 479^{a}32; *G.A.* IV. 775^{a} 13). The teleological 'end' is not necessarily the end of a cycle of activity (as Bertrand Russell held in *The Analysis of Mind*, 1921, pp. 64–5).

641ᵇ30 "they grow" (φύεται): Aristotle alludes to the root-meaning of φύσις (nature) = a growing, cf. *Met.* Δ 1014ᵇ16. The argument, however, stands without this questionable etymology. "These (i.e. the animal and its proper attributes) are natural; they grow naturally out of the seed; therefore the seed is their productive agent."

The whole argument is in three stages: (i) (ᵇ26–30) What grows from a seed is determined by the seed, not by chance (cf. *Phys.* II. 196ᵃ31); (ii) (ᵇ30–2) The seed itself is part of a process tending to a determined end; (iii) (ᵇ32–642ᵃ1) But the natural development may be upset by field conditions so that something else results: horse seed may produce a mule. Since there is no mule seed, we recognize that the seed obtained its nature not from the development but from its source, the sire horse. Moreover the seed is potentially the product; potentiality presupposes a prior actuality, and is a potentiality for that kind of actuality. Therefore natural growth tends towards an end that is already potential in the seed, namely the adult state of the sire. The final remark, "we know how potentiality is related to actuality", merely clinches the argument of ᵇ32–6. (For the priority of actuality see *Met.* Θ 8, esp. 1049ᵇ24; *G.A.* II. 734ᵇ21).

642ᵃ1–13 (*10*) *The exposition must state both causes—the teleological and the hypothetically necessary.*

This is one of Aristotle's clearest statements that all natural necessity is reducible to hypothetical necessity (cf. *Phys.* II. 199ᵇ34f. and note at 639ᵇ21). The reference to 'our philosophical treatises' (ᵃ6) cannot be certainly identified, but the likeliest is *An. Post.* II. 94ᵇ36, which distinguishes (i) movement necessitated by a natural state, as when a stone falls, (ii) movement necessitated by force, as when a stone is thrown up.

642ᵃ13–30 (*11*) *Earlier philosophers failed because they did not define what-it-is-to-be a thing.*

The nature of a thing as defined, i.e. the what-it-is-to-be-that-thing (τὸ τί ἦν εἶναι) is a more significant origin and governing principle (ἀρχή) than the necessary materials. This is the nature that Empedocles stumbles on (ᵃ18 αὐτῇ = τῇ φύσει ᾗ ἀρχῇ): cf. Emped. *fr.* 96 *VS.* Aristotle says the same of both Empedocles and Democritus at *Phys.* II. 194ᵃ20 (cf. *Met.* *A* 993ᵃ17). At *Met.* *M* 1078ᵇ17 he says that Socrates was the first to attempt definition (in ethics) and that Democritus touched upon it by giving "a sort of definition of hot and cold"—presumably by saying that hot is a sensation caused by the mobile spherical atoms (cf. *De An.* I. 405ᵃ12).

642^a31–$^b2$ (*12*) *An example of correct exposition.*

The example, which is obscure and in note form, shows how one and the same process is due to (i) finality; (ii) the necessary elementary actions of the materials; (iii) the immediate actions necessitated by (i).

(i) Breathing takes place for the sake of 'this' ($^a31$)—some end not further discussed in the example.

(ii) Because of the state and nature of the hot and of the (cold) air, the hot in the body must expand and go out through the windpipe, but must come in again on meeting resistance from the cold air outside; the hot must then retreat, and the air must flow in to fill its place. "So much is already necessary" ($^a36$)—i.e. this is their present state and nature ($^a34$).

(iii) The inner hot resists the incoming air, which cools it, causing the hot to retreat still further; therefore more air flows in. The air itself now becomes heated and, having expanded, flows out again as hot air. It meets the outside air, which is cold . . . and the cycle is repeated.

The cycle is breathing. It is necessitated both by the nature of the materials and by the end for which breathing occurs. (For the way in which both these senses of necessity are subsumed under 'hypothetical necessity' see note at 639^b21. Cf. also 645^b28–33.)

This explanation of breathing is not what Aristotle gives as his own at *Resp.* 480^a16–$^b12$. There he says that as the heat in the heart increases, it makes the chest expand like a bellows, drawing in air from outside; the incoming air cools the heat, which allows the chest to subside; the cycle begins with breathing in, not out (472^b21). Aristotle often uses examples taken not from his own theories but from common beliefs, and this one may have been a current medical orthodoxy. Plato based his own theory of breathing on a similar account of the actions of hot and cold, though in other respects there is no similarity (*Timaeus* 79DE).

Chapters 2–3

Criticism of 'Dichotomy'

Aristotle's problem is to mark off each animal species: (i) so as to show its specific attributes; (ii) so as to distinguish it from every other species. The method discussed is division *per genus et differentiam.* He criticizes a particular use of it which he calls 'dichotomy', though it will be seen that his criticism holds not necessarily against division *into two* classes as such, but against division *by one differentia at a time*—whether into two classes or more. Instead he recommends dividing at the outset by many differentiae simultaneously, then further differentiating all these differentiae as required. His method is to be contrasted with any kind of division made by single differentiae, whether dichotomous or polytomous.

Among single-differentia divisions, the advantage of dichotomy is that it makes it easier to ensure exhaustiveness. At each stage the *definiendum* is seen to be contained in one side, and to be excluded from the other. But Aristotle's case against it is that dichotomy, to be valid, must be rigorous; and if rigorous, it will be useless or even in some cases impracticable.

The least rigorous dichotomy is (1) an empirical division into two classes of any kind. If our species is a colourless fish, we might divide animals into *swimming* and *coloured*. But to this Aristotle replies (643^{a}31–4) that we must divide by opposites—he means contradictory opposites—because only opposites differentiate. *Swimming* and *coloured* are determinations of two distinct generic attributes (locomotion and coloration), and do not divide a single genus exclusively. (In our terms, there is more than one *fundamentum divisionis*.) The likely result is cross-division—there are in fact animals that both swim and are coloured. This means that any further attributes which we divide off are no longer guaranteed to belong exclusively to our species, for they may belong also to animals that are on *both* sides (the coloured swimmers).

Therefore, in order to work, dichotomy must be at least restricted to (2) division by pairs of opposed differentiae. So, if our species is a white domestic pigeon, we might now divide animals into *winged* and *wingless*, then the winged into *tame* and *wild*, then the tame winged into *white* and *coloured*. This is the kind of division that Plato illustrates in the *Sophistes* and *Politicus*. But now Aristotle objects that such a dichotomy is discontinuous and accidental (643^{b}17–23). *White* is not a kind of *tame*. Each differentia should be a determination of the previous one, for otherwise the resulting definition will not be a unity. He means that a discontinuous division fails to guarantee that the attributes belong to the species essentially rather than accidentally. A continuous division shows that the specific attribute is a determination of an attribute belonging to the whole genus to which the species belongs, for example that *biped* is a way of *having feet* which is a way of *locomotion*. To understand the biped, we need to study the principles of animal locomotion. What now of the pigeon's whiteness? We first need to know whether it flows from a generic attribute or merely from accidental causes such as climate or nutrition; but we are not told this by a division made *per accidens*.

The form of dichotomy, therefore, which Aristotle considers valid—and proceeds to attack as useless—is (3) division by successive differentiation of one differentia. This is not Plato's usage, but was presumably an Academic development. Against it Aristotle produces three main arguments, supported by reminders of certain rules of division which are needed to secure proper rigour:

(1) Dichotomy produces only one final differentia (642^{b}7–9).

(2) Dichotomy splits natural kinds by cross-division (642^{b}9–20).
(3) Dichotomy cannot use negative differentiae (642^{b}21–643^{a}27).
(4) Rule: do not divide by essential accidents (643^{a}27–31).
(5) Rule: divide by opposites (643^{a}31–4).
(6) Rule: do not divide by psychosomatic attributes (643^{a}35–^{b}8).
(7) Conclusion: division by single differentiae either fails outright or compels us to divide *per accidens*. Therefore we should divide initially by multiple differentiae (643^{b}9–26).
(8) A single final differentia, as produced by correct dichotomy, must be inadequate (643^{b}26–644^{a}11). (This section merely amplifies no. 1.)

These arguments are discussed in detail in the notes below. Nos. 1 (with 8), 2, and 3 are Aristotle's objections to dichotomy. Nos. 4, 5, and 6 are practical rules of division, which emphasize rigorous differentiation; many other rules are given elsewhere, especially in *Topics* VI. 6. No. 7 emphasizes successive differentiation, and gives Aristotle's own solution.

The method of multiple differentiation that Aristotle now recommends (643^{b}10) is to begin, not with a large simple concept like Animal, but with observed major genera such as Birds and Fishes which can be marked off straight away by various generic attributes: all birds are *winged*, *biped*, *beaked*, etc. Next he differentiates the generic differentiae, not by adding new differentiae, but by stating differences of degree within them—what he calls 'the more and less' (Chapter 4, 644^{a}17). He does not give precise examples here, but there are many in his actual practice. Thus Hawks have *long* and *narrow* wings, *thick* legs, *hooked* beaks. Then, since Hawk itself is a sub-genus having species, the Hawk-differentiae must be further differentiated for each species. By this method Aristotle can characterize a species fully, while avoiding accidental attributes. The division does not import anything new, but shows how general attributes are determined in actuality.

Multiple differentiation seems in fact to be applicable to dichotomy, for we could divide simultaneously by several pairs of opposites, and thereby preserve Aristotle's rigour while evading his criticisms. Depending on the subject matter, we may be able to divide G into $a^1b^1c^1G$ and $a^2b^2c^2G$, and these into $a^1{}_1b^1{}_1c^1{}_1G$, $a^1{}_2b^1{}_2c^1{}_2G$, $a^2{}_1b^2{}_1c^2{}_1G$, and $a^2{}_2b^2{}_2c^2{}_2G$, and so on successively. Such a dichotomy would (a) produce a multiple final differentia, (b) avoid cross-division, since e.g. *polypod* would not be taken simpliciter but as *land-polypod* or *water-polypod* (cf. 642^{b}19), (c) permit negative differentiae, which could be left undivided while the remaining differentiae were further divided (cf. 642^{b}22).

Nor, on the other hand, is it necessary that single-differentia division should generate a dichotomy. We can divide Animal *by habitat* into *land*, *sea*, and *air* animals, and then the land animals *by locomotion* into *footless*, *biped*, *quadruped*, *polypod*, and so on. This polytomy is equally vulnerable to Aristotle's arguments against dichotomy.

Aristotle's arguments in fact hold against dividing by one differentia at one stage. No doubt this was the practice of the dichotomists that he has in mind; for he speaks of 'the written divisions' and 'the dichotomists', which suggests that he is criticizing a particular actual use. Unfortunately no examples of it seem to be extant (642^b12 note).

Although his arguments in these two chapters are all in the context of zoology, Aristotle claims at one point that dichotomy cannot seize animal species 'or any other kind' (643^a17). He says this during his discussion of negative differentiae, and it is true that any dichotomy—zoological or otherwise—that uses a negative differentia must stop there (see notes at 642^b21 f.). But really simple concepts (such as some ethical concepts), which because they are not complexes have only one *fundamentum divisionis*, may well be satisfactorily divided by simple differentiae without incurring cross-division or using negatives, and the final differentia will be adequate just because the species is a simple concept itself. But where a genus is a complex of attributes, cross-division must occur in single-differentia division, unless the differentiae happen to fall into self-contained groups. For example, by Aristotle's analysis Virtue divides *both* into moral/intellectual virtues *and* into virtues of-the-mean/not-of-the-mean. But since the moral virtues are coterminous with the virtues of the mean, there is no danger of cross-division. On the other hand Animal divides *both* into land/sea animals *and* into footed/footless animals, and these divisions do not coincide. Cross-division is therefore inevitable if single-differentia division is used in zoology or similarly complex subject matters; and Aristotle's other objections also hold. But in generalizing from zoology to *all* subject matters, he has probably overstated the case.

If a complex genus is marked off by all its generic attributes simultaneously, and if these attributes are then further differentiated in parallel, the difficulties of single-differentia division are obviated. The relation between attributes is not falsified (*winged* and *coloured* are presented together, not one as the differentia of the other); there need be no cross-division; essential attributes are distinguished from accidental; negative differentiae can be used without blocking the remainder of the division; and the final differentia is a comprehensive statement of the specific attributes. Aristotle's solution is therefore of real importance. Moreover it has an immediate bearing on classification. Linnaeus' systems (although not rigorous) rely upon division by multiple differentiae.

Now it has been suggested that Aristotle's purpose was to offer this as a new method of classification, replacing the method of division; i.e. that the method which he criticizes under the name 'dichotomy' is the same that he calls 'division' in the *Topics*, *Analytics*, and *Metaphysics*, and that consequently *P.A.* I presents a development in his attitude to classification (cf. I. Düring, *Aristotle's P.A.: Critical and Literary Commentaries*, Göteborg 1943, pp. 109 f.; G. E. R. Lloyd, "The Development of

Aristotle's Theory of the Classification of Animals", *Phronesis* vi, 1961, pp. 59f.). In favour of this suggestion it can be said (i) that the arguments against dichotomy are not found elsewhere in Aristotle's works; (ii) that some of the zoological examples which Aristotle uses here to illustrate fallacious divisions are used elsewhere without his suggesting these difficulties; (iii) that Aristotle's criticism, although directed against dichotomy, holds against any division by single differentiae. As against this, however, Aristotle does seem here to be addressing himself against a particular form of division which he does not discuss elsewhere. Dichotomy is only mentioned in this passage. Aristotle's normal use of division is not dichotomous. His arguments against dichotomy only hold if one accepts the positive rules of division that he quotes, and these rules are all given elsewhere (except for the rule about psychosomatic differentiae at 643^a35, which is applicable only to zoology and is of minor importance). The method that he proposes instead is itself another form of division. It seems more likely therefore that his purpose here is to apply the logical technique of division to zoology, and to show that it must be conducted by multiple differentiae if it is to work.

Aristotle's aim in using division, again, does not seem to be classification, but definition. The first sentence states this aim—"to obtain the particular", i.e. to grasp, mark out by attributes, and so reveal the essential nature of a given *infima species*. This is always his aim in division. In the *Analytics* he denies that division can *prove*, but states that it is useful for finding definitions (*An. Pr.* I. 31; *An. Post.* II. 5 and 13). It is true that division sets up a skeletal classification as it proceeds, since each stage must show the *other* differentiae which exclude the *definiendum*. But there is no need to divide these others further, nor to state their contents. On this point Aristotle explicitly differs from those Academics (of whom we know Speusippus to have been one) who held that we cannot define one object without knowing all the other objects and differentiae in the division. Against this Aristotle says that it is unnecessary to know what other objects are being differentiated; provided that the *definiendum* falls within the differentiae taken, and that the final differentia cannot be further divided, the object will be specified (*An. Post.* II. 97^a6 f.). We track down a particular species, discarding the others as we go (cf. Joseph, *Introduction to Logic*, 2nd ed., Oxford 1916, p. 127, on '*abscissio infiniti*'). Aristotle does not criticize dichotomy as a means of classification, though a stronger case can be made against it as such than as a means of defining (e.g. it presents coordinate differentiae as subaltern). Nor does he himself propound a classification of the animal kingdom. He merely marks out the nine "greatest genera", pointing out at the same time that they exclude many important species (see note at 644^a12). Chapter 4 tells us how to proceed, but Aristotle never carried the procedure through systematically. In the *Historia Animalium* he collects and analyses animal differentiae, no doubt as a preliminary to a systematized descriptive zoology; but the latter was never achieved (see A. L. Peck's introduction to the Loeb edition of *H.A.*, and my paper on "Aristotle's Use of Differentiae in Zoology" in *Aristote et les problèmes de méthode*, Louvain 1961, pp. 195 f.).

642b5 "obtain the particular" (*λαμβάνουσι τὸ καθ' ἕκαστον*). In this first sentence Aristotle states (i) the aim in view, (ii) the method criticized. The aim is to grasp the *infima species*, both by marking it off uniquely *and* by stating its essential nature. This double aim is taken for granted by Aristotle when he considers definition. Nobody is satisfied with identifying uniquely: 'plane figure whose interior angles add up to two right angles', though true only of triangles, does not *grasp* the triangle (cf. 643a27). 'Plane figure with three angles' achieves both aims.

λαμβάνουσι is a conative present tense, having the nuance '*try* to obtain'. *τὸ καθ' ἕκαστον*, literally 'the each by each', is Aristotle's expression for (*a*) the *infima species*, (*b*) the individual member of a species, also called the 'numerically one'. In zoology he is usually referring to the species, so to avoid confusion with individual animals I have translated it 'particular' throughout this discussion.

The method criticized is called 'dividing into two differentiae' (on which see discussion above, pp. 101 f.). *διαφορά*, literally 'difference', may signify (i) a logical differentia (642b7), (ii) a class marked off by a differentia (642b6), (iii) a line of differentiation (643b23), (iv) the bifurcation made by applying a differentia (643b8, cf. *Met. Θ* 1048b4).

642b7–9 (*1*) *Dichotomy produces only one final differentia.*

Aristotle amplifies this objection at 643b26, where he argues that a single final differentia, even when it implies all its predecessors, cannot be enough to characterize an animal species (assuming that the dichotomy has been made according to the rules). 'Some' (642b7) implies that there are other species which fail to be marked off altogether, i.e. those that are shown under two separate genera (642b11) or are never reached at all (643a16).

The differentiae other than the final one are 'superfluous' because each differentia should be a determination of its predecessor and should therefore imply it (*An. Post.* II. 97a28; *Top.* VI. 144b16; *Met. Z* 1038a19–26).

The example given in the traditional Greek text at 642b8 reads baldly as 'footed, two-footed, split-footed, footless' (so in all MSS.). This cannot be taken as it stands, because (i) *split-footed* (i.e. having toes) does not imply *two-footed*, nor vice versa; (ii) *footless* excludes the others, and can only stand in the initial division *footed/footless*. Various emendations have been proposed by editors. To avoid re-writing the text, I have treated it as standing for a diagrammatic representation of two alternative lines starting from *footed/footless*. Even this requires the addition of 'or' between *two-footed* and *split-footed*, and a colon before *footless* to show that it is the other side of the bifurcation. (The same 'or' needs adding at 644a5, whereas it is given in the traditional text at 643b36.) At 642b8 'the latter' (αὔτη) can now refer to the final differentia, *two-footed* or *split-footed*.

642b10–20 (2) *Dichotomy splits natural kinds*.

This is true of a complex genus, unless the specific attributes fall into self-contained groups (see p. 104). For example, Animal divides both into *land/water* animals and into *many-footed/footless* animals, but these groups are not coterminous; therefore some many-footed animals will be shown under the sub-genus land animal, others under water animal. Why does this matter? Aristotle considers this at *Top.* VI. 144b12–30, on the premiss that one species cannot be in two genera, which he treats as self-evident. To complete his argument, we should probably say: now if in the course of division we use the differentia *many-footed*, which belongs both to land animals and to water animals, we shall not show at the end whether our many-footed species is a land or water animal. Alternatively, if *many-footed* really is a determinate form of land animal, then it cannot also be a determinate form of water animal. The dilemma is resolved by using multiple differentiae in division, as Aristotle will advise at 643b23; for then we avoid cross-division by recognizing from the outset both *many-footed land* animals and *many-footed water* animals.

In the *Topics* discussion Aristotle allows one differentia belonging to two genera if one of the genera is subordinate to the other or if both are subordinate to one higher genus. Thus, although *biped* belongs to both land-animal and flying-animal, it is allowable because both land-animal and flying-animal belong to Animal. At first sight this seems inconsistent with 642b16–20, but the cases are not parallel. In the *Topics*, *animal* exemplifies a genus (144b17), i.e. it is a division of whatever Aristotle has in mind as the universe of division here (perhaps *living things*). The universe of division is not itself a genus: every genus is a sub-division, for it is marked off from some other genus within the given universe that is being divided. If now we divide U (living things) into G^1 (animals) and G^2 (plants), and then G^1 into G^1p (*land*) and G^1q (*air*), and then wish to apply the differentia k (*biped*) to G^1, we get G^1pk over against G^1qk, i.e. a cross-division. This means that we cannot show whether our biped species is a land or air animal; but we may, according to Aristotle, by-pass the land/air division because both 'import' animal. Presumably he means that we can say that the biped is animal (either land or air) and not plant. But if, as in the *P.A.* example, U = Animal, then G^1 = *land* and G^2 = *air*. If we now say that *biped* belongs to both land and air, we get G^1k over against G^2k: the effect of this is that we simply deny the first differentiation that we have made (which said that animals must be one or the other, but not both); and we cannot bypass that differentiation because there is no higher genus. It is therefore as Aristotle says here: if we are dividing Animal dichotomously, we cannot both differentiate land and water animals and differentiate polypod and non-polypod animals. But animals *are* differentiated so in nature. Therefore dichotomy is impracticable.

642b12 "the written divisions": it is not known what Aristotle refers to here, nor at 642b22 ("the dichotomists"). Plato, who introduced logical division, commonly speaks of dividing 'in two' (δίχα), and his most elaborate divisions in the *Sophistes* and *Politicus* are dichotomous (e.g. *Polit.* 258 f.). But Plato himself makes Aristotle's point that we should not chop up natural kinds like an unskilful cook missing the joints (*Phaedrus* 265E) but should use the minimum necessary number of natural divisions in preference to dichotomy (*Polit.* 287C). Stenzel suggested Speusippus (Pauly-Wissowa, *RE* s.v. 'Speusippos'), but there is nothing in the extant fragments of Speusippus that could be Aristotle's target; nor is there anything in the *Divisiones Aristoteleae*, which probably originated in the Academy. What Plato's divisions do show is the use of a single differentia at a time, which is the real object of Aristotle's attack. Possibly this use was perpetuated in the Academy, where paradigmatic divisions may have been drawn up in dichotomous form. (See W. D. Ross, *Plato's Theory of Ideas*, Oxford, 1951, pp. 144–5.)

642b21–643a27 *(3) Dichotomy cannot use privative (negative) differentiae.*

Commentators differ over the extent of this section, and over its purport in several places. The interpretation that I suggest divides it into three arguments, which I have labelled a, b, c, all based on the premiss that a privation (στέρησις, i.e. *not-ϕ*) is not differentiable (642b22). On that premiss Aristotle argues (a) that a privation cannot stand as a general differentia, because it is not further divisible; (b) that it cannot stand as a specific differentia, because it is the same for different species; (c) that it prevents the proper one-to-one correspondence between final differentiae and species.

Aristotle introduces the section by acknowledging that privative differentiae must be used in division. It is evident from his examples and from Plato that negative differentiae were not used wholesale as they are in modern dichotomies, where every division is made into ϕ and *not-ϕ* in order to secure exhaustiveness. The dichotomists evidently divided Animal not into *land* and *not-land* but into *land* and *water*. But even if we characterize positively like this, negatives are often needed, for example *footless*, *bloodless*.

The objection is not, therefore, to negative differentiae as such; it is rather that dichotomy cannot use them properly. This argument has no connection with *Top.* VI. 143b11–144a4 (as some commentators suggest) where Aristotle puts forward an argument against dividing by a negation (ἀπόφασις). That is an *ad hominem* argument, as he tells us, directed against the Platonists on *their* premisses. It goes as follows. "If you define *line* as *length without breadth*, you are applying the differentia *without breadth* to the genus *length* to give the species *line*. But the genus *length* must itself either have breadth or not, since of everything either an affirmation or its negation is true. Therefore *length without breadth* defines the genus as well as the species." Now this argument assumes that a genus is a thing that has independent existence. In actual existence, *a* length must be either broad or not broad: so must every other *thing* in the universe. Aristotle himself does not regard a genus as a thing, but only as the mentally abstractable matter or potentiality for being a species: the genus *length* can be abstracted and considered without reference to breadth or not-breadth, even though no actual length exists without being either broad or not broad. But the Platonic form of the genus *is* said to exist by itself, and must therefore be either broad or not broad. Aristotle says (143b29) that this argument holds only against those who regard the genus as 'numerically one', i.e. an individual. He goes on to say that we have to use negations to define privations—not implying that privations cannot be defined, but that the Platonists disqualify themselves from doing so.

642b24–30 (*3a*) *Privations cannot be general differentiae.*

This argument holds if we take the differentia strictly by itself, as is proper in dichotomy. For when we claim to divide *footless animals* into fishes and snakes, what we are really dividing is not *footless* but *animals* (*less those that are footed*). But this is illicit. For whereas *footed* implies being an animal, *footless* implies nothing; and in itself it is empty and therefore undifferentiable.

The argument is severe, if not captious. Animals are not footless in the way that, say, water is footless. At *Phys.* II. 193b19 Aristotle allows that a privation is 'a form in a way' (εἶδός πως) because (presumably) it is a state of proximate matter capable of receiving the form, i.e. a privation is a positive characteristic—moles are characterized by eyes that cannot see (*De An.* III. 425a11). It is hard to see why Aristotle does not permit us to bypass the privative differentia, in the way that *biped* was bypassed at *Top.* VI. 144b12–30 (note at 642b10), and to continue dividing the higher genus—the animals that remain after the footed animals have been marked off. For footlessness in an animal implies other locomotive arrangements.

642b27 "unsplit": i.e. the insect wing (*P.A.* IV. 682b18).

642b30–643a6 (*3b*) *Privations cannot be specific differentiae.*

The general differentia is itself differentiated in each species. The two-leggedness of birds is *inward-bending*, that of man is *outward-bending* (*P.A.* IV. 693b3); *blooded* is *thin-blooded* or *fibrous-blooded* or *hot-blooded*, etc., in different species (*P.A.* II. 647b29 f.). But *bloodless* can only be the same in every bloodless species. Now if the deer's blood were the same as the lion's, we should not consider it a specific differentia: it would not be part of these animals' definitions but would merely be a generality implied by their specific differentiae, as Animal is implied by *quadruped.* The same must apply to bloodlessness. If we try to say that *bloodless* specifically differentiates both the crab and the snail, then, since *bloodless* cannot be differentiated as *blooded* can, we are saying that one and the same differentia belongs to two species—which means that it is *not* a specific differentia. But we have already shown that a privation cannot be a general differentia. Therefore it cannot be a differentia at all in dichotomy (643a6). (The argument is not yet conclusive, because there remains the possibility that only *one* species is *not-ϕ*. Aristotle seems to deal with this at 643a9.)

Some editors have emended 'bloodless' (642b35) to 'opposites' or 'contradictories' or 'indivisibles', in order to generalize the argument. But 'bloodless' (which is the unanimous reading of the MSS.) has the advantage that it makes the point by using an actual case. It is moreover important, because Aristotle divides his 'greatest genera' into the blooded and the bloodless, so that this is the primary division of animals and is super-generic. A dichotomy, then, which could not use *bloodless* as a differentia, must be impotent to differentiate animals.

643a7–27 (*3c*) *The final differentiae are equal in number to the species, if no differentia is common.*

This argument lacks a conclusion, and commentators disagree about its purport. Its premiss is that there should be a one-to-one correspondence between final differentiae and particular species (643a7, 19). This rule agrees with *Met. Z* 1038a17. It flows from two other familiar rules: (i) neither the final differentia nor the species may be further divisible; (ii) no final differentia may be common to more than one species; (643a8; cf. *Met. Z* 1038a16; *An. Post.* II. 91b32, 97a18 and 38 f.; *Top.* VI. 144b15). Aristotle then quotes further rules to show that no final differentia may be common. Then he says that *therefore* dichotomy cannot seize the species, for in dichotomy too the final differentiae must equal the species. He gives an arithmetical illustration of this, and then notes that the species is the differentia in the matter—a note which some commentators regard as a separate digression. The steps in this argument are by no means clear.

First, what does Aristotle conclude from the one-to-one correspondence of differentiae and species? Some interpret the arithmetical example as showing that the number of final differentiae in dichotomy must be a power of two, and that this is ridiculous (Peck). Le Blond takes it to show that the number must be even, and that dichotomy will therefore fail whenever the number of species is odd. But a third possibility, which I wish to suggest, is that the example merely confirms the precise numerical correspondence, while Aristotle's conclusion is that the species will nevertheless outnumber the final differentiae if any final differentia is common but undifferentiable (i.e. a privation); and that dichotomy cannot avoid this situation.

After the initial premiss and rule, lines 643a9–16 are evidently meant to establish that no final differentia may be common to more than one species. At 643a9 the MSS. all read εἰ δ' ἐνδέχεται μὴ ὑπάρχειν καὶ κοινήν, ἄτομον δέ . . . , "but if it is possible for it not to be present actually in common, but indivisibly . . .". Because this seems awkward, recent editors have deleted μή, translating "supposing it were possible to have a differentia which though indivisible was common" (Peck). This makes easy and good sense, but it seems to deny what has just been demonstrated—that we cannot use privations in dichotomy for the very reason that they are both common and indivisible (642b30–643a6). Now the Greek, though awkward, has a parallel at *An. Post.* I. 73b18, where οὐ γὰρ ἐνδέχεται μὴ ὑπάρχειν means "cannot not be present". If we retain the μή here, Aristotle may be meeting the case mentioned above (note at 642b30): could a common indivisible differentia be specific if there were only one species possessing it, i.e. if it were not *in fact* common to more than one species? The question does not arise with positive differentiae, because they are always differentiable down to species level (643a3 two-footedness and bloodedness). It was the lack of this differentiability that ruled out privations. But why cannot we allow that the one non-crested species of lark (*H.A.* IX. 617b23) is differentiated by non-crestedness, and thereby use a common differentia when it is not actually (καί, 643a9) common? To this Aristotle replies that if it is a common differentia it *does* include different species. He will not mean that there must be other non-crested larks, which would simply contradict the hypothesis that he is conceding. But he will mean one or both of: (i) This non-crestedness, though unique in larks, is the same non-crestedness in sparrows: taken by itself, as it must be in dichotomy, it does not mark off one species. (This rests upon the argument of 642b30–643a6 instead of discounting it.) (ii) Non-crestedness is undifferentiable, so that if tomorrow you find another non-crested lark species, you will be unable to differentiate the two of them, because having stated a privation you cannot proceed further in that line of differentiation; in virtue of its commonness (which is incorrigible) a privation admits other *possible* species. Of these, (i) seems more probable.

Next (643a13–16) Aristotle adduces three familiar rules of division, expressed here more tersely than elsewhere: (1) the same species must not appear under opposed differentiae; (2) different species must not appear under the same (i.e. final) differentia; (3) all must find a place under the differentiae chosen; (cf. *An. Post.* II. 97a15–38). Now (2) is enough to confirm that the final differentia must not be common, as he has just been arguing. But the three taken together establish the fact that the final differentiae are equal in number to the species. Aristotle now (643a16–19) resumes this premiss as something that, when added to the previous argument ('therefore'), shows that dichotomy cannot seize species. The reason must be that a dichotomy may end with a common differentia. The next sentence (643a20) is the arithmetical example, introduced as explaining (γὰρ) why the final differentiae ought to be equal in number to species in dichotomy: "mark off a sub-genus G^1 (the *white* species in the genus—Cornford's addition 'and the non-white ones' makes the arithmetic wrong); divide it into G^1a and G^1b, and let each of these (τούτων ἑκατέρου) be further divided; proceed dichotomously to the *infimae species*; the number of final differentiae will be four (G^1a^1, G^1a^2, G^1b^1, G^1b^2) or some other number produced by doubling, and *just so many* (τοσαῦτα) will be the species." Are we now meant to conclude more than he says, as many commentators have decided? "Obtained by doubling" is as ambiguous in the Greek as in the English. If Aristotle means doubling every number from one, the product is even numbers; if he means doubling each number produced, the product is powers of two. In a dichotomy even numbers are produced if, whenever one of a pair of differentiae is further divided, the other of that pair is also further divided (Fig. 1). Powers of two are produced if both sides of the original bifurcation are developed to the same distance (Fig. 2). The latter would of course be absurd: it would mean that if the actual species of hawk exceed eight in number (and Aristotle in fact identifies ten), there must be not fewer than sixteen to be differentiated—and if more than sixteen are found, there must be thirty-two. But if Aristotle's intention is a *reductio ad absurdum*, it is unusual for him not to say so. Nor can one see why the dichotomists should have thought it necessary to develop all lines equally far, though they might have felt that if one of a pair of differentiae is divisible its co-ordinate should be too (thus producing even numbers). In fact, however, there is no systematic need to divide both members of a pair, but dichotomy can properly produce odd numbers (Fig. 3). I would think therefore that the example is simply a self-evident little sum intended to illustrate no more than the point just made, that there will be a precise number of final differentiae and that the species cannot be of a different number. Why cannot they? Aristotle immediately explains (643a24). It is the differentia that gives form to the matter, so that if there were more species than differentiae these species would be differentiated by matter alone—which is impossible (for an animal is not formless matter, any more than it is immaterial form).

Now the one-to-one correspondence which ought to exist between final differentiae and species is upset if a division produces either more

Fig. 1: Even Numbers of Species

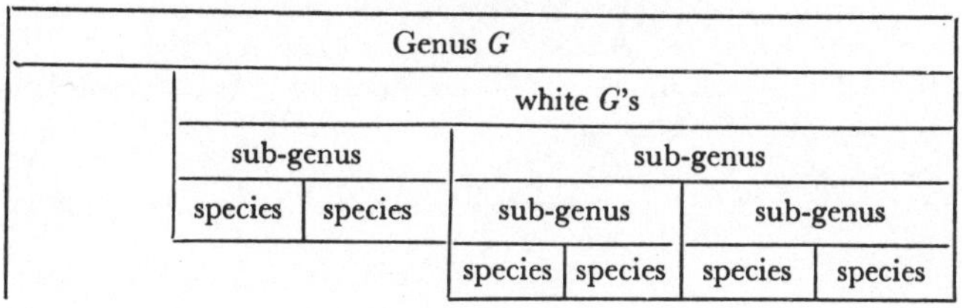
Genus *G*
white *G*'s
sub-genus
sub-genus
species
species
sub-genus
sub-genus
species
species
species
species

Fig. 2: Powers of 2

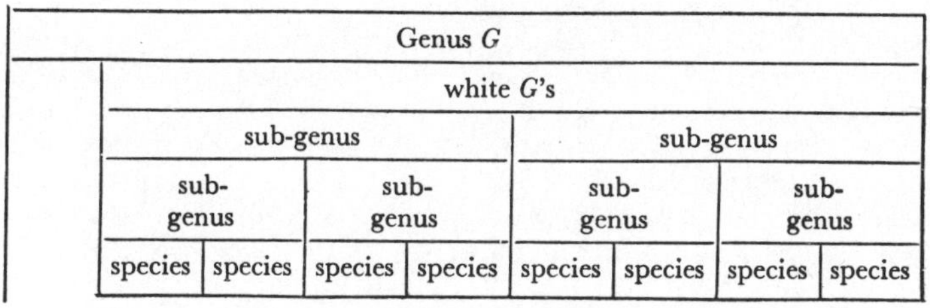
Genus *G*
white *G*'s
sub-genus
sub-genus
sub-genus
sub-genus
sub-genus
sub-genus
species
species
species
species
species
species
species
species

Fig. 3: Odd Numbers

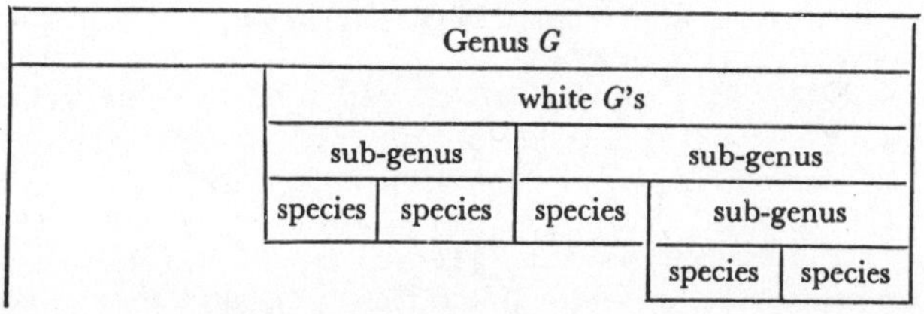
Genus *G*
white *G*'s
sub-genus
sub-genus
species
species
species
sub-genus
species
species

or fewer final differentiae than species. To produce more is not objectionable, for it means only that one has imagined possible differentiations that have not been discovered in actuality. Aristotle's objection must be the latter: that the species are not seized because they outnumber all possible differentiae produced by dichotomy. This will happen whenever a line ends with a common differentia that cannot be further divided. But the only such differentia is a privation. This section, then, including the arithmetical example and the statement about form and matter, is all part of the argument that privations are unusable in dichotomy.

The statement at 643ª17, that dichotomy cannot obtain *any kind* of species, is only true within its context, i.e. it is true if a dichotomy ends with a privation (cf. p. 104). Aristotle has said (642ᵇ21) that it *is* necessary to divide by privations, referring presumably to zoology. For instance, the significant feature of the blind mole is the privation of sight in an animal that is 'constituted to have sight' (*Top.* VI. 143ᵇ35). But we might avoid privative differentiae in dividing simpler genera, for example virtues or tools or literary genres or branches of knowledge. The advantage of using privations is to ensure exhaustiveness, through contradictory opposites. But this seems to have weighed less with Aristotle than ensuring that the *definiendum* is wholly contained within the differentia; to ensure this, it is better to characterize each of the opposed differentiae positively.

643ª24 "matter" (ὕλη): Aristotle may be referring either to the physical matter or to the logical genus (for genus as matter, cf. *Met. Δ* 1024ᵇ8, *Z* 1038ª6, *H* 1045ª23, *I* 1058ª23). But it makes no difference here (does it anywhere?). Each is one way of considering *that which is potentially X*. What determines *X* is the final differentia. The genus only exists when specified: there cannot be just blood, but it must exist as *this kind of* (e.g. fibrous) blood. Equally *fibrous* cannot exist without being fibrous something. Aristotle is confirming that there cannot be more species than differentiae; for if there were, the species would be differentiated not by form but by matter, which is nonsense. "As we have often said"—e.g. 640ᵇ22–641ª5, 31–2; *Met. Z* 1035ᵇ24, 1036ᵇ30; *G.A.* I. 722ᵇ34.

643ª27–31 (4) *We should not divide by essential accidents.*

The differentiae must be part of the animal's definition or essential nature (*An. Post.* II. 97ª23; *Top.* VI. 143ª29). This excludes accidental attributes even if they always and necessarily belong to and uniquely identify the *definiendum*, as in the present example. Self-evidently these do not seize the nature of the object (cf. note at 642ᵇ5). In zoology a definitory attribute would be e.g. bloodedness, which is 'part of the being' (643ª4, cf. *P.A.* IV. 678ª33), or the fishes' ability to swim (*P.A.* IV. 695ᵇ18). On the other hand an essential accident would be the fact that one species of octopus, which is naturally slim, has room for only one row of suckers on each tentacle, "not because this is best but because it is necessitated by the peculiar definition of its being" (*P.A.* IV. 685ᵇ15).

This is the first of three rules which Aristotle now adduces in note form, without saying why. They seem to prepare for the point to be made at 643ᵇ9, that the last differentia in a strict dichotomy must be inadequate. To make it adequate, the dichotomists evidently stretched the division to bring in heterogeneous differentiae (for example, dividing *feathered* into *tame* and *wild*, 643ᵇ20) and claimed that the last differentia imports its predecessors. Aristotle will presently argue that such division is discontinuous because *tame* is an accident of *feathered*. As a preliminary, he establishes here that even essential accidents may not be used. He probably refers to them because nobody would knowingly define by inessential accidents (like having blue eyes) which belong to some *X*'s but not to others, or belong at some times but not at other times. But the aspect that concerns his argument is their accidentalness, not their essentialness. If we divide *per accidens* in any way, we are not dividing the genus in question but another genus.

Aristotle's zoological ground for distinguishing definitory from accidental attributes is function (645^b28 f.). Lungs, heart, and liver are definitory attributes because they are for the sake of breathing and the blood; but the spleen is a necessary accident because it is present only as the counterpart of the liver (*P.A.* III. 670^a23–30). The distinction seems useful (although Aristotle has misapplied it through lack of information —for spleens do have functions). The definitory attributes are explained by the animal's basic nature, and in turn explain other attributes: by considering them we are led back to more fundamental and general attributes (blood, heat) and we are led forwards to specific attributes (this kind of blood, this consistency of lungs). The accidental attributes, on the other hand, do not inform us about the animal's nature. If we take spleen or gall-bladder as differentiae, we are not dividing the animal's nature but some other genus (the incidence of viscera). Division *per accidens* is in fact a pseudo-division. It destroys the continuity of division and consequently leaves us in the dark as to whether the differentiae are part of the animal's nature or not.

643^a31–4 (5) *We should divide by opposites.*

Aristotle means contradictory opposites, which ensure that the *definiendum* falls wholly into one or other side of the division (*An. Post.* II. 97^a20). White and black (643^a32) exhaust all colours because all are mixtures of white and black (*De Sensu* 3); strictly he should say 'whiter' and 'blacker'. Exhaustiveness, however, does not seem to be Aristotle's aim in this rule, judging from his discussion of differentiae in *Topics* VI. 6, for he does not base it on the law of excluded middle. Its aim is rather to ensure continuous division of the one genus. What we call a cross-division due to a change of *fundamentum divisionis*, Aristotle regards as a dividing of separate genera: *swimming* and *white* are determinations of two distinct generic differentiae, locomotion and coloration. He explains that to differ means to differ in a respect (not merely to be other), and therefore opposites differ and differentiate in virtue of the fact that they belong to the same genus (*Met. I* 1054^b25). That is why a genus must be divided into co-ordinate differentiae (*Top.* VI. 143^a36). In effect (though he does not say this) cross-division is another kind of accidental or pseudo-division, which imports more than one genus and thereby destroys the guarantee that one and the same genus is being divided. Like the previous rule, therefore, this one prepares the ground for arguing that dichotomy cannot produce an adequate final differentia; for it can only do so by dividing *per accidens*, which is no division.

643a35–b8 (6) *We should not divide by the common functions of body and soul.*

The sentence is in note form (we have to supply "we should not divide" from the end of the previous sentence) and is syntactically ambiguous. It may refer to either (i) functions shared by body and soul (psychosomatic), *or* (ii) functions of the body shared by other species, and functions of the soul shared by other species. The same expression elsewhere always means (i), as at *De Sensu* 436a7, but is not illustrated by the examples given here. Some commentators therefore prefer (ii) here, taking *walking* and *flying* as bodily attributes, *wild* and *tame* as psychic attributes. But since all attributes are either of the body or of the soul, this interpretation would exclude every shared or generic attribute, making division impossible. Moreover (ii) does not explain why breach of the rule entails splitting *infimae species*. But (i) may provide for this, for Aristotle holds that contrary functions like sleeping and waking belong to the same faculty of soul (*De Somno* 453b26). Sleeping and waking are psychosomatic functions (ibid. 454a5 f., cf. *De Sensu* 436a7–b2 where he also names sensation, memory, anger, appetite, desire, youth and ageing, breathing in and out, living and dying). The reason he gives for their belonging to the same faculty is that one is the privation of the other. This will apply also to *wild* and *tame*, but not necessarily to *walking* and *flying*. At 643b2, however, Aristotle shows that he is thinking of ants that are sometimes winged and sometimes wingless, in which case the walking *is* a privation of flying. We can at least say then that *some* contrary psychosomatic functions belong to the same species. The argument shows, not that we can *never* divide by psychosomatic attributes, but that we cannot do so in every case.

At 643b7 the MSS. read εἰ μὲν ὁμώνυμον, which may mean either (i) "if it has the same name", or (ii) "if it is homonymous"—i.e. if it is equivocally named, in the technical sense of ὁμώνυμον which Aristotle explains at *Cat.* 1a1 and usually intends. Neither statement seems satisfactory here. If Aristotle means (i), he is saying that if animals have the same name they are of the same kind. But he never believes this; indeed much of the *H.A.* is devoted to distinguishing species that share a common name. If (ii), he is saying (as Cherniss argues, *Aristotle's Criticism of Plato and the Academy*, p. 57 n. 47), "if each of these class names is equivocal, it has not been divided into its *infimae species*; but if on the other hand these wild and tame specimens are specifically one, then *wild* and *tame* are not specific differentiae." The argument would be a dilemma, and would hold against those (like Speusippus) who *both* regarded man, horse, etc., as *infimae species*, *and* took wild and tame as differentiae. But this would be a mere debating point. Moreover it is awkward to make ὧν ἕκαστον refer to species but ταῦτα to individuals. This is why I have suggested reading μὴ for μὲν. (Μὴ and μὲν are MSS. variants at 642b10.)

The rule, then, is: psychosomatic differences cannot safely be used as specific differentiae. It qualifies the previous rule, with which it is grammatically entangled in the Greek: the genus must be divided by opposites, but not by psychosomatic opposites. It is the only rule not found in Aristotle's other discussions of division. It prevents the dichotomists from using at least two important differences which ought to figure somewhere in zoological characterization (both are used by Plato). Aristotle's own method of simultaneous differentiation enables him to use them, and in practice he often does.

643b9–26 (7) *Division by single differentiae either fails for these reasons or compels us to divide per accidens; therefore we should divide initially by many differentiae.*

What is the 'necessary result' (643b9)? 'This' has no grammatical reference, but presumably means 'all this'—pointing back to the previous arguments. Aristotle recapitulates them at b14–16. He has now pointed out the basic defect of dichotomy, that it proceeds 'by dividing any one differentia by one differentia' (retain the MSS. reading at 643b9, ὁποιανοῦν διαφορὰν μιᾷ, with Bekker and Langkavel). At b17 he makes the point that he seems to have prepared for by citing the three rules at 643a27–b8: each differentia must be a determination of its predecessor, not an accident of it. The argument is signposted by the particles μὲν at b13 and δὲ at b17, which contrast a properly conducted dichotomy with an accidental division.

This contrast is an essential part of Aristotle's case. If, *per impossibile*, accidental division were made, then even a dichotomy could produce a varied list of differentiae, which could all be recited together as the definition: Plato, who regularly divides *per accidens*, collects all the differentiae at the end (e.g. *Sophistes* 223B, 224D, 226A). At *Met. Z* 1038a12 Aristotle says that accidental division is improper, and goes on at 1038a26 to say that dividing by the differentia of a differentia produces one final differentia, but dividing *per accidens* produces as many differentiae as 'cuts' (stages of division). It now follows inevitably that dividing by one differentia is inadequate. Aristotle adds (643b25) that multiple differentiation enables one to use privations, i.e. by taking them in combination with positive differentiae which *are* further divisible. If G^1 is marked off straight away as *a*, *b*, *not-c*, we can continue dividing *a* and *b* while carrying down *not-c*.

Aristotle might seem unduly narrow over this. Modern dichotomists do not feel that successive differentiation is essential (cf. Jevons's defence of dichotomy, *Principles of Science*, ch. xxx). Moreover a zoologist could object that featheredness is not just about feathers, and footlessness implies other locomotive equipment. But, if anything, this strengthens Aristotle's argument that clusters of differentiae, which belong together, should be taken together. Rather than adding other qualities arbitrarily to the quality *feathered* when we pretend to divide it into *tame* or *white*, we should recognize from the start that every feathered animal must also have a disposition and a colour (and locomotion and reproduction, etc.). If we can show that these are attributes of the whole genus, and then divide each scrupulously down to the species, we shall end with a cluster of final differentiae that belong together, because they are all determinations of more fundamental qualities common to this genus. If we divide *per accidens*, we may empirically light upon the right differentiae, but we shall have no general grounds for thinking so. This is not to claim, however, that strict division ensures the right initial differentiation. As Aristotle points out, it does not prove the differentiae; but it helps to find them (*An. Post.* II. 91^b12, 96^b27).

643^b26–644^a11 (*8*) *A single final differentia is inadequate, whether it is simple or compound.*

By 'compound' Aristotle means a differentia taken together with its superordinates (e.g. *biped* together with *footed*, 644^a5).

At 643^b31–2 the MSS. offer two quite different versions, between which editors have been divided. The majority (but excepting the important E) offer the version accepted by Bekker and translated here. According to it a simple differentia is exemplified by *split-footedness*, while a compound differentia is exemplified by *the many-split-footed in relation to the split-footed*. The former 'does not have a differentia' (643^b31) while the latter does. To 'have a differentia' may signify either to be differentiated *from* a genus or to be differentiated *into* species. The first, which is the commoner, must be intended here, since *many-split-footed* is in fact differentiated from *split-footed*. How then does the 'simple' *split-footedness* differ from the compound? Not because it is not *in fact* differentiated from a genus, since it is clearly a differentiation of *footed*. But in its case the differentiation is not expressed in words: it is a single word, while the other is a list of words. Similarly at 644^a4 'the whole compound' is exemplified by 'putting together' *footed* with *biped* or *split-footed*. Here then the compound differentia is the whole expression giving the differentia together with its superordinates. (At 643^b32 Platt, followed by Ogle, rewrote πρὸς τὸ as πρὸς τῷ: 'the many-split-footed *in addition to* the split-footed'. But the MS. reading is right, for the differentia is not an addition to its superordinate but a determination of it: it bears a logical relationship to it as species to genus.) The point at issue, then, is whether the whole line of division should be recited. If the dichotomists divided *per accidens*, they would have to recite all the stages like Plato. But Aristotle now shows that if the dichotomy has been conducted according to the rules, by successive differentiation, it makes no difference to recite the superordinates, since all are implied by the last differentia. This MSS. version therefore gives good sense. The only awkwardness is that *split-footed* represents a final differentia in the first example, but a superordinate in the second.

The reading of E, which Langkavel and Le Blond prefer, is : "I call simple (whether or not they have a differentia) such as the *many-split-footed* in relation to the *split-footed*, but compounded such as *many-split-footedness*." Here the compound differentia is a single word, so its compoundedness must lie in the fact that it implies its superordinates, as explained in the next sentence. The simple differentia on the other hand is taken by itself, whether it has sub-divisions (as *split-footed* is differentiated into *many-split-footed*) or not (as *many-split-footed* in comparison with *split-footed*). That is to say, the simple differentia does *not* imply its superordinates. But this contravenes Aristotle's rule (*An. Post.* II. 97a28; *Top.* VI. 144b16) which is recalled in the next sentence. The reading of E is therefore wrong.

644a1 "many-footed" (*πολύπουν*) is read by all MSS. and by Michael of Ephesus, but was queried by Meyer (*Aristotelische Thierkunde*, p. 79, note) because in Aristotle's normal practice it signifies 'having more than four feet'; hence Ogle, followed by Düring, rewrote 'split-footed' (*σχιζόπουν*). But in this essentially logical discussion *many-footed* is a satisfactory example of a differentia more determinate than *footed* but less determinate than *biped*, and is therefore acceptable.

644a3 "(though not . . . species)": these words interrupt, since 'this' in the next sentence must refer back to 'the last differentia' (a2); hence Peck secludes them. But the argument needs the distinction between the inadequate last differentia of a dichotomy and the true final differentia which in a successful division renders the species (*Met. Z* 1038a25); therefore I have retained these words as a parenthesis.

644a5 "or": cf. note at 642b8.

Chapter 4

Generic and Specific Differentiae

644a12–23 *Within a genus, the species differ by the more-and-less; between genera the similarity is by analogy; higher groupings of genera are not practicable.*

From the rigorous view of division that Aristotle has maintained in Chapter 3, it follows that the species of one genus all possess basically the same attributes, because each is a determination of a generic attribute. They differ only in degree—in size, shape, consistency (examples at 644b13)—differences that Aristotle calls 'the more and less', corresponding roughly to what we call homologies. The distinction between these and 'analogies' is illustrated in more detail at *H.A.* I. 486a15 f. Aristotle bases his homologies on common function, not on any theory of common descent, still less on evolution from a common ancestor (for he has no theory of evolution). He recognizes them chiefly by morphology, supported by comparisons of 'activities, lives, and characters' (644b7 note). These are his criteria for identifying a genus. He may also, however, have been influenced by the root-meaning of *genus* (γένος) as a kinship-group. He explains that an offspring which fails to resemble its parents will nevertheless retain a specific or generic likeness (as something heritable); cross-breeding is possible only between animals that are close in kind; (*G.A.* II. 746a29, IV. 767a36 f.).

Aristotle's genera (which he sometimes calls 'major genera', μέγιστα γένη, *H.A.* I. 490b7, II. 505b26) are: birds, fishes, cetaceans, viviparous quadrupeds, oviparous quadrupeds, (the 'blooded' genera—i.e. red-blooded); crustaceans, testaceans, molluscs (i.e. cephalopods), insects, (the 'bloodless' genera). He occasionally discusses the possibility of sub-genera within these (cf. *H.A.*, l.c.), but none emerge in practice. Outside these genera there are other important species (man, snakes, various marine animals, and peculiarities such as the bat, the seal, the ostrich) which he says must be treated separately (644b6).

These genera cannot be grouped in larger overarching genera, presumably because their attributes are not basically the same but are merely analogous, as feathers are to scales. Analogous attributes cannot be shown as differentiae of a single attribute. It is not enough that *some* attributes are common to different genera (e.g. breathing). Aristotle indicates sometimes that he would like to recognize larger genera such as *lung-possessors* (*P.A.* III. 669b9), and *G.A.* II 732b27 f. shows him groping towards a basic differentiation by bodily heat which he regards as the underlying cause of differences in reproduction, respiration, posture, locomotion, and psychology (cf. A. L. Peck, Loeb edn. of *H.A.*,

Introd. p. xv). The *blooded* and *bloodless* are not higher genera, but groupings of genera; blood is a symptom of heat.

644a15 "and so have all the other animals": the Greek is syntactically ambiguous and could signify that water animals and fliers share common characteristics with all other animals; but this would of course destroy the point. Either the words must be removed (Ogle, Peck), or they must be taken as a careless way of saying "there are certain affections common to these, and there are certain affections common to all other animals". Aristotle probably has in mind such differentiae as *walking* (πεζόν) with the associated affections of the limbs: animals that fly or swim have wings or fins in place of legs.

644a22 "to do this": i.e. to link under kinds (644a18).

644a23–b7 *Common attributes should be spoken of by genera; ungrouped species should be treated separately.*

Having solved how to mark off genera and species, Aristotle uses his solution to answer the question raised at 639a15: should we first state specific attributes or generic attributes?

644a24: The natural way to read the Greek is to make *tauta* refer back to *eide*, as I now translate it. Some interpreters find this difficult because it seems to make Socrates and Coriscus stand for *infimae species*, implying that individuals *are* formally differentiated (Ogle; cf. A. C. Lloyd in *Mind*, 1970, p. 519. Le Blond ad loc., however, denies that it need have that implication). But Aristotle does not notice the difficulty about individuation which Zeller first raised—that Socrates and Coriscus visibly differ, but that all differences are formal, and that therefore the individual has a form other than the specific form (or that we must allow that matter differentiates, which is surely a contradiction). To Aristotle the perceptible form *is* the specific form (cf. *An. Post.* 100a16); Socrates and Coriscus are the same in form, but other in matter (cf. *Met. Z* 1034a5). Since he cannot have pretended that individuals are carbon copies (in fact much of *G.A.* V is about the causes of sub-specific variables like coloration and voice; cf. also his view that the birth of females, or of offspring not resembling the sire, requires explanation, *G.A.* IV), he must have subsumed individual differences within the definition of the specific form—i.e. the form of man must be expressed as a long disjunction, just as modern naturalists describe species: so Man must be said to have eyes that are coloured (blue or brown or . . .), a nose that is straight or aquiline or snub, and so on.

644a31 "so of bird": the expression is condensed, but there is no need to emend the text. The argument is: 'as in the case of man we survey the undifferentiated *infima species*, so we should do in the case of bird because there are undifferentiated species of bird: I mean we should survey each and every particular kind of bird—sparrow, crane, and all." At a32 ἀλλὰ ('but') does not oppose what has just been said but picks it up and qualifies it—'but of course what I mean is . . .'.

644b5 "unnamed": Aristotle means that it lacks a denotative general name like Bird. Such are the blooded and the bloodless (642b15). Among the genera that he accepts as co-ordinate with birds, the crustaceans are 'unnamed' (*H.A.* I. 490b11): 'crustacean' is not a name but a description (see my paper in *Classical Quarterly*, 1962, p. 90).

644b7–15 *The genera have been marked off chiefly by similarity of parts.*

Aristotle attributes primary importance to morphology again at *H.A.* I. 491a15, but it should be borne in mind that he recognizes similarity of parts mainly by similarity of function (cf. 645b20). In *H.A.*, where he collects and compares differentiae, the 'parts' are only one of the four main divisions. The others are (2) activities (πράξεις), including reproduction and general bodily functions; (3) lives (βίοι), i.e. habitat, feeding, etc.; (4) characters (ἤθη), i.e. psychology and intelligence.

644b15–21: an editorial connective that may not be original. The words translated 'beginning as follows' may alternatively signify 'having made this beginning'.

Chapter 5

The Interest of Zoology

644b22–645a36: This famous passage reads like an independent composition. It begins without connecting particle, like the opening of a book or speech. It is carefully written out in full, unlike the jottings in parts of the previous chapters, and the sentences run easily for reading aloud—they fall into parts that are convenient in length, and balance each other, and lead to a natural conclusion both rhythmically and syntactically. The diction is very slightly elevated (for example, 644b27 ποθοῦμεν, 'we long for', and the rather stately presentation of the argument), but it is nearer to ordinary than to purple language. For instance, Aristotle does not avoid hiatus (a stylish feature introduced by Isocrates and practised by Plato in some later dialogues), nor does he distort the order of thought for the sake of sound effects. It is in fact very beautiful natural Greek, similar to the best parts of the *Politics*, well deserving the compliment that Cicero paid to Aristotle's writing (to the surprise of later readers of the treatises)—"a golden river of discourse", *flumen orationis aureum* (Cicero, *Acad.* II. 119).

644^b22: The opening sentence is in indirect speech lacking an introductory verb. While this happens sometimes in Aristotle's lecture-note style, it is unlikely here. Editors have therefore proposed various additions such as 'we say that'. It may be that whoever edited it with the preceding papers remodelled the syntax to fit in with 644^b21: 'beginning as follows, that...'.

644^b26: The ungenerated and imperishable objects are the heavenly bodies, which Aristotle deals with principally in *De Caelo* (referred to at 645^a4–5). For their 'value' cf. 639^a2 note. The 'starting points of the inquiry' are presumably the data (the physical components, movements, interrelations) that one needs to establish by observation before theorizing about causes. But the planets and stars are too far away or too rarely seen. Aristotle expresses the same difficulty at *De Caelo* II. 12. 292^a15, and in that chapter he elaborates the kind of problem that demands answering —probably what he here calls 'the things we long to know about': for example, why are the apparent motions of the planets more complex than those of the sun and moon? At *De Caelo* 291^b27 he also uses rather emotive language, 'thirst for philosophy'.

645^a8 "in the same way": reading ὁμοίως with the MSS. That is, in the same way as in the study of divine things, because causes are revealed. Bekker, followed by many editors, emended it to ὅμως ('nevertheless') which seems to lose a point.

645^a19 "warming himself at the oven": possibly a polite euphemism for visiting the lavatory (Robertson, *Proc. Cambr. Philol. Soc.* clxix–clxxi, 1938, p. 10). Alternatively, the anecdote might allude to Heraclitus' cosmic principle of fire. In the context the former perhaps makes a better point.

645^a23 "beautiful" (καλοῦ): this ordinary word connotes *good* as well as *beautiful*, and both senses are present here. In saying that non-randomness (τὸ μὴ τυχόντως) characterizes nature more, Aristotle refers to the contrast with artefacts, not with divine objects (645^a11, cf. 639^b19, 641^b19). The visual arts aim at beautiful representations of animals; real animals may not have such beauty, but instead they are composed for the sake of ends, which is even more wonderful. Since the 'end' is often called the 'good' (ἀγαθόν or καλόν), it is easy to say that it occupies the position of the beautiful or good (καλοῦ, ^{a}25).

Functions and Parts

645^{a}36–646^{a}4: How to consider the bodily parts in their proper relationships, having regard to interdependent functions. This part of the chapter is in the same style as Chapter 4, which it naturally follows, becoming more scrappy towards the end.

645^{a}36–^{b}14 (*1*) *Distinguish first the common essential attributes, then their causes.*

This recapitulates 644^{a}23–^{b}7 and 639^{a}15–^{b}10, but adds that we should next state the causes of the common attributes, i.e. before going on to those peculiar to genera or to species.

645^{b}14–28 (*2*) *Bodily parts are for activities; therefore the activities must be stated first.*

This follows from the teleological arguments of Chapter 1 (cf. 642^{a}11). It corrects the popular over-emphasis on morphology (644^{b}7 note).

645^{b}17 "full" (πλήρους): complete and comprehensive, i.e. the co-ordinated activity of the animal as a whole organism, not merely the aggregation of the activities of the parts (hence the variant πολυμεροῦς is wrong).

645^{b}28–33 (*3*) *Distinguish* (*i*) *activities and parts that are subordinate to others as instruments to ends;* (*ii*) *activities and parts that are prior, as ends;* (*iii*) *things that necessitate attributes.*

Class (iii) is obscurely expressed, but by comparison with *An. Post.* II. 94^{a}24 (τὸ οὗ ὄντος τοδὶ ἀνάγκη εἶναι) must mean "things whose existence necessitates the presence ⟨*sc.* of other things⟩". It is the same threefold analysis as at 642^{a}31–^{b}2 but now applied generally and not to a single process. Class (i) contains breathing and lungs, or seeing and eyes. Class (ii) contains cooling and blood, or cognition and soul. Class (iii) contains the proximate matter and the necessary consequentials, which are of *two* sorts: (a) attributes due to the proximate matter *and* necessitated by classes (i) and (ii)—inflow and outflow of air, or the eyeball's translucence, (b) attributes due to the proximate matter alone—the behaviour of hot and cold air, or the eye's colour and other qualities. Some editors, thinking of (iii) (a), emend ὧν to ἃ τούτων "things whose presence is necessitated by the above things", which is supported by another threefold analysis at *G.A.* II. 742a28. But the received text here, though more difficult, has the advantage of covering both the senses of 'necessary' given in Chapter 1 as relevant to biology, i.e. both kinds of consequential or concomitant attribute (on which see 639b21 note, p. 78).

646a1 "member . . . the other parts": i.e. the non-homoeomerous and the homoeomerous parts respectively. At *H.A.* I. 486a9 Aristotle distinguishes 'members' (μέλη) as a sub-division of non-homoeomerous 'parts' (μέρη) but makes no further use of the distinction. Here he more probably means the homoeomerous parts: flesh is for noses, which are for functions.

646a1–4 (*4*) *The causes must be stated in the same order: first the causes of common attributes, then the causes of specific attributes.*

The sentence ends with words preparing the hearer to start the inquiry proper, like the words at *De Sensu* 436a5–6. Nevertheless it seems to be more than an editorial connective, for it adds the necessary last point: the statement of causes, which must come after statements of phenomena (639b8), will follow the same order for the same reasons. Aristotle does in practice follow this procedure, taking first the general attributes and then the specific, and giving the causes after each item as he goes along.

DE GENERATIONE ANIMALIUM I

Aristotle sets out his general theory of reproduction in a long but connected argument which continues to the end of II. 3. Then he takes the development of the embryo genus by genus. The argument is 'dialectical': it moves from agreed starting points to uncover more basic principles. Aristotle starts from the sexes and shows that a common pattern underlies the differences in generative organs. From this he argues that in all cases the male contributes formative movements to the female material, and finally that the real cause of generation is the conveyance of vital movements into appropriate material (with or without sexual differentiation).

Book I is a theoretical discussion from first to last, but its thread has been obscured by some ancient editor who believed it to be a descriptive anatomy. Hence some strange chapter divisions and irrelevant linking sentences; the former are best ignored, and the latter have been printed within square brackets in the translation.

715ᵃ1–18 *Having spoken of the other parts, we now speak of the generative parts and of the efficient cause.*

This stylized preamble, so different from the pointed introduction to *P.A.* I, may be post-Aristotelian. Its reference to *P.A.* shows that *G.A.* has been placed later in the *corpus*. It is true that little is said about the generative parts in *P.A.* (cf. IV. 689ᵃ3 f. where there are editorial cross-references to *G.A.*). But it is wrong to say that *P.A.* has dealt with only three of the four causes, since it is fundamental that all four must be brought into every explanation of biological phenomena, and of course *P.A.* is full of explanations involving efficient causes.

In saying (ᵃ15) that the inquiry into generation and into the moving cause is all one, the writer probably means that nutritive soul is the source of both generation and growth (cf. *P.A.* I. 641ᵇ5 note, *G.A.* II. 3). The generative parts are analysed in the first sixteen chapters (to 721ᵃ30), followed by the theory of generation.

See the glossary and index for the technical terms used here—cause, definition, being, source, homoeomerous parts.

715ᵃ18–716ᵃ1 *Most animals are generated by coition of male and female; the remainder are spontaneous.*

Aristotle is not simply distinguishing between sexual and asexual reproduction, but establishing sexual reproduction as the norm. From that he will conclude that the sexes are the chief sources (ἀρχαί) of generation (716^{a}4). By analysing the contribution that comes from these sources he will argue to a cause that is even more fundamental than the sexes, i.e. nutritive soul. This approach enables Aristotle to start from common sense (for the Greeks, unlike some peoples, held that coition is essential to reproduction, though they disagreed as to what each parent contributes). It also enables him to apply a hylomorphic analysis, whereby the male seed conveys form while the female provides the proximate matter. Finally, when his explanation goes beyond the sexes to a psychic source associated with vital heat and *pneuma*, it becomes necessary for him to explain why there are separate sexes at all (731^{a}30, 732^{a}3–11). Asexual reproduction turns out to be consistent with theory, for the same factors are present as in sexual reproduction: a suitable material (warm mud) and an active source of soul happen to coincide (*G.A.* III. 11). Since it is in each case a chance coincidence, spontaneous generation is (like all spontaneity) the accidental occurrence of a sequence normally due to natural teleology (*P.A.* I. 640^{a}27). But Aristotle does not mean that a given species of animal is produced sometimes from seed and sometimes spontaneously: each species is either always spontaneous or never (cf. my paper in *Phronesis*, 1962, p. 97).

The types of generation that Aristotle distinguishes are:

1. Separated sexes, which generate their own kind: most blooded and some bloodless species, 715^{a}20.
2. Separated sexes, which generate a different, asexual kind (i.e. grubs which develop no further, as he thought) and themselves develop out of other grubs generated spontaneously: certain insects, 715^{a}23, ^{b}6, 721^{a}2 (note on p. 139).
3. Sexes combined in one organism, which produces an embryo direct: most plants (762^{b}11), and to a limited extent the honey bee (759 ^{b}30).
4. Sexless animals which can bud off: certain testaceans, 761^{b}25.
5. Sexless animals, which generate nothing and are generated spontaneously: some fishes, most testaceans, many insects, 721^{a}9, 762^{b}21.
6. Plants (sexless?) generated spontaneously: "some, e.g. mistletoe", 715^{b}25.

As peculiarities, he also recognizes:

7. Animals which are only female and produce their own kind: the fishes *channa* and *erythrinos* (two species of sea-perch, *Serranus*, now known to be hermaphrodite), 741^{a}35, 755^{b}21.
8. Plants which, although containing the sexes combined, lack enough 'residue' to produce seed and are generated spontaneously: willow and poplar, 726^{a}7.

715^{a}21 "perfected": the sexes are fully developed. The implication is that they are imperfectly developed in insects that generate grubs (a23), i.e. fleas, flies, beetles (721a6 note). At 715a23–4 the expression is condensed: Aristotle does not mean that all spontaneous insects generate grubs, for he denies this at 721a9 and often, but that those spontaneous insects which generate something generate grubs. (Similarly at 715b4.)

715a25 "residue": in this case, excreta; (cf. notes at *P.A.* I. 640b14, *G.A.* I. 717a30).

715a26: The connection between locomotion and the separation of sexes is suggested, rather than fully worked out, at *G.A.* I. 730b33, 731a24, II. 732a3–9. The function of the blooded animals, and of some of the bloodless, includes some cognition, unlike plants; the male source is less material than the female, and therefore an animal that is purely male can function better than if the sexes are mingled; locomotion makes it feasible for the sexes to be separate and yet to unite for reproduction; since they can be separate, and it is better for them to be separate, therefore they *are* separate. Aristotle does not explain the causal connection in more detail. At *G.A.* II. 732b26 he points out that differences in locomotion do not tally with differences in method of reproduction, and seeks a more basic cause (heat). Animals were traditionally grouped by differences in locomotion, which were probably used in the Academic classifications as a *fundamentum divisionis*. Aristotle may therefore be taking locomotion as a familiar starting point in which he sees a limited significance.

715b7–16: This argument does not rely directly on infinite regress (as Michael of Ephesus, 4. 19, implies, "ad infinitum, which is impossible"), for the notion of an endless series of different offspring is not logically absurd. Such a series, however, would lack a final cause, for an infinite series cannot be hypothetically necessitated unless it is cyclical and has an absolutely necessitated final cause (*G.C.* II. 11, cf. *P.A.* I. 640a6 note). If the changes are endless and non-repeating, so that neither the series itself nor any member of it remains or recurs, then the series takes place for the sake of nothing: it is this that is impossible. Aristotle's gnomic expression "nature flees from the unlimited . . ." gives the appearance of confusing the endless with the goalless and thus begging the question; but on the premiss that he argues for in *P.A.* I, that final causes do govern natural sequences, it follows that an endless non-repeating series of changes would be contrary to nature.

715b16–25: The comparison with plants in these lines rests on the fact that plants have only a quasi-sexual difference, as Aristotle held. Popularly the fruit-bearing varieties were called female, and the non-fruit-bearing male. Aristotle compares this 'small, analogical differentiation' with that of mussels which produce young like sideshoots, and whelks which produce a slimy 'honeycomb' which he holds is not seed but a residue that develops directly into new animals (*G.A.* III. 761^b29–35). So in all these cases what looks like sexual reproduction is really a direct production of young. He then quotes the caprifig as the most striking example of quasi-sexual differentiation, where the non-fruit-bearing tree actually assists in the ripening of another tree's fruit. Further than this the comparison does not hold, for Aristotle believes that plants are not sexless like testaceans, but contain male and female factors mingled (731^a1, 27); plant seeds are already embryos (728^b32). Hence at 715^b19 "no male and female" means no *separate* sexes in the case of plants. On caprification see Theophrastus, *Historia Plantarum* II. 8 (Loeb edition by Hort, entitled *Theophrastus, Enquiry into Plants*).

715^b24 "concocting" (*πέττειν*): *pepsis* is the physiological concept that Aristotle relies on most. It means ripening, bringing material to a higher state of refinement or organization through the natural operation of heat. It applies to crops, and to the cooking of food. Bodily heat concocts nutriment into blood, and blood into flesh (i.e. muscle) or fat or marrow, etc. —in particular into semen or into an embryo. The opposite of pepsis is *sēpsis* or *syntēxis* (726^a21), rotting or disintegration into simpler constituents, a process that is always morbid in living things and is brought about by disproportion between hot, cold, wet, dry. The proper action of cold, on the other hand, is to congeal or solidify, also a constructive process though not invoked by Aristotle so often as heat. Although cold is strictly no more than the lack of heat (*sterēsis, Met. Λ* 1070^b12), Aristotle always treats it as having its own capability: cf. *G.A.* II. 743^a36 "Cold is privation of heat. Nature uses both, for they have of necessity the capability, the one to do this, the other to do that", and *P.A.* II. 649^a18, "In such cases the cold is a sort of nature, not a privation." Aristotle presumably means that materials which act in a certain way when they are hot, act in a certain other way when they lack heat; if, when hot, they concoct, then when cold they congeal. The privation is a sort of form, as he says at *Phys.* II. 193^b19: it is a certain state of proximate matter.

715^b25–30: Here the comparison with plants makes a different point. They can be divided into those produced from seed and those produced spontaneously. This corresponds to the distinction between sexually generated and spontaneous animals, marked at 715^a26 and $^b16$ by *ὅσα μὲν . . . ὅσα δὲ*.

The paragraph is added abruptly, but this is not unusual; there seems no real need to suspect its authenticity or position as some editors have done.

715b29 "constitute" (συνιστάναι): to put materials together so as to make a new thing out of them, another important concept in Aristotle's physiology. He applies it to the forming of an embryo out of the inchoate menstrual material, an action which he compares with that of rennet upon milk—it 'sets' the material, gives it form (729a9–13). (Cf. Peck, *G.A.* lxi–ii.)

716a1: It is doubtful whether Aristotle wrote a treatise on plants. He expresses a great many views on them in the course of his zoology. The extant work *De Plantis* is now known to have been written by Nicolaus of Damascus in the first century A.D. The references in Aristotle's treatises were probably inserted by an editor, and refer to Theophrastus' botanical works.

716a2–721a25: *The Male and Female Parts, their Functions and Causes*

In this long section Aristotle analyses the types of generative apparatus, explaining why they vary from a basic pattern. The basic male organ is the pair of 'spermatic passages' within the body, where seed is 'concocted'. The basic female organ is the uterus in which the embryo is 'constituted', nourished, and protected. This analysis is preliminary to his discussion of seed, from which will come his explanation of what brings about generation (721a30–end).

At a2 the 'other animals' are animals other than those spontaneously generated.

716a4–17 *Male and female are the sources of seed and therefore of generation.*

Aristotle now sets out what he has to demonstrate: that the male contributes the generative movement to the female material (at a6 "movement *and* generation" is hendiadys, cf. 726b21). 'The male' may refer to (i) the male animal, 716a9; (ii) maleness, 716a28; (iii) the differentiating male factor, 716a5. Sometimes (ii) and (iii) are intended together. Since 'sex' is even vaguer, it has only been used for τὰ ἀφροδίσια (indulgence in sex) but not for ἄρρεν καὶ θῆλυ ('male and female').

'Seed' (σπέρμα) may refer to (i) seed of a plant; (ii) the male semen (strictly γονή); (iii) the female contribution to generation; (iv) the first stage of the foetus (strictly κύημα, foetus or conception). At this stage of the argument 'seed' is necessarily vague because Aristotle has not yet analysed for the reader what exactly comes from the female and what from the male. This is the question he refers to at a9–10, where "*how* this comes to be produced" does not mean the mechanics of it but "what does the male produce by way of seed, and what does the female produce by way of seed?" (See also 724b12–21.)

At a9 "produced naturally' is contrasted with spontaneous generation as *not* natural; for although it is normal—and therefore in a general sense natural—for certain species to be generated spontaneously, each instance of spontaneous generation occurs by chance (cf. note at 715^a18). It is not contrary to nature, but it is accidental.

716^a17–$^b12$ *Male and female differ by capability, and accordingly by organs.*

The relation of organs to functions has been explained at *P.A.* I. 640 $^a10$ f., 645^b14 f. Organs do not create functions, as the atomists argued; but equally functions do not create organs—Aristotle would not have thought that the giraffe owes its long neck to straining after foliage. He says that functions *necessitate* organs, and organs are *for* functions. If the functions are present, this fact *implies* that the organs are present; if the organs are present, their presence is *explained by* the functions (cf. note at *P.A.* I. 639^b21, p. 77 and at 641^b10, p. 98).

716^a22 "the generator": i.e. the mother. To take it as the father, as Peck suggests, seems to anticipate too much of what Aristotle has still to explain.

716^a27: By arguing that the male–female differentiation resides in the generative organs and not in the whole animal, Aristotle makes a necessary distinction between source and consequentials, and can now restrict the inquiry to the source. But eventually he will conclude that the generative organs too are consequentials, and that the real source of sex-differentiation is in the heart (*G.A.* IV. 764^b36). His final remark at 716^b11 leaves room for this more precise identification of the source. There is no important contradiction here, for he says at 766^b5 that although the source is in the heart, animals are not male and female until they have the sexual organs.

716^b13–717^a12 *General differences in generative organs of blooded animals.*

From here to 720^b1 Aristotle compares the generative organs of blooded animals, and from 720^b2 to 721^a25 those of bloodless animals. By exhibiting the reasons for the differences, he isolates the essential common functions. First he summarizes the differences in this paragraph.

716^b17 "channels": these are in fact the testes which Aristotle did not recognize as such. This empirical mistake leads him to conclude that testes are not present in all males, and are therefore no more than ancillary to generation (717^a17).

716^b26 "front": Aristotle's words for bodily orientation are related to man's posture. The translation preserves them, and the key is as follows:

"upright"	=	standing on hind legs
"front"	=	ventral
"back"	=	dorsal
"above"	=	forward
"below"	=	hindward

"Right" and "left" are related to the direction in which the animal naturally looks, which is not always the direction in which it naturally moves (cf. crab, octopus). The "diaphragm" is not only the actual tissue that mammals have between thorax and abdomen, but also a corresponding imaginary line in all animals separating the higher from the lower functions, i.e. just aft of the heart.

716b31: There is no "more precise clarification" in *H.A.*, but Books III–V occasionally quote animals not quoted in *G.A.* *H.A.* III. 1 summarizes the differences in generative organs in the same terms as *G.A.*, but adds a description, with diagram, taken from a dissection of an unnamed viviparous animal. Since *H.A.* as a whole appears to have been compiled after *G.A.*, references to it in *G.A.* are probably editorial insertions.

716b32 "uterus": Aristotle's concept needs to be understood in the context of his medical contemporaries. He was moving away from their opinion, but not so far as modern opinion has moved. The term is now confined to mammals, and to the expanded part of the whole oviduct in which embryos develop; its function is regarded as primarily nutritive. Aristotle's contemporaries included the whole oviduct, and applied the concept of uterus to all animals. They considered its primary function to be conception and delivery (cf. Plato, *Timaeus* 91B–D). They thought it virtually independent of the mother and able to move about in the mother's body. An atomist theory of the origin of animals even held that 'wombs' were formed by chance in the primeval mud (Lucretius V. 808; Diodorus Siculus I. 7. 3). Aristotle instead emphasizes its function as the mother's instrument for concocting and nourishing the embryo, and he also points out that it is fixed within the body (719a33, 720a12). But he still regards it as the female sexual organ of all animals (716a33, cf. IV. 766a4) corresponding to testes and spermatic channels in the male. He calls it 'paired' because he includes the whole oviduct. (There was of course no recognition yet of the mammalian *egg*; the question was whether the female contributes *seed* comparable with the male seed.) In order to extend the concept to 'bloodless' animals, Aristotle takes the protective membranes enclosing the eggs to be 'uterine' (717a5), and rightly says that in crustaceans this 'uterus'—i.e. the ovarian ducts—can be seen 'divided on either side of the gut' (720b14). In the cephalopods it is in fact not the poulps but the sepia and squid which have only one oviduct:

Aristotle puts this the wrong way round whenever he mentions it (717^{a}6, III. 758^{a}6, *H.A.* IV. 525^{a}2–6, *al.*). As to function, although he puts more emphasis than his contemporaries on nutrition, he evidently sees the uterus as primarily a protective structure in which four functions take place: conception, concoction, nutrition, delivery. He says that it completes its function at its terminus (718^{b}27). And the reason that he gives for its being internal is not that this facilitates nutrition but that it affords greater protection and heat (719^{a}33).

716^{b}35 "viviparous within themselves": as distinct from the ovoviviparous which first form an egg but then hatch it within the body, e.g. vipers and certain selachian fishes (718^{b}32).

717^{a}12–718^{a}34 *Reasons for differences in male spermatic organs.*

The common point that emerges is that semen must be in the right state of concoction and heat, and the different sorts of genital apparatus are all for the sake of ensuring this in different animals' circumstances, by regulating the speed of coition and emission.

At ^{a}12 "differentiation of" is ambiguous in the Greek, and may mean (i) "differentiation consisting in", (ii) "difference between".

This section contains two apparent interpolations (717^{b}23–6 and 26–31).

717^{a}19 "for they have been seen": i.e. snakes and fishes *do* generate sexually. At III. 755^{b}1 Aristotle argues against those who held that all fishes are female.

717^{a}23: For the effect of convoluted intestines upon appetite cf. *P.A.* III. 675^{b}23 and context.

717^{a}30 "residue": *perittōma* is an unused surplus. Bodily heat concocts food into blood, leaving as by-products phlegm, serum, and useless excreta (725^{a}15, cf. 715^{a}25, *P.A.* I. 640^{b}14). The blood is further concocted into the homoeomerous parts: the wetter constituent is concocted into flesh, fat, marrow, the earthier into hair, bones, sinews, nails, teeth, horns. At the final stage of concoction, when blood is about to be particularized into these tissues, it can be concocted into semen (726^{b}10). All these products are 'useful residues' or 'residues of useful nutriment' (725^{a}3 f.).

717^{a}33 "doubling-back": the epididymis including the *vas deferens*, cf. 718^{a}11, *H.A.* III. 510^{a}20.

717^{b}4 "In birds . . .": this passage gives two reasons why testes are internal in some animals. Having shown in 717a12–b4 that in vivipara external testes slow down the movement of seed, Aristotle now says (i) that internal testes make coition slower than where there are no testes, but quicker than where they are external (b4–13); (ii) that if there is no external penis there can be no external testes (b14–23). (He is of course mistaken in thinking that the penis is absent in snakes and some birds, but the observation is difficult. *H.A.* III. 509b30 corrects this: "in the small birds the penis is not clearly visible, but in the larger, such as the goose, it is more evident." The *H.A.* observation destroys the *G.A.* argument, but was no doubt later.)

717b23–26: Besides being irrelevant, this puts the Hippocratic view which is rejected at 724b36. Aristotle's view is that these animals concoct the seed during coition (718a6).

717b26–31: Another addition to the text, but not necessarily non-Aristotelian. It qualifies the statement at 716b26 that all vivipara have the testes ventrally, and should have been inserted either there or at 717b4. (Cf. 719b15, where the note about elephant and hedgehog also looks like an afterthought.) At b28–9 the reason why birds have internal testes is given as speed of coition, ignoring the lack of penis (b11, b21). Possibly this represents a later correction of theory, necessitated by the *H.A.* observation of the penis in birds (cf. note at 717b4). There is another interpolation about speed of coition in birds at *G.A.* IV. 769b34.

717b33–718a34: This section shows that in fishes and snakes, whose coition is necessarily quick in the former case but slow in the latter, the heat and concoction of seed is safeguarded in both cases by simpler spermatic channels.

The section, like the next (718a35–720b1), has been broken up by the early editor who took it as a series of descriptions of animal testes and coition.

718a1: In fact the oviparous fishes do not copulate, but the male sprinkles the eggs with semen after they are laid. Aristotle mistakenly insists that they do copulate (cf. 717a19), and at III. 756a33 goes so far as to criticize the fishermen for failing to observe it 'through lack of desire for knowledge'. *H.A.* V. 540b6 and 541a11 f. distinguish pairing methods in oviparous fishes and selachians. Undoubtedly Aristotle was sure that it had been observed; nevertheless it was also necessary to his theory, for he held that where there are male and female there must be coition (715a18, II. 741b2, *H.A.* V. 539a27). He regards the later sprinkling as a second stage: coition constitutes the eggs within the female, and the sprinkling makes them fertile after they have been laid (730a20, III. 755b5, 757a25).

"Are detached" (^{a}1 ἀπολύονται): Peck, followed by Louis, translates 'ejaculate' here and at ^{a}14 and 32. This would give good sense, but it does not seem to be paralleled elsewhere and is not recognized by the article in Liddell and Scott's Greek Lexicon (ed. Jones and McKenzie, 9th ed., Oxford 1940). From the observer's viewpoint it is not the ejaculation but the separation of the two animals that is evident.

At ^{a}11 the 'doubling-back' is the epididymis, of which the 'bloodless section' is the *vas deferens* (cf. 717^{a}33).

At ^{a}23 ("whose penis is large") the reference is possibly to the ass and the horse (cf. II. 748^{b}8 f.).

718^{a}35–720^{b}1 *Reasons for differences in uterus.*

The puzzle (^{a}35) is that the uterus is placed differently although its function is the same. The vivipara have it in its natural position, where its function takes place, near the outlet of the generative channel (718^{b}27). But the other animals have it extending in various directions for which Aristotle gives reasons in this section. He reduces the arrangements to a schema. As before (716^{b}26 note), "high" means forward, in this case by the diaphragm; "low" means rearward, by the groin; "front" means ventrally by the stomach; "back" means dorsally in the loin or lower part of the back. The schema is:

Vivipara: rearward ventral.
Ovo-vivipara: forward dorsal extending to rearward ventral.
Ovipara (perfected eggs): forward dorsal.
Ovipara (unperfected eggs): rearward dorsal.

As will be seen at 719^{b}21, there is a muddle over the ovipara which is insoluble, because the whole schema is unreal and cannot be related to some of the facts. The summary of it at *H.A.* III. 511^{a}22–7 is even more muddled, because it has been written by somebody who mistook Aristotle's use of 'high' and 'low', and these words have to be removed before the passage can even be understood.

718^{b}1: Aristotle mistakenly classed *all* the selachians except the fishing-frog as viviparous; that is, all the cartilaginous fishes such as sharks, dogfishes, rays, skates.

718^{b}7: The 'perfecting' of eggs means both fertilizing by the sprinkling with semen (718^{a}1 note) and completion of their growth from a residue within them (III. 755^{a}22). The function of fishes is to be prolific because so many eggs get destroyed: "nature retrieves the wastage by quantity" (III. 755^{a}31; on the teleological implication see p. 96).

718^{b}11 "each of the two sections": i.e. each oviduct (716^{b}32 note).

718b13 "a nature analogous": i.e. the nature of a *small* animal or plant (cf. 725a30, II. 749b26, IV. 771a17f.).

718b27 "terminus . . . function" (πέρας, ἔργον): the convenient location for an organ is where it completes its function. Aristotle's observations of embryos *in utero* seem to have been mostly carried out in birds and fishes, especially the ovo-viviparous dogfishes. He may therefore have been impressed with the action of the oviduct as a channel down which the embryo moves as it grows, culminating at the point of delivery where the function is completed. (He does report seeing mammalian embryos *in utero*, but does not record their progress in the way that he records the progress of eggs and fish embryos, cf. *G.A.* III. 2–3, IV. 771b30.)

718b36 "as some say": e.g. Empedocles, cf. *Resp.* 477b1.

719a2: Aristotle later points out important differences between the eggs of birds and of fishes (III. 754b20). Here he is concerned only with the arrangement of the uterus. Both birds and the viviparous selachians perfect the eggs within, and must do this in the forward part near the diaphragm where there is enough heat to concoct the eggs fully. Then in the selachians the eggs descend to the rearward part and are hatched; the young are thereafter developed in the position corresponding to that of viviparous quadrupeds. Aristotle gives more details, including the peculiar placentoid structure in *Mustelus mustelus*, at III. 754b27, *H.A.* VI. 564b30–565a11, 565b2–17. The 'Dissections', a collection of anatomical drawings referred to at a10, is not extant.

719a14: Such a 'function of nature' would be the concocting of a perfected egg, which requires a more forward position of the uterus (718b20, 26). It is the ovo-viviparous selachians that "generate in two stages" (literally 'generate doubly', διττογονεῖ).

719a22 "fleshy": by 'flesh' (σάρξ) Aristotle refers to muscle, but since he has not recognized its action (which he attributes wholly to 'sinews', νεῦρα) the translation 'flesh' has been kept. But the argument sometimes requires the connotation of 'muscular', as here and at 725b32. 'Flesh' excludes fat.

719a30–b17: This section interrupts the discussion and looks like a later insertion by Aristotle, possibly displaced from 720b1. Its final sentence (719b15–17) may be later still. At 719a35 Platt and Lulofs mark a lacuna after "internal in others"; but the text as it stands, although clumsy, is not impossible. Testes too need shelter, and whether they are external or internal depends upon the nature of the shelter available: animals with skin unsuited to forming this shelter must have the testes internally.

719ᵇ17–720ᵇ1: Having distinguished between the rearward and forward *arrangement* of the uterus in 718ᵃ35–719ᵃ27, Aristotle now distinguishes between ventral and dorsal *position*. Some editors seclude parts of this section on the grounds that it repeats what was said in the other (Platt, Peck). But it really makes a new point, as Michael of Ephesus suggested (17. 20). Aristotle seems to show this by calling the ventral/dorsal difference a difference of 'position' (*θέσις*, 719ᵇ18), while the rearward/forward difference was one of 'manner' (*τρόπος*, 718ᵃ36). For since the uterus terminates in the same place in all cases, the difference between rearward and forward is not one of position but one of prolongation and shape: in reality it is the difference between the simple oviduct of egg-layers and the uterine enlargement in mammals, where the latter gives the impression that the duct as a whole is rearward compared with the others. The ventral/dorsal difference on the other hand can properly be called one of position.

The schema however is artificial and now breaks down in the case of ovipara. 719ᵇ21 and 720ᵃ1 clearly imply that birds and oviparous quadrupeds have the uterus in the ventral position as distinct from oviparous fishes which have it dorsally. But at 720ᵃ16 Aristotle says that ovipara (without distinction) have the uterus dorsally, and goes on to argue that the ovo-vivipara have the egg-producing part dorsally because that is the position for ovipara. *H.A.* III. 511ᵃ24, in an admittedly muddled summary of the schema, says that all ovipara have the uterus dorsally. Since the distinction is difficult to relate to actual facts, there is no way of knowing which of these apparently contradictory statements Aristotle intended. It is noticeable that the schema (for which see note at 718ᵃ35) contains no occupant of the forward ventral position: possibly Aristotle felt this must be filled by the ovipara of perfected eggs, but then failed to reconcile it with his argument for the dorsal position in ovo-vivipara.

719ᵇ34: Some editors seclude or transpose 719ᵇ34–720ᵃ3, but the passage seems to make satisfactory sense (and in the Greek *οὔτε* at ᵃ2 looks forward to *τε* at ᵃ3). The two reasons given at 719ᵇ 24–34 for the ventral position in vivipara, namely the embryo's growth and the position of the outlet, are now shown to be inapplicable to ovipara, in which the outlet is dorsal and there is no reason against a dorsal uterus.

720ᵇ2–721ᵃ25 *General differences in generative organs of bloodless animals.*

Aristotle merely summarizes the generative methods of these four classes of animals, extracting the data that he needs for his coming discussion of the male and female contributions in general. He gives more details at *G.A.* III. 757ᵇ31–763ᵇ16.

In the testaceans, most or all of which he holds to be spontaneously generated, he reports that coition has been observed only in snails, but that it is not known whether generation results (III. 762a33, cf. I. 731b8).

At 720b9 the description is apparently drawn from a long-tailed crustacean. *H.A.* V. 541b19–22 is more precise and goes on with details of the crabs. Aristotle here makes his points that there is coition, that the males have spermatic channels, and that the eggs are first produced within the female. By 'uterus' he refers to the ovarian ducts (cf. 716b32 note).

In cephalopods (720b15) Aristotle is evidently uncertain about the generative mechanism, but again extracts his necessary points: there is coition during which the male contributes something, and there is a 'uterine' part where the eggs are first constituted. At 720b32 he rejects the possibility of generation by means of the tentacle, because it is 'outside the channel and the body', i.e. it is not connected through the male generative channel to the inner spermatic parts. His words show that the fishermen had correctly reported the method, rediscovered in modern times and known as hectocotylization, by which a modified sperm-carrying tentacle is detached from the male and left behind in the female's mantle-cavity. Aristotle has put his finger on the difficulty that is not yet solved—how the sperms get on to the tentacle. At b20 the reference is to *P.A.* IV. 684b34f.

The division of insect reproduction into three types (721a2) has already been implied at 715b2, but is more precisely stated here and with a different emphasis. There Aristotle was arguing that spontaneous insects which have sexes produce no fertile offspring. Here his point is that sexually generated insects perpetuate their own kind. This is necessary to his later argument that the male contributes its own form (*eidos*) to the foetus. Aristotle's theory of insect larvae shows knowledge of some life cycles but ignorance of others. He says at *G.A.* III. 758b7f. that all insects, the sexually generated and the spontaneous, originate as larvae. He regards the larva as the first stage of the embryo in all types of generation including viviparous. Although the first stage of insects' offspring may resemble an egg, it is really a motionless larva. Some insect larvae then go through an egg stage (here he equates the pupa with an egg). But the larvae that some spontaneous insects produce do not develop into animals: these insects develop from *other* larvae which are produced spontaneously in various materials (details in *H.A.* V. 19).

The second point that Aristotle makes about insects here is that the male inserts no part into the female. 'Part' may signify an organ or a tissue or any spermatic substance (cf. 716a11, 720b31). This point becomes important later, as showing that the male need contribute nothing somatic (723b19, 729b22). The observation is of course mistaken: the female part in question was presumably the ovipositor. Nor is Aristotle's inference valid; for he has not shown that the male does not pass seed into the female organ, but assumes that the female carries the generative material to the male source of movement, obviating the need for semen (730b26).

A third point is that, as in other animals, the embryos are produced first within the female, even though they are bulky larvae: hence his remark that the females are big in proportion (721a11, which I have transposed to what seems its proper position). The relative smallness and weakness of the males becomes relevant at 730b27.

721a26–30 This linking sentence, evidently interpolated, corresponds to cross-references at *P.A.* II. 653b16 and 655b25. It is more than usually inept, for milk is of negligible significance in Aristotle's theory: it is discussed only at *G.A.* IV. 776a15–777a27, where it is held to be a residue from the material of the embryo. A mention of the menses would have been more to the point. The sentence may have replaced an original phrase indicating that the next step is to consider what seed is: hence possibly the connecting word 'for' (*γὰρ*) at 721a30.

721a30–731b14 *The Male and Female Contributions to Generation*

The questions raised at 721a30–b6 occupy the rest of Book I. Aristotle approaches them by refuting pangenesis.

721a32 "in which of the two ways" (*ποτέρως*): i.e. whether by visible seed or by some invisible means. "Some evidently emit" (a30) means that it is visibly evident, and implies that the others do not emit visibly.

721b6–724a13 *Seed is not drawn from all parts of the body.*

Aristotle begins as usual from an accepted starting-point; then by refuting current theories he prepares the ground for his own. He cannot start from male seed, because of the doubt about cephalopods and insects (above); nor can he prove directly that the female contributes no seed. The common ground is that animals which are sexually generated (= 'they all' at 721b6) develop from a small beginning within the female —a 'seed' in this sense—which has derived from one or both of the parents. The current view was that this seed must somehow contain all the bodily parts, drawn from the corresponding parts of one or both parents—a combination of the views later known as preformationism and pangenesis, whereby the embryo's development is merely the enlargement and manifestation of structures already present and fully diversified in the seed. This view is found in some Hippocratic treatises which are generally believed to belong to the period just before Aristotle: e.g. *On Airs, Waters, Places* 14 (II. 60, Littré), *Sacred Malady* 2 (VI. 364, L), *On Generation* 3 and 8 (VII. 474, 480, L), *Maladies* IV. 1 (VII. 542, L).

By showing that seed cannot consist crudely of bits of each part, Aristotle clears the ground for arguing (a) that seed need only be something capable of *becoming* such parts—like blood when it is being particularized into bodily parts: i.e. seed is a final residue of blood; (b) that the corresponding female residue must be the menses, and cannot be another seed like the male's; (c) that the change from potential to actual parts necessitates the presence of both a material cause and a moving cause, and these must be the female and the male respectively.

721^b13 "four pieces of evidence": for these traditional arguments and the data adduced see the Hippocratic treatises mentioned above, with *H.A.* VII. 585^b29, discussed by E. Lesky, *Die Zeugungs- und Vererbungslehren der Antike und ihr Nachwirken* (Abhandlungen der Akademie der Wissenschaften und der Literatur in Mainz) (Wiesbaden 1950), 1294f.

Aristotle replies to the first and second argument at 723^b32–724^a7, and to the third and fourth at 722^a4–$^b3$. To judge from these exchanges, the preformationist theory must have been modified since Anaxagoras' reported remark "For how could hair come from not-hair?" (*VS* 59 B 10). Anaxagoras presumably held that the seed contains every part, in a crude sense. But Aristotle mentions nails and hair among things from which nothing comes away, and his objection would only have weight if his opponents agreed to this fact. Aetius (based ultimately on sources close to Aristotle) reports that Democritus considered the seed to originate from "the most important parts such as bones, flesh, sinews" (*VS* 68 A 141). The Hippocratic treatise *On Generation*, 1, says that it originates from all the fluid parts (VII. 470, L). The pseudo-Aristotelian *Problems* has a version in which seed comes only from the parts to which blood vessels extend (878^b5). It is likely therefore that Aristotle knew the theory in a modified form which could not explain the inheritance of resemblances in voice, hair and nails, movement, or remoter ancestral characteristics. Epicurus seems to have answered Aristotle, for Lucretius specifically mentions that even ancestors' facial expressions, voices, and hair are transmitted by atom-groups in the seed (IV. 1218–26).

Aristotle's objection about beards (722^a7) has more force: the offspring can develop parts that had not yet been developed by the parent at the time of generation. This should compel the preformationist to admit that the seed is not completely diversified. The Epicureans do not meet this explicitly, but their hypothesis of atom-groups could be made to account for it in the same way that it accounted for growth. The parent who has not yet grown a beard has within him the nucleus of the appropriate atom-group, which will become a visible beard when enough similar atoms have joined it; he need only hand on, in the seed, a part of this nucleus to enable his son to grow a beard too. This is how ancestral traits remain concealed through several generations of descent (Lucretius IV.

1221). Evidently Aristotle had not encountered this development of atomism, for he does not reply to it.

722a16–b3: If each part contributes seed, what composes the parts into a *whole*? Aristotle's analogy of syllables and letters (722a30–35), which recalls *Met.* Z 17, shows in particular the difficulty that the fourth 'piece of evidence' (721b25) gets into: a whole is not merely an aggregation of parts.

722b3–30: Nor does the theory account for the *parts*. Here Aristotle puts up six objections:

(i) 722b3–4. The seed is not a miniature animal (as in the 'homuncule' theory of the seventeenth century). In saying this Aristotle presumably relies on the visible evidence (cf. *G.A.* II. 740a17, 741b25, *H.A.* VI. 3 and 10). Therefore the parts, if present, must be unconnected. But if so, they are not capable of living and functioning but are only homonymously parts (cf. 722b17 and *P.A.* I. 640b29f.). That is, they are not present as actual, completed hands and feet, but as something from which hands and feet will be completed. But to admit this would remove the ground for believing that the seed comes from all parts, cf. 723a1 f.

(ii) 722b5–6. How could female organs come from the male parent, and vice versa? The theory fails to account for resemblance between daughter and father, or son and mother. Democritus dealt with this by saying that each parent contributes a complete set of parts, of which the stronger prevails in each case. Aristotle replies in the next section.

(iii) 722b6–12. If both parents contribute all parts, the product should be two animals. Aristotle allows that Empedocles' theory of the 'tally' avoids this difficulty, though it is illogical on other grounds (cf. b17–30). It is not known how exactly Empedocles pictured the *half* that each parent contributes.

(iv) 722b13–14. On Democritus' theory a female ought to be able to produce a complete offspring by herself. Why does Aristotle not make more of this, and argue that males are shown to be needed? Possibly because the existence of the parthenogenetic *channa* and *erythrinos* (note at 715a18) weakens his ground by showing that males are not always necessary. What he tries to maintain, therefore, is that where there *are* separate sexes, both are needed for generation; in *channa* and *erythrinos* no males exist (741a35).

(v) 722b14–28. Either the separate parts are not living, in which case they must disintegrate; or they are living, in which case they cannot join together any more than living animals can. To be alive necessitates being either a complete organism or an integral part of an organism—able to perform its function (cf. *P.A.* I. 640b30f.).

(vi) 722b28–30. The use of Empedocles' word 'sundered' (διέσπασται, as in the fragment quoted at 722^b12) suggests that this objection is again aimed at the tally theory. Possibly, in the missing continuation of the fragment, Empedocles said that the superior parts come from the male and the inferior from the female (so Michael of Ephesus, 27. 8 and 26, τὰ κυριώτερα), the superior parts being the upper and right-hand and front (cf. *Inc. An.* 706^b12; Michael's interpretation of the superior parts as head, heart, etc., is less workable in terms of a tally). But such a division is illogical, because these dimensions cut across each other.

722^b30–723^a23: Seed does not consist of actual blood and bones, for it lacks their defining characteristics. But if it is granted that seed, without being blood, can produce blood, why not grant (a) that it can produce the other parts too, (b) that it can come from a single source?

At 722^b35 'synonymous' means 'having the same name and nature' (*Cat.* 1^a6). At 723^a8 "all things" recalls Anaxagoras' repeated statements (*VS* 59 B 1, 4, 6, etc.).

723^a23–$^b2$: If sex-differentiation does not depend on the seed's contents but on what happens to the seed, so that a given seed may become either male or female, then there is no reason to say that the seed contains parts drawn from the sex organs; *a fortiori* it need not contain parts from remoter organs. At 723^b1 the uterus stands for the characteristic female organ, not for the receptacle of conception: if the female element in seed does not come from the parent's female characteristic, then why should any other element come from the corresponding part in the parent?

723^b3–8: cf. 721^a7. Flies and fleas are generated spontaneously, and generate larvae unlike the parents.

723^b9–15: Pangenesis does not explain multiple births. Each fruit-bud is a foetus, which by the pangenesis theory ought to contain a secretion from each part of the tree; the same applies to each cub in a litter. But there has been only one act of coition (one 'movement' in the tree), producing one separating-off or discharge of seed, i.e. one secretion from each part according to pangenesis. There has been no cause of multiple secretions. When each secretion reaches the uterus, all are immediately combined in a foetus. But a foetus cannot be divided; hence multiplication at this stage is impossible. When Aristotle repeats the argument at 729^a 6–8 below, he adds that one part would not give off separated secretions; as Michael of Ephesus comments (56. 29), there is no reason for one foot to give off five foot-parts. Darwin's version of pangenesis avoids this objection, because the foot consists of cells, each of which sends a 'gemmule' to each germ-cell.

$723^{b}16$–19: If a complete fruit can be produced from a cutting, this shows that the rest of the tree from which it was cut did not contribute to the fruit.

$723^{b}19$–32: cf. notes at $721^{a}2$, $729^{b}22$. If the male insect generates without transmitting physical seed, then even the preformationists ought to look beyond seed for the effective agent of generation in each part. Aristotle prepares the way for his own theory. On the analogy with crafts see notes at $730^{b}19$ and *P.A.* I. $641^{b}10$.

$723^{b}32$–$724^{a}3$: Aristotle replies to the argument of $721^{b}15$. If the seed arrives at the outlet simultaneously from all parts both far and near, it must have started out earlier from some than from others.

$724^{a}3$–7: Aristotle replies to $721^{b}17$. Though he casts doubt on the evidence of the inheritance of acquired characteristics, he accepts some of it and accounts for it by his explanation of inherited resemblances (*G.A.* IV. 3). Cf. $722^{a}8$, *H.A.* VII. $585^{b}28$–$586^{a}8$.

$724^{a}14$–$^{b}12$ *Definition of seed.*

The Greek at $^{a}19$–20 has been marked as corrupt by most editors but, though clumsy, it is translatable and seems to be needed by the argument. The seed is the first thing in the generative sequence: it is not the box out of which the first thing comes (the parent is the box). Whether or not the seed actually becomes (turns into) the embryo, is yet to be argued; but meanwhile Aristotle makes the point that the seed is the beginning or first item of a continuous physical development.

From $^{a}21$ to $^{b}12$ Aristotle considers some ways in which a thing can be the starting-point of a continuous sequence. The section is expository, not rigorous: he does not try to establish the function of seed by exhausting the meanings of 'out of' (which would be futile), but picks out the two meanings that he wants to use by contrasting two others that he wants to discard. (Elsewhere he uses the same examples to pick out other meanings of 'out of'. At *Met.* *α* $994^{a}25$ man-out-of-boy exemplifies *A* turning into *B*; at *Met.* *Δ* $1023^{b}8$ night-out-of-day exemplifies reciprocal change. *Met.* *N* $1092^{a}24$ gives 'mixture' and 'synthesis' as two other ways of coming out of. *Met.* *Δ* 24 purports to list all the ways, but is far from complete. Cf. Bonitz, *Index Aristotelicus*, $225^{a}45$.) The two ways that Aristotle discards here are (i) that seed is an intermediate stage in a longer sequence that has a remoter cause (like day–night, boy–man, or the voyage of the sacred ship to Delos following the Panathenaea in the annual religious programme); (ii) that seed is an 'opposite', i.e. a formed product which must lose its own properties to become the embryo—as some appearances might suggest (grubs, eggs); here Aristotle chooses his examples well, for musical-to-unmusical and healthy-to-sick indicate changes from a positive qualification into its opposite (better than the more usual unmusical-to-musical and sick-to-healthy, which suggest potential states becoming actual). Either of these ways would imply that seed is not the real origin. Other possible ways such as mixture or synthesis (i.e. juxtaposition of parts) have been in effect discarded in the refutation of pangenesis.

The two ways that are retained are those of the proximate matter and the proximate mover. Aristotle seems to assume the hylomorphic analysis as known. Insult–abuse–battle admirably illustrates a proximate mover which (a) has no somatic component, (b) exists within the things being moved; both these features will be shown to belong to the role played by male seed. But the crafts (^{a}34) better illustrate how the proximate mover also shapes the material and gives it a specific form (^{b}6); cf. *P.A.* I. 641 ^{a}26, *Phys.* II. 3, *Met. Z* 7. This too is done by the male seed, cf. 729^{a}10 f., II. 1–3. In so far as form and matter are complementary aspects of a thing, they can be called opposites; and therefore in so far as the form and matter are conveyed by the male and the female respectively, generation takes place out of two separate opposites (^{b}7–12). But this is not the same as generation out of *an* opposite, which would imply that something sheds one property and takes on another (^{b}3–4). Aristotle has not properly distinguished these two kinds of generation out of opposites, but the confusion does not seem to cause trouble (cf. the same confusion at *Met. N* 1092^{a}34, with Ross's note).

At 724^{a}36 πρῶτος ('first') means 'proximate', i.e. counting from where you stand, as it often does; only the context can determine whether it means this or 'the ultimate origin'.

724^{b}12–21 *Difference between semen, seed, and fruit.*

Aristotle unfortunately does not adhere to these valid and useful distinctions: cf. 728^{b}33 where 'seed' (*sperma*) stands for all three in turn. This note is probably an insertion, but need not be non-Aristotelian.

724^{b}23–726^{b}30 *Physical composition of seed: a residue of blood.*

Aristotle now sets out to show that the male semen and its female counterpart (menses) are residues from the blood in its final stage of concoction before it is particularized into tissues: the spermatic residues are produced by a further concoction that occurs in coition. This will explain why the seed contains the embryo's parts potentially, just as blood contains potentially the parts that it nourishes. Further, differences in concoction will explain differences in embryos' development, such as their resemblance or lack of resemblance to parents. More generally, differences of reproductive method between one species and another, and differences of 'perfection', are due to differences of concoction and of heat. This argument therefore is fundamental to Aristotle's biological theory. Hence the importance of this first section in which he establishes that seed is a concocted residue and not a colliquation.

'Colliquation' (*σύντηγμα* or *σύντηξις* in Aristotle and in Hippocratic medicine, *ῥύσις* in Galen: Latinized traditionally as *colliquatio*) is a morbid breaking-down of tissues into noxious fluids which force their way through the body, causing pus and abscesses. It was chiefly associated with the kidneys and bladder, but was also thought to occur in stomach and lungs. At 726^{b}24 the 'spermatic colliquation' may be gonorrhoea. Aristotle quotes Empedocles (who was connected with a medical fraternity) as comparing milk with pus, and criticizes him on the grounds that milk is a concoction, not a corruption (*G.A.* IV. 777^{a}10). The extant Hippocratic writings do not call seed a colliquation, but Aristotle considers their view tantamount to it (724^{b}35, cf. Hippocrates, *On Generation* 1, VII. 470, L).

After arguing the case theoretically at 724^{b}23–725^{a}24, Aristotle gives items of additional evidence:

(i) 725^{a}24–8: The seed produces a resemblance to the parent because it is a residue of the material that becomes the parent's parts. If it were a colliquation of that material, it would be disintegrating and would have lost its character.

(ii) 725^{a}28–33: Large animals are less prolific than small animals, as we should expect if seed is a residue but not if it is a colliquation.

(iii) 725^{a}33–^{b}4: There are natural places in the body for the spermatic fluids, as there are for all residues but for no colliquations.

(iv) 725^{b}4–18: Loss of seed causes weakness, indicating that it is a concentrated product of nutriment.

(v) 725^{b}19–25: Infertility in youth, old age, and sickness is due to insufficient concoction of residue.

(vi) 725^{b}25–726^{a}15: Variations of fertility all fit the hypothesis that seed is a residue:

Little seed, due to weakness (as above)
Little seed, due to strength—725^{b}31
No seed, due to weakness—726^{a}6
No seed, due to strength—726^{a}9
Much seed, due to strength—726^{a}10
Much seed, due to weakness—726^{a}11

(The existence of this pattern of argument is a reason for accepting 726^a 11 f., which some editors have secluded.)

(vii) 726^{a}16–21: Seed has the same regular outlet as the excreted residue, suggesting that it too is a residue. (These lines may be displaced from 725^{b}4.)

(viii) 726^a21–5: Discharge of seed is partly beneficial like the discharge of residue, whereas discharge of colliquation is always harmful. Aristotle probably means that the flow of a colliquation implies the breaking-down of a tissue, and is therefore harmful; the beneficial thing is not to discharge the colliquation but to stop it by curing its cause. On the other hand a residue is produced naturally, and is a surplus.

(ix) See 726^b24–9 which has apparently been displaced from 726^a25. Even the morbid discharge of seed is such as to show that it is a residue.

726^a26–$^b24$: Aristotle now makes his point that the seed is a residue of blood. He is still discussing it in terms applicable to both male and female, but will show in the next section (726^b30f.) that the female is incapable of the final concoction that produces semen. He has not 'said before' (726^b1) that blood is the last stage of nutriment, though it is possibly implied at 725^a12; it is stated at *P.A.* II. 650^a34.

726^b24–9: these lines belong after 726^a25 (so Peck, who however regards both passages as interpolations).

The spermatic colliquation is probably gonorrhoea (cf. Mich. Eph. 47. 3, Galen XIX. 426, K). Aristotle's explanation seems to be that newly secreted seed, if it is added to seed already in the spermatic channels, is not retained there: just as a fresh coat of plaster falls off if it is applied before the previous coat has set. The implication is that over-production of seed may be self-perpetuating, producing a continuous morbid discharge of seed; normally seed would not be replaced in the channels until they have been emptied. But as in the case of plaster it does not follow that what falls away is not plaster, so the seed that is constantly discharged as a colliquation is still the same stuff as normal seed. It is therefore in the initial stage of colliquescence, before any loss of the seed's nature. This fact, so far from showing that seed altogether is a colliquation, tends to the contrary. (Michael of Ephesus takes 726^a14–15 as also referring to gonorrhoea; but there Aristotle is speaking not of a colliquation of seed but of the mixing of seed with alien residues and colliquations.)

726^b30–729^a33 *The female contributes the menses as matter.*

The condensed argument at 726^b30–727^a2 shows that the menses are a spermatic residue, but not that all of the female's spermatic residue is menses. The latter point is taken at 727^a25.

That females are colder than males has not been 'previously stated' (726^b34) but is a commonplace which Aristotle accepts from tradition (cf. *G.A.* IV. 765^b15 f., *P.A.* II. 648^a12, *Resp.* 466^b16). By 'hot' and 'cold' he refers to other things besides sensible temperature. At *P.A.* II. 648^a20 he says that a thing that is hot in itself, such as blood, is hotter than a thing that has received heat incidentally, while a thing that causes a sensation of heat does not necessarily contain more heat. He had of course no means of measuring temperature objectively; but in any case that would measure only the 'hot according to touch', which is not necessarily an index of the amount of heat within the object. Wine contains more heat than water contains (*Meteor.* IV. 389^{a}27); anything that has been concocted by heat contains heat (ibid. 389^{b}8). Aristotle's concept of heat is that it is a 'power' (δύναμις) possessed primarily by fire, which is mixed with the other elements of things,—not unlike the later concept of 'phlogiston'. (See also C. Strang, 'The Perception of Heat', *Proceedings of the Aristotelian Society*, vol. lxi (1961), pp. 239–52, where Aristotle's discussion in *P.A.* II is compared with modern concepts of temperature, conductivity, specific heat, and radiant heat.)

In saying that the menses are 'analogous' to semen (727^{a}3), Aristotle means homologous: he has not adhered (and rarely does adhere) to the distinction drawn at *P.A.* I. 644^{a}17 between analogy and 'the more and less'—that the former holds between genera, the latter between species of one genus. But although he speaks of analogy at all levels of taxonomy, he is strict in confining it to equivalent parts as judged by function, so that the analogue of blood is not merely *a* comparable fluid but *the* functional counterpart which excludes other fluids from this role. So if menses are the analogue of semen, Aristotle assumes that there is no other analogue. The supporting evidence now follows:

(i) 727^{a}4–10. Evidence that the menses are the analogue of semen: both begin at puberty and cease at the decline of life.

(ii) 727^{a}10–25. Evidence that the menses are residue:

(a) while they occur, other flows of excess blood cease;

(b) female bodily characteristics show a comparative lack of residue, suggesting that it has been diverted to the menses. For 'blood-flows' (^{a}12) see 728^{a}23 note.

(iii) 727^{a}25–30. Since there cannot be two (i.e. different) spermatic residues simultaneously, the existence of menses precludes the production of semen in females. Why not two? Presumably because spermatic residue comes from a regular source or set of sources; all that Aristotle has said above about the female residue will apply to all the production from these sources; there cannot also be other sources, or other conditions of production. At ^{a}29–30 the contrast between coming into being and existing seems to be merely a play on words (unlike *P.A*, I. 640^{a}10 f.).

(iv) 727^{a}31–^{b}5. Circumstantial evidence in bloodless animals. The argument of this section (which Susemihl secludes) seems to be: (a) well-nourished blooded males produce fat instead of semen (cf. 726^{a}3); (b) well-nourished blooded females are also infertile (ibid., suggesting that they too divert spermatic residue to fat; (c) now, well-nourished bloodless females, which are constitutionally unable to produce fat, produce extra eggs; (d) hence these eggs are formed from surplus nutriment, i.e. residue; (e) hence the analogous embryos of blooded females are formed from residue too; (f) since the residue which blooded males divert to fat is spermatic, the residue which blooded females divert is also spermatic. It now remains to be shown that the blooded embryo is formed from the menses, and this point follows at once. (The bloodless animals, unlike the blooded, are 'best' (727^b3)—i.e. healthiest and most edible—when breeding, e.g. lobsters and squids, *H.A.* VIII. 607^b3.)

(v) 727^b5–30. Evidence that the female does not contribute seed of the male kind, but instead the menses as matter of the embryo: conception may occur without sensation of pleasure (i.e. orgasm) in the female, but not without the presence of the menses in due proportion.

727^b33–728^a14. Explanation of female's sensation of pleasure and fluid discharge in coition. Aristotle refers to a vaginal discharge, not to leucorrhoea (which is mentioned at *G.A.* II. 738^a25, *H.A.* VII. 581^b2). For pneuma see note at II. 736^b29.

728^a14–30 The menses are incompletely concocted seed. This section belongs with 727^a2–$^b12$. From here to 728^b32 there are some signs of disorder.

At 728^a23 'blood-flows' (*αἱμορροΐδες*) was a concept common to medical theories at Aristotle's time. It was held that blood normally stands in the blood-vessels like water in irrigation channels, percolating into the tissues as needed (*P.A.* III. 668^a14). But under the pressure of pneuma in the vessels, the blood may flow and cause nose-bleeds, varicose veins, haemorrhoids, and the menses.

At 728^a26–30 it is not certain what process is being compared, but the point is clear enough. Menses cannot generate by themselves because they are insufficiently concocted, but become generative when mixed with semen; in the same way nutriment which has been insufficiently worked upon can become nutritious when mixed with fully worked nutriment. Michael of Ephesus (53.27) thinks Aristotle refers to the mixing of refined with unrefined flour in breadmaking. Modern interpreters have taken the 'crops' ($^a28$ *καρποί*) to be fruit, but without explanation. Cf. 725^a17, IV. 765^b30, and Newman's note at *Pol.* III. 1281^b36.

728^a31–$^b32$. Three further arguments, which look like later additions by Aristotle.

(i) 728^a31–33. The menses are not discharged from the place where the sensation of pleasure occurs, whereas in males the semen is discharged there. (Hence the menses are not semen.)

(ii) 728^a34–$^b21$. The external discharge of menses occurs only in females with a great amount of residue; in males the discharge of semen is greatest in those with most residue. (Hence the menses, though not semen, are an analogous residue.)

At $^{a}35$ *αἱματικὰ* is translated 'having plenty of blood' (cf. *P.A.* II. $647^{b}7$, III. $673^{b}27$), referring to only some of the class of blooded animals; it will mean the same at *G.A.* II. $738^{b}5$, IV. $776^{b}12$. Michael of Ephesus, however, and some modern editors take it as a synonym of *ἔναιμα*, 'blooded'.

At $^{b}1$–2 (if it is not an interpolated gloss) the point must be that the bloodless animals have an analogue of blood and could therefore produce an equivalent of menses; the fact that they do not is another sign that the menses are not a discharge of semen but merely of unused residue in those animals that concoct a great deal (bloodless animals, being colder, concoct less).

At $^{b}4$ most MSS. have "the purgation is produced neither in them nor in the above-mentioned blooded animals (those that have the uterus below . . .)", which contradicts $728^{a}36$ and $^{b}7$. Some MSS. and editors correct the sense by omitting or re-writing the parenthesis. Since Michael of Ephesus (55. 4) gives *τισι τῶν ἐναίμων*, I have suggested that something like *τισὶ πλὴν* may have fallen out; at any rate this restores the required sense.

At $^{b}7$–9 the parenthesis '(these are man . . . egg)' looks like a defining gloss that has no relevance here. 'Inwards' means that the leg is bent so that the foot is brought in towards the body (*P.A.* IV. $693^{b}3$, *I.A.* $704^{a}23$).

At $^{b}10$ Aristotle is distinguishing between the internal secretion of menses, produced by all viviparous quadrupeds, and the external 'purgation' (menstruation) which he says is most abundant in women (in fact it is limited to women and certain primates, while other mammals have a slight discharge when on heat). At $^{b}12$ cf. *H.A.* VI. $572^{b}29$, $574^{a}31$.

At $^{b}17$ the point is that the more perfect animals, being wetter and hotter (cf. II. $732^{b}31$), concoct the nutriment more completely, so that the blood is finer and its residue contains least of the coarse kind but most of the finest (i.e. spermatic); cf. *G.A.* II. $745^{b}18$, *P.A.* II. $650^{b}19$, $655^{b}14$, $660^{a}12$.

(iii) $728^{b}21$–31. (Nevertheless) the menses are spermatic.

The style of the first sentence suggests that this is a note added later. It is however a necessary corrective to the previous section. Menses are not semen, but they *are* seed of a kind (cf. $728^{a}26$). In spite of his theory, Aristotle can speak of female seed, presumably in this limited sense: cf. $725^{b}3$, II. $737^{a}28$, IV. $766^{b}14$.

At $728^{b}25$ *διισταμένων* is translated 'drawn apart' as at *G.A.* II. $742^{a}9$, *H.A.* III. $518^{b}9$, i.e. not just a differentiation (as Peck takes it) but a physical lessening of compactness which allows hair to grow through.

The argument assumes that axillary hair appears with the pubic hair (cf. *G.A.* V. 784a10).

728b32–729a20. Multiple births, which cannot be explained by pangenesis, are explainable if the male contributes the form and movement to the female matter.

728b32: for this distinction between plant embryo and animal semen cf. 724b12–18.

729a6–8: for this argument cf. 723b9–15 note. Aristotle's solution is that the semen does not convey bodily parts but a set of movements which start the foetal material on a process of development (*G.A.* II. 737a18). If the semen is divided into separate parcels, each will bring about the same set of movements in the surrounding parcel of material, resulting in as many offspring as there are parcels. At *G.A.* IV. 771a17–b12 Aristotle explains the factors controlling such a division. Each animal has natural limits of size, and develops from a definite quantity of material, requiring a proportionate quantity of semen to 'set' or 'constitute' it. When these quantities are exceeded, more than one offspring may be produced. Animals with more heat and less earth regularly concoct enough residue for multiple offspring (772b3). For this explanation to work, it is important to distinguish the physical semen from the setting agent within it, as Aristotle does at 729a19–20. The setting agent is the capability, which remains the same in each parcel of semen. In however many parcels, the setting agent in each is indivisible and complete, and will produce one offspring. This avoids the difficulty that was fatal to pangenesis—how to divide up semen so that each parcel will contain one complete set of bodily parts.

729a20–33. Semen and menses are related as agent to patient. Aristotle now confirms his analysis from the general principle that in every change that which causes movement is distinguishable from that which is moved (cf. *Phys.* VIII. 257b2f., *G.C.* I. 324a24f.). But this principle would still hold even if he had accepted the view that male and female each produce semen, both combining to form the foetus—or supposing that he had a microscope and were able to see the fusion of living cells: his question would still be, should we distinguish an active source from that which is acted upon in each seed or cell? He would answer affirmatively on the same grounds that he answered Empedocles in *P.A.* I (640a10, 641b10 note): the automatic actions of the cell's elements are not enough to account for the cell's development into an ordered organism, from which it follows that two separate causes are distinguishable even though they coexist in a single natural process. This teleological view would apply equally to the theory that the female provides merely shelter and nutrition for the growth of the male sperm. One could not say therefore that the hylomorphic theory has necessitated Aristotle's particular theory of generation.

729a32 "in accordance with" (κατὰ): the menses have the character of proximate matter, for they are residue that has not been fully worked upon but is still in a state of potentiality.

729a34–b33 *The body of the semen does not become physically part of the embryo.*

This question was left open at 726b20. Aristotle will explain at II. 734b5 how the semen can convey a capability without adding an active substance to the material.

At 729b14 "the extremes" (τὰ ἄκρα) may mean the widest generalization, as it does at *Met.* Γ 1003a26, (so Platt, Peck). But, perhaps better, it may mean the most exact respects in which two commensurates are commensurate or two opposites are opposite. So at *Phys.* II. 195b22 "the most extreme cause" (τὸ ἀκρότατον αἴτιον) of a house is not a man but a builder, or rather a builder in respect of the art of building. Equally strictly, in generation the male acts not *qua* animal nor even physical body, but *qua* agent and mover in the change that takes place in the female matter. Substituting mover for male, we may now ask: does a product necessarily contain part of its mover? The answer is, obviously, no more than a bed contains part of the carpenter. If the male's contribution consists in forming the matter into a specific kind, then *as such* it does not add anything material.

At 729b22 Aristotle answers the question about the mating of insects (cf. 723b27, 721a13). The male impulse is transmitted direct, without the intermediary of semen (cf. 730b30). At b27 most MSS. read not 'heat' but 'moisture'; but Galen IV. 519 K paraphrases these words as 'gives some soul-heat', which agrees better with Aristotle's theory of generative heat and pneuma in semen (II. 736b30, cf. 730a16). Aristotle's false belief about insects has hardly determined his theory, which is evidently founded on the preceding argument (729b14–22); but no doubt it clinched it. For insect 'grubs' (b32) see note at 721a2.

729b33–730a23 *Further evidence from birds and fishes.*

Aristotle regards fertilization as a comparatively gradual process. He holds that in the bird's egg the yolk is formed first, and is incompletely concocted; next is formed the hotter and completely concocted white, which collects round the yolk. Before it completely surrounds the yolk, and while it is being secreted, the white—if fertilized—receives certain movements from the male semen; these movements 'constitute' and diversify the embryo, which uses the yolk as food and concocts it into blood and bodily parts. By the time the white is complete, it is too late for a further fertilization to influence the growth; the animal is now being formed, and possesses its perceptive soul (potentially) as well as its nutritive soul (*G.A.* III. 757b1–30). Fishes' eggs are fertilized in two stages. They are constituted, but not made fertile, by the semen in coition (cf. 718a1 note); after spawning they are made fertile by a further sprinkling of semen (*G.A.* III. 756a24). Such evidence (unfortunately false) is certainly easier to account for on Aristotle's theory than on the theory that semen becomes a physical part of the embryo. But as in the case of the insect evidence (729a34 note), it is doubtful whether it did more than clinch Aristotle's theory.

730a24–32 *Our theory explains why* (*i*) *the female cannot generate without the male.*

Wind-eggs (a32) are explained in *G.A.* III. 1: the female material has nutritive soul which enables it to develop so far, but lacking perceptive soul it cannot become an animal.

730a32–b8 (*ii*) *generation must take place initially in the female.*

The female contains the matter without which generation cannot take place.

730b8–32 (*iii*) *the male can fertilize with or without semen.*

Aristotle expands what he said at 729b14, now distinguishing the significant male contribution (the movement) from the instrument used (semen). For his use of the analogy between nature and craft see note at *P.A.* I. 641b10. His language is imprecise: at 729b14f. 'the male' was compared indifferently with the craftsman (b16), the form (b17), and the craft (b21). Here at 730b19 it is 'the nature in the male' that is compared with the user of an instrument, while the real user is not the craftsman but the craft—for it is the 'art's movement' that resides in the instruments (730b22).

730b33–731a24 (*iv*) *the sexes must unite for generation.*

For the connection between locomotion and the separation of the sexes see note at 715a26. For plant seeds as embryos cf. 724b14, 728b33.

731a24–b14 *Animal sexes are separate for the sake of cognition.*

Aristotle completes this argument in the first section of Book II by saying that the male is superior, and that it is better for the superior to be separated from the inferior—presumably because the male can function better as a cognitive animal when not combined with the more material female nature (732a3).

At 731b8–14 the point about testaceans is that they are intermediate between animals and plants, which explains why they have neither separated nor combined sexes. There are of course other sexless and spontaneous animals (insects 721a9, fishes II. 741b1), but in their case the condition is due to weakness and imperfection as compared with other insects and fishes. In testaceans it is a universal condition due to their intermediate status, which is also indicated by their minimal perception and locomotion. Aristotle explains various ways in which mussels, whelks, oysters, etc., are spontaneously reproduced, and comments that "compared with animals they are like plants, but compared with plants they are like animals" (*G.A.* III. 761a15). Nature is continuous from plants to animals (*P.A.* IV. 681a9, *H.A.* VIII. 588b4). Testaceans come at the point on the scale where the change occurs from mingled sexes to separate sexes, and are not therefore a counter-instance to what he has been saying about separation of sexes in animals.

DE GENERATIONE ANIMALIUM II

The argument follows straight on from the end of Book I. Aristotle completes his explanation of the separation of sexes by explaining why there are sexes at all. Then he speaks of the significance of vital heat, and explains how the male semen physically brings about the change from foetal material to foetus. The general theory is completed in Chapter 3, and Chapter 4 begins a consideration of embryology genus by genus.

731^{b}18–732^{a}1 *Reproduction is for the perpetuation of kinds.*

For the argument cf. *De An.* II. 415^{a}25, *G.C.* II. 336^{b}25, and note at *P.A.* I. 641^{b}10 (p. 96 above).

731^{a}22 "as our argument proceeds": Aristotle begins shortly to explain the development of the embryo, and reaches the question of sexual differentiation at IV. 1.

731^{b}23 "prior" (ἄνωθεν): literally 'from above'. Peck interprets it as a reference to the prime mover of the universe (God). But Aristotle regularly says 'above' to denote a prior member of a series, especially a prior postulate or a more general or comprehensive premiss (cf. Bonitz, *Index Aristotelicus* 68^{b}44, 69^{a}20). Here he refers, as the next sentence shows, to a more general final cause.

731^{b}24f.: All existing things (^{b}24 τῶν ὄντων) are divided into (i) the eternal and divine, e.g. stars, (ii) those capable of being and not being, i.e. those that come into being and perish—animals and other sublunary objects. In (ii), the qualities of goodness and divineness (^{b}25) are a cause in the sense that animals and plants naturally strive towards them (cf. *De An.* II. 415^{a}29). In this sense even perishable living things have a share in 'the divine' especially if their nature is conspicuously well organized (e.g. bees, *G.A.* III. 761^{a}5). At ^{b}26 "according to its own nature" may mean simply *ipso facto*, or it may mean "according to the circumstances of a particular animal". At ^{b}27 "capable" may mean "capable of the good and divine" (Peck), or preferably "capable of being and not being" as in the previous line. At ^{b}27–8 Platt's addition '⟨and not being⟩' which is accepted in the O.C.T., is probably wrong, because the argument has moved on: in calling these things 'non-eternal' Aristotle grants that they must perish, but he now says that in spite of being non-eternal they are nevertheless capable of being. (He will explain this at $^{b}31$ f. as the continued being not of individuals but of species.) The "worse" here is not non-being but being-worse, e.g. being a soulless body. At $^{b}30$ the context requires that 'not-being' means 'being dead', as at $731^{b}4$. Granted that it is better to have a soul (for the reason given at $731^{a}30$ f.), what is the connection between having a soul and being as eternal as possible? Aristotle does not explain this step, but presumably the connection is that soul makes reproduction possible, as he will presently argue.

$731^{b}33$ f.: The argument presupposes the division of existing things into eternal things and things capable of not being ($^{b}24$); the latter are now called things that 'come into being' ($^{b}33$). At $^{b}34$ 'existing things' (*τῶν ὄντων*) comprises both classes, as at $^{b}24$:

1. All beings either are eternals or come into being;
2. What a thing is, it is as a particular;
   Therefore if a thing is eternal in number, i.e. as a particular, it is an eternal;
3. But things that come into being are not eternals;
   Therefore things that come into being are not eternal in number.

The question "What is this thing?" (i.e. what is its 'being', $^{b}34$) is answered by "*a* man"—not by "*Man*" (its kind). Now if things that come into being could be numerically eternal, it would follow that Smith could be eternal: which is impossible. What is possible is that Man could be eternal, if Smith's kind is continually reproduced.

$732^{a}1$–7 *The sexes are separate because the male is superior.*

This completes the arguments of I. $715^{a}26$, $731^{a}24$ (cf. notes there).

$732^{a}29$–32 The development of eggs and of larvae is explained at *G.A.* III. $752^{a}24$ f. and $758^{b}6$ f., where this distinction is repeated.

$732^{b}15$–$733^{b}16$ *Animals should be divided by differences of heat.*

For the points raised here see Index under 'Classification', 'Division', 'Heat'.

$733^{b}31$ *What makes the embryo develop from the material?*

Aristotle is now asking what is the proximate efficient (mechanical) cause, what physically moves the material in the uterus. His observational evidence probably comes chiefly from birds' eggs: he describes the daily opening of eggs in one clutch (*G.A.* III. 2, *H.A.* VI. 3), and his frequent statement that the heart appears first is probably based on the early appearance of blood spots and vessels. The 'plaiting of the net' ($734^{a}20$ = Orphic *frg.* 26, Kern) may also have been suggested by the appearance of an egg during the first few days, when the vitelline arteries and veins of the chick embryo spread like a net over the surface of the yolk.

At 734^b4 f. Aristotle's problem is to explain how the movement is maintained after the semen loses contact with the sire's body, for he held that movement does not continue unless sustained by a mover either within or outside the moving body (*Phys.* VII. 2). The seed is ensouled (735^a5) and therefore potentially self-moving, but this is not enough to explain how the particular movements initiated by the sire are maintained. The 'marvels' which he compares were probably not the puppets of Plato, *Republic* VII. 514B, but robots which would continue to move after being set going (cf. *G.A.* II. 741^b9; *Mot. An.* 701^b2 with Farquharson's note in the Oxford translation of *Mot. An.*, 1912).

734^b21–735^a26 *The semen, which contains movement and soul, causes the first foetal part to be formed (heart).*

The movement by which foetal material is transformed into an actual animal must have been implanted by a previous actual animal (cf. *P.A.* I. 640^a23–6). The sire implants movement in the semen, which conveys it to the material; the semen's movement ceases when the material begins to move itself and when the somatic part of the semen evaporates (737^a11, 21). (At 734^b23 παυομένης, queried by Platt and Peck, is acceptable.) For the argument at 734^b24 f. cf. *P.A.* I. 640^b22–641^a32. The 'same argument' applies to semen (735^a5): (a) soul is not an entity itself, but is the activity of a living animal or part; (b) a living part cannot be devoid of soul. What sort of soul has the semen? Its activity is to generate, that is to initiate such movements in the material as will transform it into a growing embryo. It does so by causing the heart to be formed, containing movements which will continue the foetal development, i.e. containing a source of soul. From that moment the foetus has its own soul. The semen therefore has potentially the embryo's activity, and exists as a potential embryo. But it is at a further remove from actuality than is the first stage of the embryo, which is itself only potentially an animal. Since the first activity of the embryo is to nourish itself, the kind of soul that the semen first produces in the material is nutritive soul. This is the same as generative soul (cf. *P.A.* I. 641^b5 note, and *G.A.* II. 740^b29–37). The semen's soul therefore is nutritive soul, in a state of potentiality. But since animals are characterized by perception, and humans by intellect too, the embryo must also possess these faculties potentially, and therefore the semen must somehow contain and convey them. This problem is dealt with below at 736^a29 f. The foetal material in the female, however, possesses in itself no more than nutritive soul (II. 741^a6 f.).

735^a29–736^a23 *The somatic characteristics of semen.*

The active part is the pneuma (discussed below), which Aristotle defines simply as 'hot air'. In the next section he distinguishes its heat, as generative, from heat that cannot generate; this too is discussed below (for his concept of heat in general see note at 726b30).

736a24–737a34 *What becomes of the somatic part of semen, and how does the embryo acquire the perceptive and intellective powers of soul?*

The relation between these two questions becomes apparent during the discussion. The pneuma in the semen conveys heat of a special quality, such as to organize the foetal material into an animal capable of perception (and, if human, of intellect). In losing its heat to the foetus, the water of the semen evaporates in accordance with Aristotle's normal theory (cf. *G.A.* V. 783a16, 35). Both questions therefore lead to the more basic question, how does the semen *physically* convey the higher faculties of soul?

The question arises because the foetal material is not at first equipped with even the beginnings of organs of perception, and therefore cannot possess perceptive powers even potentially in the way that it can immediately possess nutritive powers (it can immediately grow, 735a15). Aristotle has explained at 734b9 f. that nutritive soul is conveyed from the sire as a set of movements by the seed acting like a pre-set automaton, and these movements are at once taken up by the material. What now of the perceptive movements—how are they *later* originated in the embryo? At 736a24–b8 Aristotle sets out the problem. The parenthesis at a36 must be an editorial insertion (referring to *De An.* II. 4), for Aristotle has just argued the point at 735a13. At b1 some words may have dropped out, to the effect that a further acquisition is intellective soul which differentiates man (see note in OCT), but the argument can be read without that supposition.

At 736b8–15 Aristotle establishes, as his first point, that the perceptive and intellective powers must exist potentially in the embryo before they are actualized (i.e. at birth or later). In the same way the nutritive power was present potentially while the foetal material was being formed into an embryo, and became actual when the embryo became quasi-independent within the uterus, comparably with a 'separated foetus' (e.g. plant seed, 731a3). At 736b13 ἑπομένως may mean either 'conformably' or 'next' in a temporal sense. We may now think of these higher faculties as potentially present while the embryo forms the organs of perception. But where have they come from?

At 736b16–20 Aristotle tabulates the possible answers:

(i) b16–17. Any faculty of soul that is produced in the embryo must either have existed previously or not.

(ii) b17–18. When it is produced, it must be produced either in the female contribution or in the male contribution.

He does not consider further the possibility that these faculties are produced in the female contribution (i.e. originate there), since this has been ruled out by the whole argument of Books I and II so far. Nor does he even mention the possibility (laboured by later commentators) that any faculty of soul enters the embryo after conception. Much of the difficulty that has been seen in this chapter arises from allowing this possibility in the case of intellect, and it is important to observe that Aristotle himself does not allow it: if he had, he must have mentioned it at 736^b18–19. But since he has already demonstrated that the male is the source of soul, it follows that if any faculty enters from outside, the place into which it enters can only be the male semen. Hence he proceeds:

(iii) $^b19$–20. Any faculty that is produced in the male seed either comes into it from outside or not.

The next lines, $^b21$–9, therefore concern only the production of soul faculties in the male seed: each faculty either enters the male seed from outside or does not. Now if a faculty requires body (as walking requires feet) it cannot exist before its body; therefore it cannot enter the seed in a disembodied state. But it cannot enter embodied either, for the seed is not a mixture of bodies but a residue of nutriment obtained by concoction. Hence no faculty that is an activity of body (i.e. the nutritive and perceptive faculties) can enter the seed from outside. What possibility remains for them? Only that they are produced in the seed when the seed itself is produced, and are somehow embodied in it. He will proceed at once to show how they can be in the seed (736^b29f.).

But the faculty of intellect does not require body, because it is not the activity of a body. Since it is immaterial, it is incapable of not-being (hence 'divine'; cf. *De An.* II. 413^b26), and consequently pre-exists. Therefore it has entered the seed from outside. Its transmission too is accounted for in the following section (esp. 737^a10).

The above passage, 736^b16–29, has been suspected by recent commentators on two chief grounds: (i) that the argument seems to ignore the distinction between potential and actual states, which has just been emphasized at 736^b15; (ii) that the expression 'enter from outside' in $^b21$–6 is ambiguous, for in each case it could mean entering either (a) the female material, or (b) the male seed, or (c) the embryo after conception.

Now the passage as a whole is unlikely to be spurious, since its conclusion—that the intellect enters from outside—is authenticated by Theophrastus (*fr.* 53B Wimmer) and therefore rests on better authority than much of Aristotle's works. It could be misplaced; but there is no other obvious place for it. This establishes some claim for it to be interpreted in its context.

The reason why the argument does not use the distinction between potentiality and actuality must be that it is only the embryo that is being considered, and in this there is no question of actualization of the perceptive faculty, still less of the intellective. Aristotle discusses the perceptive state of the embryo at *G.A.* V. 778^{b}22 f., and likens it to sleep, that is a potential state. The question considered in these lines, then, is how and whence and when these potential faculties are produced.

If 'enter from outside' in ^{b}24–6 means either 'enter the female material' or 'enter the embryo after conception' (unlike its meaning at ^{b}19), then Aristotle is saying that these faculties do not enter with the seed. And if they enter neither in the seed nor in any other body nor independently, they do not enter the embryo at all. So interpreted, the passage would lead to an impasse (Moraux 1955, p. 274; Solmsen 1957, p. 121). But this interpretation contradicts what Aristotle has already shown, that the male seed is the source of soul for the female material (cf. 734^{a}1). The only question left is how the male seed comes to possess and convey the faculties of soul.

Now the possibilities are not exhausted by (i) pre-exist, (ii) enter independently, (iii) enter within a body, as has been assumed by some who interpret this passage as a *reductio ad impossibile*. Aristotle also mentions (iv) come to be without pre-existing (^{b}16) and without entering from outside (^{b}20). This is the possibility remaining for the nutritive and perceptive faculties which require body: they come to be in the seed when the seed itself comes to be. The intellect, on the other hand, both pre-exists (because it is everlasting) and enters the seed from outside (which it can do because it is not in body). "The intellect is already a kind of being (*ousia*) when it is born within us" (*De An.* I. 408^{b}18).

The position reached at 736^{b}29, therefore, is that both the perceptive and the intellective faculties are brought by the seed in a state of potentiality, the former embodied in the seed and the latter disembodied (cf. 737^{a}7–10). But now Aristotle must explain (a) how the perceptive faculty can be embodied even potentially in something that is not equipped to perceive, (b) how the intellect, which is not capable of being embodied, can be conveyed by body. He answers these questions in the next sentences, which should be read as following on without a break (736^{b}29 f.).

Every faculty of soul, whether or not it is associated with a bodily activity, is associated with a certain diviner sort of body (*pneuma*). Aristotle is not saying that soul is the activity of this body. His point is not to distinguish between this body and the animal body (as implied by Lulofs's reading at ^{b}29, '*the* bodily actuality'). The distinction lies rather between being associated with a *bodily activity* and being associated with a *body*. Even the intellect has some association with body: among animals, it requires a living human to be present in; it presupposes the presence of perception, which is a function of body; though itself unaffected by body, its activity is increased or diminished by bodily circumstances (cf. *De An.* I. 408^{b}24). It is not impossible, therefore, for Aristotle to recognize a physical association between intellect and body. Now he goes on to say that the heat in pneuma has the special property of being able to convey soul, including intellect. He does not explain this in physical terms, but judging from 737a18–19 we may guess that he conceived it as a conveying of movements superimposed upon the heat's own movements—perhaps as a liquid conveys waves.

Because of the strange after-history of the concept *pneuma*, this passage (736b29–737a12) has elicited mystical interpretations from some and suspicion from others. But there is no other reason to doubt its authenticity, for it is integral with the preceding argument. Its apparent uniqueness lies in the statement that *pneuma* contains a generative heat that is different from the heat of fire but is analogous to the element of the stars (i.e. *aithēr*, cf. *de Caelo* I. 3). Yet its expression does not suggest that Aristotle intended something novel. The interpretation that I suggest below treats this statement as not out of accord with Aristotle's normal views, but as a more accurate definition in a particular context, such as he often provides. But there is room for wide disagreement here, and it may be useful to give a summary of the problem.

At Aristotle's time '*pneuma*' was the ordinary word for wind; when used of animals it meant breath and also internal wind. But in medical theory it was fast developing special connotations, which led to the Stoic conception (soon after Aristotle) of an indwelling divine spirit. The 'pneumatist' medical school after Aristotle came to systematize three kinds of *pneuma* in the body (known to Renaissance medicine as the natural spirits, vital spirits, and animal spirits) to account respectively for life, for sensory and motor impulses, and for the higher faculties. Where Aristotle stood in this development is not clear. It began before him with Diogenes of Apollonia and Philistion (Plato's medical contemporary); and it was much advanced by Diocles of Carystus, who used to be thought a contemporary of Philistion but has been plausibly dated by Jaeger as a younger contemporary of Aristotle.

Aristotle gives no extensive analysis of *pneuma* as he does of heat (*P.A.* II. 648b12 f.). Outside a biological context he means only wind, and it never appears in discussions of the elements. In the biological works it appears to do different things, raising the question whether Aristotle had systematized any doctrine of *pneuma* at all. (Bonitz, *Index Arist.* 605b31 s.v. πνεῦμα gives a good collection of the usages. For a systematized account see Peck's Loeb edition of *G.A.*, Appendix B.) Aristotle's primary and most frequent reference is to breath. But a doctrine of his, on which he much relies, is that the breath is not only innate in the embryo before it begins to breathe at birth (Philistion too had spoken of innate *pneuma*) but that it is also present in non-breathing animals: by means of it insects can buzz, smell, move (*De Somno* 456a19, *P.A.* II. 659b18). It is a source of strength in them, as it is in men who hold their breath to make an effort (*De Somno* 456a16). It is the internal medium of hearing and smelling, and connects with the outside air (*G.A.* II. 744a3,

V. 781a23). The pulse is caused by pneumatization of the blood, the *pneuma* being transmitted from lungs to heart and thence through the blood vessels (*Resp.* 480a14, *P.A.* III. 667a29, *H.A.* I. 495b14). In these functions there is not necessarily anything to distinguish *pneuma* qualitatively from the air breathed in. *De An.* II. 420b20 identifies it with atmospheric air.

Air in Aristotle's analysis consists of the hot and the wet, but the hot element in *pneuma* is not significant in explanations outside *G.A.* On the contrary the chief function of breath, both indrawn and innate, is to cool the excess heat (*De Somno* 456a6–13). In *G.A.*, however, Aristotle attributes to *pneuma* some functions that do not obviously belong to air. At V. 789b8 he says that nature uses *pneuma* generally as an instrument that has many uses, like hammer and anvil. At II. 741b37 f. he says that the embryo is articulated by *pneuma*, not the mother's breath but *pneuma* that is present because of the presence of the hot and the wet: this seems to imply that *pneuma* can be formed within the body (possibly implied also at *Resp.* 480a15). Its hot element is exploited at II. 735b33 and V. 786a6: the whiteness of semen and of fair hair is in both cases due to the heat of *pneuma*. At 736a1 (above) *pneuma* was defined as 'hot air', implying that air, which is already hot, has additional heat when it is *pneuma*.

But the association of *pneuma* with generation appears only in the present passage (736b29–37) and in the account of spontaneous generation at III. 11. 762a18: "Animals and plants are produced in earth and in wet because in earth water is present, and in water *pneuma* is present, and in all *pneuma* soul-heat is present, so that in a way all things are full of soul; that is why they are quickly constituted once it has been enclosed. It gets enclosed and, as the somatic liquids become heated, it becomes like a foamy bubble . . . (762b13) The seasonal heat in the surroundings compounds and constitutes by concoction, out of sea-water and earth, that which in the case of animals the heat present in them produces out of the nourishment. And that portion of the soul-principle (ἀρχή) which gets enclosed or separated off within the pneuma makes a foetus and implants movement in it." There Aristotle seems to imply the distinction, which he makes explicit at 737a1, between generative heat and other heat; and in both passages he connects *pneuma* with soul. Finally, in *M.A.* 10, which may be a late work of Aristotle or even post-Aristotelian, the innate *pneuma* in its role as source of strength is said to be the soul's instrument for moving limbs. This is the only other passage which connects pneuma with soul, unless we include its function as medium of perception (so Peck, loc. cit., and Beare, *Greek Theories of Elementary Cognition*, 1906, p. 333).

At 736b29 f. the argument is:

soul associates with a diviner body, whose nature varies in value;

for in seed there is generative heat, which is not fire but the *pneuma* in the seed, or rather it is the nature in the pneuma, something comparable with *aither*;
it is this heat that generates.

From this the following points seem to emerge:

(i) It is not *pneuma* but the generative heat that is comparable with *aither*. At ᵇ35–7 Aristotle at first identifies the heat with the *pneuma* but then qualifies it. In the words 'the *pneuma* . . . *and* (καὶ) the nature in the *pneuma*' καὶ cannot be simply connective, since the heat cannot be both; καὶ must mean not 'and' but 'i.e.' as it often does (cf. *P.A.* I. 644ᵃ3; Bonitz, *Index* 357ᵇ13; Moraux, p. 276 translates it 'et plus exactement' here). From 737ᵃ1 Aristotle speaks only of the heat, and does not mention the pneuma again in this discussion.

(ii) The nature *in* the pneuma (ᵇ37) is not the nature *of* the pneuma, which consists of air as well as heat. 'Nature' here must therefore mean 'a stuff', as often—i.e. this heat.

(iii) It is not clear whether it is the pneuma or the heat that varies in value (ᵇ31–2); but it comes to the same thing. Aristotle clearly means that soul can be conveyed in varying grades, according as man or a higher or lower animal is generated. (It seems therefore unnecessary to construe the sentence in a less natural way, as Moraux does in order to confine the reference to heat: 'en connexion avec toute âme se trouve la vertu d'un élément différent des éléments vulgaires et plus divin qu'eux.') Both the generative heat and, by consequence, the *pneuma* that contains it, vary in quality.

(iv) The generative heat is not identified with *aither*: if they are analogous, they must be different. In calling the *pneuma* (or the heat within it) divine, Aristotle need not imply a connection with the divine stars or the unmoved mover. The very use of the comparative 'divin*er*' excludes a definite boundary between divine and non-divine. He need only mean here what he meant at 732ᵃ3 and often: less grossly material, purer, superior.

(v) It is not all *pneuma* but 'the *pneuma* in the seed' (ᵇ36) that contains generative heat. The other functions of *pneuma* do not imply this quality of heat.

Aristotle is saying, then, (a) that *some* heat differs in being generative; (b) that *some pneuma* differs in containing generative heat.

Elsewhere Aristotle calls the warmth of an animal vital, innate, natural, or 'belonging to soul' (ψυχικός), without suggesting that it differs from other warmth. At *Resp.* 479ᵃ29 he says simply 'Generation is the first participation in nutritive soul, taking place in the hot'. At *Resp.* 474ᵃ28 he equates animal heat with fire (cf. *De An.* II. 416ᵃ9; *Resp.* 474ᵇ12; *P.A.* II. 652ᵇ7, where he says that soul is not identical with fire but works through it). Now for most purposes animal heat *is* indistinguishable from the warmth of fire. But when it generates new life, it is doing something that fire cannot do, that only the sun's heat can do besides. Then animal heat conveys soul-movements (737a19). What enables it to do this sometimes? Probably a state of superior 'purity'. The fact that man has intellect is attributable to the purity of the heat in his heart (*G.A.* II. 744a29). The differences in value of souls (736b31) are not only the general differences between nutrition, perception and intellect, but also the differences in fineness of perception and intelligence and in qualities of character; also differences in the grades of animals as measured by modes of reproduction; all these differences are attributed to heat (*P.A.* II. 648a2 f., *G.A.* II. 732a18 f.). Gradations in heat (not, of course, temperature, but quality, cf. 726b30 note) account for gradations in the *scala naturae*. Since nature is continuous from non-living to living (*H.A.* VIII. 588b4 f., *P.A.* IV. 681a12 f.), animal heat need not be an altogether different element from other heat, nor generative heat from the rest of animal heat. Similarly *pneuma* is basically atmospheric air. But when it is breathed in, it participates in the animal's heat, which will be at varying levels of purity, giving various grades of *pneuma*. If the *pneuma* is formed from the hot and wet within the body, the same considerations apply.

Therefore it is unnecessary to hold that Aristotle is innovating here, or contradicting what he says elsewhere. It is rather that, having to consider the implications of generation (particularly the conveying of soul-movements), he finds these more precise distinctions necessary. This is not uncommon. For example, the *De Anima* draws many distinctions regarding the soul which are ignored in the biology, while the biology works with the tripartite soul and the *Ethics* needs only a distinction between rational and non-rational soul. These differences of precision do not lead to contradictions. The distinctions necessitated by one subject matter could be misleading in another. When Aristotle is attending to the problem of generation and the conveyance of soul from one organism to another, he must distinguish generative from non-generative residues, and what distinguishes them is the quality of heat in their concoction. But when he considers living phenomena in general, their distinctive property is vital or psychic heat (of which some part is generative). To distinguish there between the generative and non-generative heats would be not only irrelevant but probably impracticable. For while Aristotle's theory of generation necessitates his theory of generative heat, he may be in no position to say where exactly in the body the heat is of the purity required for generation. All that he can say is that some of it must be so.

At 737a7–12 the text is corrupt but the sense is not in doubt: the semen brings with it both disembodied intellect and embodied nutritive and perceptive potentialities; the somatic part of the semen (foam made of pneuma and water, 736a1, 14) then evaporates. At both a8 and a11 the MSS. and Galen read *τὸ σπέρμα* ('the seed'). This must be wrong at a11, and Lulofs has accepted Wimmer's reasonable conjecture *τὸ σῶμα* ('the body') which recalls a7. At a8 'the seed' would have to be a metaphor (the *germ* of the soul-source), which seems gratuitously confusing. Platt's conjecture 'the *pneuma*' is wrong because *pneuma* is body. Probably it should be omitted (with P, Wimmer, Peck), leaving *τὸ τῆς ψυχικῆς ἀρχῆς*, 'that which consists in the soul-source', cf. 762b16.

737a14: The analogy with a curdling agent was used at I. 729a12, and is pursued in more detail at II. 739b22.

737a18: The seed is concocted out of blood at the stage at which blood is being particularized into the various tissues (I. 726b9). Why the parts are not reproduced exactly (why family likeness is disturbed) is considered at *G.A.* IV. 767a36 f.

737a25: i.e. the female material contains potentially *both* sets of parts by which the sexes are distinguished.

737a30 "the parts of both": i.e. of both sexes. Wind-eggs can be fertilized later, and may then be of either sex. Sex is determined by the relative strength of male seed and female material (*G.A.* IV. 766a18).

737a33: When Aristotle considers how unfertilized eggs can come about (II. 741a18, III. 757b16), he concludes that the female material itself also has nutritive soul potentially; but until it receives perceptive soul from the male it cannot develop animal parts (from which it follows that it cannot nourish itself and so cannot have nutritive soul in actuality). Otherwise Aristotle usually speaks as he does here: the male contributes the source of soul, including nutritive (cf. *Resp.* 479a29). This is another case of discrepancy between his more precise statements and his general statements, where no contradiction need be found.

SELECT BIBLIOGRAPHY

Aristotelis Opera, ed. I. Bekker. 5 vols., Berlin, 1831, H. Bonitz, *Index Aristotelicus* (vol. v of the Berlin edition, 1831), repr. 1955.

The Works of Aristotle translated into English, ed. W. D. Ross. Vol. v, Oxford, 1912 (containing *De Partibus Animalium* trans. W. Ogle; *De Motu Animalium* and *De Incessu Animalium* trans. A. S. L. Farquharson; *De Generatione Animalium* trans. A. Platt).

J.-M. Le Blond, *Aristote, Philosophe de la Vie* (text, transl., introd., commentary, *P.A.* I). Aubier, 1945.

A. L. Peck, *Aristotle, Parts of Animals* (text, transl., introd.). Loeb. London, 1955.

—— *Aristotle, Generation of Animals* (text, transl., introd., appendices). Loeb. London, 1953.

Michael of Ephesus (= Pseudo-Philoponus), *Comm. in libros de generatione animalium*, ed. W. Hayduck, *Commentaria in Aristotelem Graeca*, vol. xiv. 3. Berlin, 1901.

A. L. Peck, *Aristotle, Historia Animalium* (text, transl., introd.). Loeb, 3 vols. London, 1965– .

D. W. Thompson, *Aristotle, Historia Animalium* (transl. with notes) (vol. iv of the Oxford translation, ed. W. D. Ross). Oxford, 1910.

W. D. Ross, *Aristotle's Prior and Posterior Analytics* (text, introd., commentary). Oxford, 1949.

Die Fragmente der Vorsokratiker, ed. H. Diels–W. Kranz. 3 vols., 6th ed., Berlin, 1951 (cited as *VS*).

Hippocrates, *Œuvres*, ed. E. Littré (text, French transl.). 10 vols., Paris, 1839–61.

Galen, *Opera Omnia*, ed. C. G. Kühn (text, Latin transl.). 20 vols., Leipzig 1821–33, repr. 1964.

F. J. Ayala, 'Biology as an autonomous science', *American Scientist*, 1968, p. 207.

D. M. Balme, 'GENOS and EIDOS in Aristotle's Biology', *Classical Quarterly*, N.S. xii (1962), 81.

H. F. Cherniss, *Aristotle's Criticism of Plato and the Academy*. Johns Hopkins 1944, repr. 1962 (Chapter 1 on Division).

A. Diès, *Platon, Le Politique*. Paris, 1950 (introd. on Division).

M. Grene, *A Portrait of Aristotle*. Faber, 1963.

W. F. R. Hardie, 'Aristotle's Treatment of the Relation between Soul and Body', *Philosophical Quarterly* (1964), 63.

W. Jaeger, *Diokles von Karystos*. 2nd ed., Berlin, 1963 (on *pneuma*).

A. C. Lloyd, 'Genus, Species and Ordered Series in Aristotle', *Phronesis*, vii (1962), 67.

J. B. Meyer, *Aristoteles Thierkunde*. Berlin, 1855.

P. Moraux, 'A propos du ΝΟΥΣ ΘΥΡΑΘΕΝ chez Aristote', *Autour d'Aristote*, p. 255, Louvain 1955.

A. Preuss, 'Science and philosophy in Aristotle's *G.A.*', *Journ. Hist. Biology* 1970, p. 1.

F. Solmsen, 'The Vital Heat, the Inborn Pneuma and the Aether', *Journal of Hellenic Studies*, lxxvii (1957), 119.

J. Stenzel, art. 'Speusippos' in Pauly–Wissowa, *Real-Encyclopädie der klassischen Altertumswissenschaft*, Bd. IIIb, col. 1636.

REPORT ON RECENT WORK

ALLAN GOTTHELF

DAVID BALME's volume continues to be invaluable for all those who are interested in Aristotle's biological works and their philosophical significance. Since its publication in 1972 there has been much discussion of the relevant texts and topics, and I have been asked to write a brief report on this recent work.[1] I have necessarily been very selective. Balme's own work has been highlighted.[2] Many of the papers cited are contained in three collections: Gotthelf 1985*a*, Gotthelf and Lennox 1987, Devereux and Pellegrin 1990.

After a comment on 'Text and Translation', I will proceed, under 'Issues', by isolating most of the topics to which Balme devoted a significant amount of attention in his notes, in the order in which he treated them. Numbers in parentheses after each heading refer to the pages on which his commentary appears. Discussions of particular passages are cited under the appropriate topic-heading. My remarks are intended to be read along with Balme's notes on the relevant topic or text.

Text and Translation

There have been no editions or English translations of *P.A.* or *G.A.* since 1972. (Slightly revised versions of the Oxford translations, *sans* notes, appeared in Barnes 1984.) The translation in the present volume has been changed in a few places (in accordance with Balme's own request): *P.A.* I. 4 644^{a}23–5 (see Longrigg 1977), with consequent changes at ^{a}29 ('form' replaces 'species') and ^{a}31 ('formally' replaces 'specifically'); *G.A.* II. 3 736^{b}1 (lacuna no longer read); and *G.A.* II. 1 730^{b}35 ('form' replaces 'kind').

This last item exemplifies to some extent a change Balme would have made throughout: a consistent rendering of *eidos* as 'form' (rather than as 'species' or 'kind') and *genos* as 'kind' (rather than as 'genus'); this is an increasingly common practice among specialists in Aristotle's biology, and is explained in Balme 1987*c*: 306, Lennox 1987*b*: 339 n., and Pellegrin 1987, *passim*.

[1] I would like to thank James Lennox, Jennifer Powell, Kelly Rogers, and the editors of the Clarendon Aristotle Series for helpful comments on an earlier version of this report.

[2] A full bibliography of his writings on ancient philosophy up to 1985 may be found in Gotthelf 1985*a*; with the works cited here it is complete to date.

REPORT ON RECENT WORK

Issues

1. *Aims of Aristotle's biological works* (v, 69–70, 127): In recent work Balme argued that Aristotle's entire 'biological' enterprise is more closely connected with his philosophical work (in our sense of 'philosophical') than many have thought (Balme 1987*a*; cf. 1987*c*). Others have stressed Aristotle's claim to be developing a body of scientific understanding (*episteme*) about animals (cf. Gotthelf 1987*a*: 170 ff., and Balme himself in 1987*b*: 80), and there has been much discussion of the relationship of Aristotle's practice (and the methodology advocated in *P.A.* I) to the theory of science presented in the *Posterior Analytics* (e.g. Barnes 1975, Balme 1987*b*, Bolton 1987, Gotthelf 1987*a*, Lennox 1987*a*, 1990, 1991, Charles 1990, Lloyd 1990, all with additional references). These two perspectives are not incompatible—an Aristotelian work can certainly have both 'scientific' and 'philosophical' dimensions—but it is as yet unclear (i) whether Aristotle saw both dimensions as *aims* of his biological treatises, and if so, (ii) which aim he saw as primary, and (iii) how he saw the relationship of these two aims, given that he did not separate 'science' and 'philosophy' as firmly as we do.

The nature of the 'educatedness' (*paideia*) referred to in the opening paragraph of *P.A.* I is discussed extensively in Kullmann 1974.

2. *The distinction between arriving at and judging explanations, and the question of method in biology generally* (69–70): Lennox (1987*a*, 1991) and Bolton (1987) have argued that *An. Post.* is as much concerned with the *establishment* of causes as with their organized presentation; the same is implied for *P.A.* I. 1, the methodological principles (*horoi*, 639ᵃ13) of which are, on this view, to be seen as applicable to the judging of inquiry as well as of exposition. Even if that is so, Balme is certainly right that there are aspects of scientific *method*—i.e. of scientific inquiry itself—which the principles given in I. 1 do not address. They do not, for instance, address (*a*) how, if at all, dialectic is to be used; nor (*b*) how the data are to be initially collected and sifted; nor (*c*) how the precise causes of specific biological phenomena are to be determined.

(*a*) The role of dialectic in biology is considered in Bolton 1987; most of the large recent literature on the role of dialectic in Aristotelian inquiry has not examined the biological works in any detail, but biological passages are more frequently cited now (e.g. in Irwin 1988). (*b*) Aristotle's programme of empirical research and, more generally, his collecting and sifting of data (including reports from others), are discussed in Lloyd 1978 and 1987.

In regard to topic (*c*), although there has been much work on Aristotle's insistence that the study of nature must make use of the final cause (see below under 'Natural teleology'), comparatively little attention has been given either to Aristotle's view of how the scientist should proceed in determining what the precise final cause of some structure or process *is*, or to Aristotle's own practice in this regard (although the papers cited in the previous paragraph all bear on this question). Lloyd 1983 argues that Aristotle's results in his biology are significantly influenced and sometimes distorted by pre-philosophical beliefs and cultural biases. Balme would have substantially disagreed with both parts of this thesis, especially the second part, and aspects of both parts are questioned in Parker 1984 and Lennox 1985.

On first principles of Aristotle's biology (p. 70), cf. Kullmann 1974, Bolton 1987, and Gotthelf 1987*a*, with dissent in Lloyd 1990.

3. *Starting explanation at the generic level* (72–4, 121–2, 124–5): Recent work has followed Balme's lead in connecting this first methodological principle with aspects of the theory of scientific understanding presented in the *Posterior Analytics*, and in treating the principle as important for Aristotle's biological work. *An. Post.* distinguishes between knowledge *that* something is and knowledge *why* (and thereby *what*) it is, and describes the progression from the former to the latter in terms of the discovery of causes (*An. Post.* I. 13, II. 1–2, 8–10, and *passim*). Proper explanation is of attributes that belong to their subjects *in virtue of themselves* (*An. Post.* I. 4–5 and *passim*). Lennox 1987*a* and 1991, building on Balme's suggestion here that this first methodological principle in *P.A.* I. 1 is connected with the theory of *An. Post.* II. 14 (and ff.) regarding the role of generic attributes in explanation, argues that securing the widest subject to which an attribute to be explained belongs 'in virtue of itself' is a central part of the pre-explanatory, 'that'-stage of science. Both Lennox (in these papers) and Gotthelf (1988) have argued that the *Historia Animalium* is to a significant extent aimed at providing such 'widest-class generalizations', as a preliminary to scientific explanation and perhaps, via explanation, to formal definitions (although see Balme 1987*a*, 1990*b*, for the hypothesis that Aristotle eventually abandoned the aim of formal definition). Charles 1990, focusing on the *An. Post.* account of the route from knowledge of the 'that' to knowledge of the 'what', gives a somewhat different account of both the aims and procedure at the 'that'-stage, and of the practice in *H.A.*, to which Lennox 1990 is a response.

Attention to generic attributes raised for Balme the question of the place of classification in Aristotle's enterprise (p. 71). His work published in the early 1960s had established that there is no systematic hierarchical classification (i.e. no taxonomy) of animals to be found in the biological corpus, but he continued to think that such a classification was an ultimate aim of Aristotle's biological work. The development, and eventual change, of his views on this matter is traced in Gotthelf 1988. The change was in part influenced by Pellegrin's argument that the concepts of *genos* ('kind'), *eidos* ('form'), *diaphora* ('differentia'), and *to analogon* ('analogy') are used consistently in the logical and the biological works without taxonomic import and with a specific set of logical/ ontological interrelationships to each other (Pellegrin 1986, esp. ch. 2; 1987). Recently the classification issue has been reopened by Charles 1990, critically discussed in Lennox 1990. Pellegrin's views are discussed, and some of them criticized, in Lennox 1984, and in Lloyd 1990, to which Pellegrin 1990 is a reply.

4. *Necessity in nature* (76–85, 100, 101): In his complicated argument for the view that all necessity involved in natural coming to be is hypothetical, an argument which raises many important issues, Balme defends, among others, the following four theses: (i) animals and their organs do not come to be of absolute necessity; (ii) the coming to be of features of animals or their organs that come to be by material necessity is conditional upon the coming to be of things which do not come to be by absolute necessity (viz., from (i), animals and their organs); (iii) material necessity is a type of *hypothetical* necessity; (iv) 'the very existence and properties of the elements' (p. 82) are hypothetically necessitated. ((iii) is argued partly, but not only, from (i) and (ii).)

Cooper 1985 defends theses (i) and (ii) but rejects (iii) and (iv), arguing that material necessity is (sometimes) included under absolute necessity by Aristotle. Balme had himself come to question (iii) and (iv), and in 1987*c* presented his revised view, briefly indicating areas of agreement and disagreement with Cooper.

Thesis (i) (and thus (ii)) was questioned in Nussbaum 1978 and Sorabji 1980 (criticized respectively in Balme 1982 and Gotthelf 1980, and Gotthelf 1987*b*), and by several scholars since. Their view that animals and their parts come to be of *material* necessity gets its best defence perhaps in Charles 1988. Charles, however, maintains that such necessities are not absolute but are 'forward-looking hypothetical necessities'. The issues remain controversial.

These and related topics concerning the role of necessity in biological explanation are also discussed in most of the studies cited under 'Natural teleology' below.

5. *The order of explanation, from being to parts to generation* (86–7): Balme's view that the important passage at 640ᵃ33 ff. identifies for animal parts three teleological and one (relatively) non-teleological mode of explanation, is supported and amplified in Cooper 1985 and Gotthelf 1985*b*, 1987*b* (sec. III of 'Postscript 1986'). Kullmann 1974: 37 suggests that for animal parts we are given here two teleological modes of explanation and one non-teleological mode; Sorabji 1980: 155 proposes that for parts we are given altogether only two teleological modes. All interpreters agree with Balme that there is in addition one teleological mode given for generation.

640ᵃ27–33: Aristotle's theory of spontaneous generation, and its connection with his natural teleology, are discussed in Lennox 1982 and Gotthelf 1989*b*.

6. *Soul and its place in natural philosophy* (88–93): Balme's intriguing inference from the *G.A.* theory to Aristotle's conception of soul has not to my knowledge been remarked on in subsequent literature. Connections between Aristotle's biological studies and his views about the nature of soul are made in Charlton 1985, 1987 (which also considers the claim at 641^{a}32 ff. that natural philosophy does not study intellect), Code 1987, and Furth 1988. Balme amplified his views in a paper published posthumously (1990*a*).

7. *Natural teleology* (93–101): This issue has received more discussion than any other of the major topics treated in Balme's commentary. There is a review of some of the key studies to 1983 in Bradie and Miller 1984, and mention of others in the 'Postscript 1986' to Gotthelf 1987*b*. Studies that make most use of biological texts include: Kullmann 1979, Cooper 1982, Bradie and Miller 1984, Charlton 1985, Gotthelf 1987*b*, Charles 1988, Cohen 1989, Matthen 1989, and Balme's own reconsideration in 1987*c* (remarked on above, under 'Necessity in nature'). The topic most discussed has been the first of the two Balme singled out (pp. 93–4), that of the nature of the 'teleological control' and its relation to 'the hot and the cold and the "necessary" causes', with discussion centred around the question whether, according to Aristotle, the applicability of teleological explanation to nature is conditional upon the unavailability of a full material-efficient account (however defined) of organic development. Cooper, Charlton, Gotthelf, and Cohen, along with Waterlow [Broadie] 1982 in different ways argue the affirmative; Charles and Matthen in different ways argue the negative. With his 'cybernetic' interpretation of Aristotle's teleology (1987*b*), Balme moved towards the view that the applicability of teleological explanation to nature is *consistent* with the thesis that the coming to be of animals and their parts is in some sense materially necessitated, but continued to think that such a thesis was not within the reach of 'the state of observational science in [Aristotle's] day' (Balme 1987*c*: 285; a similar view is presented in Bradie and Miller 1984).

On the set of issues Balme gathers under his second topic, 'over-all teleology', Furley 1985 and Sedley 1991 consider aspects of 'the question whether particular ends are subordinated to general ends' (p. 95), Gotthelf 1989*a* discusses the role of normative concepts in teleological explanation, and Lennox 1985 discusses the eternality and fixity of species. On the nature of an Aristotelian 'species' (p. 97), see now Balme 1987*c* and Lennox 1987*b*.

8. *Division and the criticism of 'dichotomy'* (101–19): *P.A.* I. 2–3 is discussed at some length in Kullmann 1974 and in Tarán 1981 (where the object of criticism in these chapters is taken to be Speusippus). That the aim of Aristotelian division is definition and not classification, and that the

logical interrelationships among Aristotle's concepts of *genos*, *eidos*, and *diaphora* are to be understood by reference to the divisional process, is argued in Pellegrin 1986. Aristotle's successive reforms of Academic division (of which the ones introduced at 643^{b}9–26 are the culmination), and their implications for the nature of definition and its role in the study of animals, are discussed in Balme 1987*b*; some problems that Aristotle's reforms raise for him are usefully laid out in Deslauriers 1990 (although Aristotle's ability to deal with them is perhaps underestimated). The connection between these reforms and the enterprise which is the *H.A.* is discussed in Balme 1987*b* and in the Introduction to Balme 1991. The metaphysical issues surrounding definition are discussed in Balme 1987*c*; this discussion is criticized in Lloyd 1990, to which Balme 1990*b* is a reply. The role of division in facilitating the search foı explanations is considered in Lennox 1987*a* and 1991.

643^{a}35–8: See now Balme 1987*b*: 76 n. 6.

9. *Identifying natural kinds* (120–2): The question of what counts as a kind (*genos*) for purposes of division, definition, and/or explanation, and of how such kinds are identified, is discussed in Gotthelf 1985*b*, Charles 1990, and Lennox 1990.

644^{a}24: We print here, in place of Balme's original note, the substitute he requested (see Longrigg 1977).

10. *The argument of* G.A. *I–II. 3: structure and starting-points* (127–32): The aims of this part of *G.A.*, and the roles of dialectic and empirical investigation in its argument, are discussed in Bolton 1987 and Furth 1988.

11. *The male and female contributions to generation and the transmission of form* (140–65): There is a substantial discussion of Aristotle's theory and its metaphysical significance in Furth 1988, including a lengthy discussion of the refutation of pangenesis. Balme has drawn heavily on *G.A.* for his own recent account (1987*c*) of central metaphysical themes in Aristotle. On the compatibility of the *G.A.* IV. 3 theory of parental 'movements' with the theory of I–II. 3 (and ff.), and the implications of *G.A.* for the issue of individual forms, see, in addition to Balme and Furth, Cooper 1988. Most of the studies cited above under 'Soul and its place in natural philosophy' and 'Natural teleology' draw implications for these topics from the *G.A.* theory, and thus contain discussion of various passages in *G.A.* I. 17–II. 3 (and ff.).

731^{b}18 ff. (155–6): This passage is examined in Lennox 1985.

736^{a}24 ff. (158–60): Both the text and interpretation of this notorious passage on the 'entrance' of intellect (*nous*) into the human embryo are discussed in Charlton 1987, and in Balme 1990*a*, where Balme elaborates the view defended here and connects it with the *De Anima* discussions of *nous*. *Pneuma*, vital heat, and their capacities are discussed in Nussbaum 1978, Gotthelf 1987*b*, Charles 1988, and Matthen 1989.

ADDITIONAL BIBLIOGRAPHY

BALME, D. M. 1982. Review of Nussbaum 1978. *Journal of the History of Philosophy*, 20: 91–5.

—— 1987*a*. 'The Place of Biology in Aristotle's Philosophy', in Gotthelf and Lennox 1987, pp. 9–20.

—— 1987*b*. 'Aristotle's Use of Division and Differentiae', in Gotthelf and Lennox 1987, pp. 69–89.

—— 1987*c*. 'Teleology and Necessity', in Gotthelf and Lennox 1987, pp. 275–86.

—— 1987*d*. 'Aristotle's Biology was not Essentialist', in Gotthelf and Lennox 1987, pp. 291–312.

—— 1990*a*. '*Anthropos anthropon gennai*: Human is Generated by Human', in *The Human Embryo: Aristotle and the Arabic and European Traditions*, ed. G. R. Dunstan, Exeter, pp. 20–31.

—— 1990*b*. 'Matter in the Definition: A Reply to G. E. R. Lloyd', in Devereux and Pellegrin 1990, pp. 49–54.

—— 1991. *Aristotle, History of Animals, Books VII–X*. Prepared for publication by A. Gotthelf, Loeb Classical Library, London and Cambridge, Mass.

BARNES, J. 1975. 'Aristotle's Theory of Demonstration', in *Articles on Aristotle*, i. *Science*, ed. J. Barnes, M. Schofield, R. Sorabji, London, pp. 65–87.

—— ed. 1984. *The Complete Works of Aristotle: The Revised Oxford Translation*. Princeton, NJ.

BOLTON, R. 1987. 'Definition and Scientific Method in Aristotle's *Posterior Analytics* and *Generation of Animals*', in Gotthelf and Lennox 1987, pp. 120–66.

BRADIE, M., and MILLER, F. D., JR. 1984. 'Teleology and Natural Necessity in Aristotle', *History of Philosophy Quarterly*, 1: 133–45.

CHARLES, D. 1988. 'Aristotle on Hypothetical Necessity and Irreducibility', *Pacific Philosophical Quarterly*, 69: 1–53.

—— 1990. 'Aristotle on Meaning, Natural Kinds and Natural History', in Devereux and Pellegrin 1990, pp. 145–67.

CHARLTON, W. 1985. 'Aristotle and the *Harmonia* Theory', in Gotthelf 1985*a*, pp. 131–50.

—— 1987. 'Aristotle on the Place of Mind in Nature', in Gotthelf and Lennox 1987, pp. 408–23.

CODE, A. 1987. 'Soul as Efficient Cause in Aristotle's Embryology', *Philosophical Topics*, 15/2: 51–60.

ADDITIONAL BIBLIOGRAPHY

COHEN, S. 1989. 'Aristotle on Hot, Cold, and Teleological Explanation', *Ancient Philosophy*, 9: 255–70.

COOPER, J. M. 1982. 'Aristotle on Natural Teleology', in *Language and Logos: Studies in Ancient Greek Philosophy presented to G. E. L. Owen*, ed. M. Schofield and M. C. Nussbaum, Cambridge, pp. 197–222.

—— 1985. 'Hypothetical Necessity', in Gotthelf 1985*a*, pp. 151–67.

—— 1987. 'Hypothetical Necessity and Natural Teleology', in Gotthelf and Lennox 1987, pp. 243–74. (An amalgamation of most of Cooper 1982 with all of Cooper 1985.)

—— 1988. 'Metaphysics in Aristotle's Embryology', *Proceedings of the Cambridge Philological Society*, 214: 14–41. (Repr. in Devereux and Pellegrin 1990, pp. 55–84.)

DESLAURIERS, M. 1990. 'Plato and Aristotle on Division and Definition', *Ancient Philosophy*, 10: 203–19.

DEVEREUX, D. and PELLEGRIN, P., eds. 1990. *Biologie, logique et métaphysique chez Aristote*. Paris.

FURLEY, D. J. 1985. 'The Rainfall Example in *Physics* ii 8', in Gotthelf 1985*a*, pp. 177–82.

FURTH, M. 1988. *Substance, Form, and Psyche: An Aristotelean Metaphysics*. Cambridge.

GOTTHELF, A. 1980. Review of Nussbaum 1978. *Journal of Philosophy*, 77: 365–78. (Additional discussion in *Review of Metaphysics*, 35 (1981–2), 619–23.)

—— ed. 1985*a*. *Aristotle on Nature and Living Things: Philosophical and Historical Studies presented to David M. Balme on his Seventieth Birthday*. Pittsburgh and Bristol.

—— 1985*b*. 'Notes toward a Study of Substance and Essence in Aristotle's *Parts of Animals* II–IV', in Gotthelf 1985*a*, pp. 27–54.

—— 1987*a*. 'First Principles in Aristotle's *Parts of Animals*', in Gotthelf and Lennox 1987, pp. 167–98.

—— 1987*b*. 'Aristotle's Conception of Final Causality', in Gotthelf and Lennox 1987, pp. 204–42.

—— 1988. '*Historiae* I: *Plantarum* et *Animalium*', in *Theophrastean Studies*, ed. W. W. Fortenbaugh and R. W. Sharples, Rutgers Studies in Classical Humanities III, New Brunswick, NJ, pp. 100–35.

—— 1989*a*. 'The Place of the Good in Aristotle's Natural Teleology', in *Proceedings of the Boston Area Colloquium on Ancient Philosophy*, Vol. iv, ed. J. J. Cleary and D. C. Shartin, Lanham, Md., pp. 113–39.

—— 1989*b*. 'Teleology and Spontaneous Generation: A Discussion', in *Nature, Knowledge and Virtue: Essays in Memory of Joan Kung*, ed. R. Kraut and T. Penner, *Apeiron* Special Issue 22/4: 181–93.

—— and LENNOX, J. G., eds. 1987. *Philosophical Issues in Aristotle's Biology*. Cambridge.

ADDITIONAL BIBLIOGRAPHY

IRWIN, T. H. 1988. *Aristotle's First Principles*. Oxford.

KULLMANN, W. 1974. *Wissenschaft und Methode: Interpretationen zur aristotelischen Theorie der Naturwissenschaft*. Berlin and New York.

—— 1979. *Die Teleologie in der aristotelischen Biologie: Aristoteles als Zoologe, Embryologe und Genetiker*. Heidelberg.

LENNOX, J. G. 1982. 'Teleology, Chance, and Aristotle's Theory of Spontaneous Generation', *Journal of the History of Philosophy*, 20: 219–38.

—— 1984. 'Recent Philosophical Studies of Aristotle's Biology', *Ancient Philosophy*, 4: 73–82.

—— 1985. 'Demarcating Ancient Science: A Discussion of G. E. R. Lloyd, *Science, Folklore, and Ideology: The Life Sciences in Ancient Greece*', *Oxford Studies in Ancient Philosophy*, 3: 307–24.

—— 1987*a*. 'Divide and Explain: The *Posterior Analytics* in Practice', in Gotthelf and Lennox 1987, pp. 90–119.

—— 1987*b*. 'Kinds, Forms of Kinds, and the More and the Less in Aristotle's Biology', in Gotthelf and Lennox 1987, pp. 339–59.

—— 1990. 'Notes on David Charles on *HA*', in Devereux and Pellegrin 1990, pp. 169–83.

—— 1991. 'Between Data and Demonstration; The *Analytics* and the *Historia Animalium*, in *Science and Philosophy in Classical Greece*, ed. A. C. Bowen, New York, pp. 1–37.

LLOYD, G. E. R. 1978. 'The Empirical Basis of the Physiology of the *Parva Naturalia*', in *Aristotle on Mind and the Senses*, ed. G. E. R. Lloyd and G. E. L. Owen, Cambridge, pp. 215–39. (Repr. with a new foreword in Lloyd, *Methods and Problems in Greek Science* (Cambridge, 1991), pp. 224–47.)

—— 1983. *Science, Folklore, and Ideology: Studies in the Life Sciences in Ancient Greece*. Cambridge.

—— 1987. 'Empirical Research in Aristotle's Biology', in Gotthelf and Lennox 1987, pp. 53–63. (Repr. from *Magic, Reason and Experience* (Cambridge, 1979), pp. 211–20.)

—— 1990. 'Aristotle's Zoology and his Metaphysics: The *status questionis*—a Critical Review of Some Recent Theories', in Devereux and Pellegrin 1990, pp. 7–35. (Repr. in Lloyd, *Methods and Problems in Greek Science* (Cambridge, 1991), pp. 372–97.)

LONGRIGG, J. 1977. Review of D. M. Balme: *Aristotle's De Partibus Animalium I and De Generatione Animalium I (with passages from II 1–3)* (Oxford, 1972), *Classical Review*, NS 27: 38–9.

MATTHEN, M. 1989. 'The Four Causes in Aristotle's Embryology', in *Nature, Knowledge and Virtue: Essays in Memory of Joan Kung*, ed. R. Kraut and T. Penner, *Apeiron* Special Issue 22/4: 159–80.

NUSSBAUM, M. C. 1978. *Aristotle's De Motu Animalium: Text with Translation, Commentary, and Interpretive Essays*. Princeton, NJ.

ADDITIONAL BIBLIOGRAPHY

Parker, R. 1984. 'Sex, Women, and Ambiguous Animals', *Phronesis*, 29: 174–87.

Pellegrin, P. 1986. *Aristotle's Classification of Animals: Biology and the Conceptual Unity of the Aristotelian Corpus*, tr. A. Preus, Berkeley, Calif. (Rev. edn. of *La Classification des animaux chez Aristote: Statut de la biologie et unité de l'aristotélisme*, Paris, 1982.)

—— 1987. 'Logical Difference and Biological Difference: The Unity of Aristotle's Thought', in Gotthelf and Lennox 1987, pp. 313–38.

—— 1990. 'Taxinomie, moriologie, division', in Devereux and Pellegrin 1990, pp. 37–47.

Sedley, D. 1991. 'Is Aristotle's Teleology Anthropocentric?', *Phronesis*, 36: 179–96.

Sorabji, R. 1980. *Necessity, Cause, and Blame: Perspectives on Aristotle's Theory*. London.

Tarán, L. 1981. *Speusippus of Athens: A Critical Study with a Collection of the Related Texts and Commentary*. Leiden.

Waterlow [Broadie], S. 1982. *Nature, Change, and Agency in Aristotle's* Physics. Oxford. (Repr. 1988.)

GLOSSARY

References are to passages discussed in the notes

αἱμορροΐδες: 'blood-flows' 728^{a}23.

αἴσθησις: 'perception' 641^{b}5; 'observation' dist. 'theory'.

αἰτία: 'cause' 639^{b}5, 11; 'reason'.

ἀλλοίωσις: 'alteration' 641^{b}5.

ἀνάλογον: 'analogously' 644^{a}12, 727^{a}3.

ἀνομοιομερῆ: 'non-homoeomerous' parts 640^{b}19.

ἄνω: 'above'; 'forward' in an animal's body 716^{b}26; 'prior' in a series 731^{b}23.

ἁπλοῦς: 'simple' 643^{b}31; 'unambiguous'.

ἀρχή: 'beginning'; 'source'; 'governing principle'; 639^{b}12.

γένεσις: 'coming-to-be'; 'generation' (reproduction).

γένος: 'kind'; 'genus'; 639^{a}20.

διάθεσις: 'condition'.

διαίρεσις: logical 'division' pp. 101–6, 642^{b}12.

διαφορά: 'difference'; logical 'differentia'; 'differentiation'; 642^{b}5.

δύναμις: 'power' 641^{a}6; 'capability'; 'potentiality' 641^{b}36.

εἶδος: 'form'; 'kind'; 'species'; 639^{a}28, 640^{b}26, 644^{a}24.

ἔναιμα: 'blooded' genera (i.e. red-blooded).

ἐνέργεια: 'actuality'; 'actualization'.

θερμός: 'hot' 726^{b}33.

θέσις: 'position' 719^{b}18.

θεωρεῖν, θεωρία: 'study'; 'survey'; 639^{a}1.

θρεπτική: 'nutritive' soul 641^{b}5.

καθ' ἕκαστον: 'particular'; 'individual'; 642^{b}5.

καθόλου: 'in general' dist. 'particular'.

καταμήνια: 'menses'.

κάτω: 'below'; 'hindward' in an animal's body 716^{b}26.

κύημα: 'foetus'.

λόγος: 'account'; 'speech'; 'argument'; 'reason'; 'definition' 639^{b}11.

μαλάκια: 'cephalopods' (lit. 'molluscs').

μαλακόστρακα: 'crustaceans'.

μᾶλλον καὶ ἧττον: 'the more and less' 644^{a}17.

μέθοδος: 'investigation' 639^{a}1.

νοῦς: 'intellect' 641^{a}22.

ὅλως: 'generally'.

ὁμοιομερῆ: 'homoeomerous' parts 640^{b}19.

ὁμώνυμος: 'equivocal' (i.e. equivocally named) 643^{b}7.

ὀστρακόδερμα: 'testaceans'.

οὐσία: 'being' 639^{a}16.

πάθος: 'affection' 639^{a}22, 641^{b}5.

περίττωμα: 'residue' 717^{a}30.

πέττειν, πέψις: 'concoct, concoction' 715^{b}24.

πνεῦμα: '*pneuma*' p. 161.

πρῶτος: 'first'; 'proximate'; 'ultimate'; 724^{a}36.

σάρξ: 'flesh' (i.e. muscle) 719^{a}22.

σκώληξ: 'grub'; 'larva'; 721^{a}2, 732^{a}29.

σπέρμα: 'seed' 716^{a}4, 724^{b}14.

στέρησις: 'privation' 642^{b}21.

συμβεβηκός: 'concomitant fact'; 'accident'; 'attribute'; 643^{a}27, cf. p. 117.

συμπεπλεγμένον: 'compounded' dist. 'simple' 643^{b}26.

συνιστάναι: 'constitute'; 'compose'; 'set'; 715^{b}29.

σύνολον: 'composite' 640^{b}26.

σύντηγμα: 'colliquation'; σύντηξις: 'colliquescence'; 724^{b}23.

σῶμα: 'body' 640^{b}16.

τέλειος, τελειωθείς: 'perfected'.

GLOSSARY

τέλος: 'end' 641b24.
τὸ τί ἦν εἶναι: 'the what-it-is-to-be' 642a13.
τρόπος: 'manner'.
ὕλη: 'matter'.
φαινόμενα: 'appearances' 639b5.
φύσις: 'nature' 641b30, cf. p. 93.
ψυχή: 'soul' 641a17, 27.

INDEX

(See also Glossary)

INDEX